THE INTERNATIONAL BLADE COLLECTORS ASSOCIATION PRICE GUIDE TO

COMMEMORATIVE KNIVES

1960-1990

J. Bruce Voyles

Dedication

This book is dedicated to the very few that produce commemorative knives without the first priority being a dollar in their pocket—to those who make high quality collectible knives and then price them at an honest price.

The funny thing is that many of the players in the commemorative game will think this dedication applies to themselves—when it doesn't.

Published by

 **krause publications**

700 E. State Street • Iola, WI 54990-0001
Telephone: 715/445-2214

Please call or write for our free catalog of firearms/knives publications. Our toll-free number to place an order or obtain a free catalog is 800-258-0929 or please use our regular business telephone 715-445-2214 for editorial comment and further information.

Library of Congress Catalog Number: 95-81620
ISBN: 0-87341-420-9

Printed in the United States of America

Contents

About this book

What this book originally set out to do was tell everything there is to know about every single commemorative knife. But as the book progressed I found that impossible. Simply there are so many knives being produced by both knife manufacturers and private enterprises that it is impossible to find them all.

I did try. I started collecting the flyers on the various commemoratives when the very first ones came out in the 1970s. The various ads in the knife magazines have always been a primary means of research, but even within those materials in some instances the flyers left off a quantity made, or whether they were serial numbered, etc. Sometimes we could discover that information, and sometimes we could not. And sometimes we could give absolute documentation, because we witnessed it.

The Genella "Little Buddy" and "Spike" I named. The Voyles Cutlery knives of 1977 and 1978 I had made on contract. The 1978, 1979, and 1980 NKCA club knives: I sat in the room when they were selected. The 1976 NKCA club knives were unwrapped by me, handed to Ben Kelley who serial numbered them, and then rewrapped by me. I think Ben paid me $100 for helping him those four days. It was my junior year in college.

While still in college I made sales calls on Beck & Gregg Hardware in Atlanta on behalf of the Eagle Set series. I had two samples of the 13 colonies sets, but the sets were sold out before I could sell any to wholesalers.

There have been others in which I was there when they started, but for most of the facts recorded here I had to rely on what raw material I could find.

Naturally I would appreciate your help in filling in the gaps for future editions. If there is a commemorative you own but is not listed in this book please let us know. We need to know the following: Who made it, what it was commemorating, when it was issued, how many were made, the original cost, what you would value it at today. Every addition will be appreciated and acknowledged in the future editions.

Just write to Bruce Voyles, Commemorative Book info., in care of Krause Publications, 700 East State Street, Iola, WI 54990-001.

Is this book complete? No. But it is as complete as I could make it.

What is a Commemorative Knife?

A commemorative knife should commemorate something, usually issued on the anniversary of a historical event such as the American Bicentennial in 1976 or the 500th Anniversary of Columbus' discovery of America.

These knives will usually have a special etching, a specified number serial numbered at some place on the knife, and an attractive box housing the entire package. At times the pattern, handle material, or blade configuration will be exclusive to the edition

That's the strict definition, but demand for boxed, serial numbered knives extends beyond commemoratives, and those knives that do not commemorate some event are termed "limited editions".

To make a knife a limited edition all that is required is to manufacture a finite number of them, but the reality is that many manufacturers start on limited editions when they run out of things to commemorate.

Honoring the "Moon" simply because the manufacturer needs to sell one more knife is hardly justification for another limited edition. Also under the heading of limited editions comes wildlife series, military branches of service, and sports teams.

Most collectors of commemoratives collect a lot of limited editions. All commemoratives are just that, limited editions. But not all limited editions are commemoratives.

In our experience a true commemorative (commemorating something) has a tendency to be more valuable in the long haul than the more common limited edition.

Belknap Hdw. & Mfg. Co. of Louisville, Ky, in the heart of knife country, offered a series of commemoratives featuring hardware & tools as shields. Here's the "Ax" version.

To make a knife a limited edition all that is required is to manufacture a finite number of them, but the reality is that the many manufacturers start on limited editions when they run out of things to commemorate.

There's so much more to knife collecting than simple return on investment.

Why Collect Commemoratives?

Commemoratives have a lot going for them. Unusual variety, often elaborate decoration and packaging, and one of the few items in knife collecting of which you usually know how many were produced.

Some dealers and authors have rapped commemoratives. I used to be alarmed until I realized that many of the doomsayers of the future of commemorative collecting are usually die-hard antique knife collectors and dealers who look down with contempt on any knife made after 1965.

They don't collect commemoratives, they aren't in the commemorative market. In other words, they don't know anything about commemoratives. But they still consider themselves qualified to pass judgement on commemoratives.

When you hear an evaluation on commemorative knives, consider the source. Would you heed the advice of a surgeon about brain surgery if all operations the surgeon had conducted had been heart surgery?

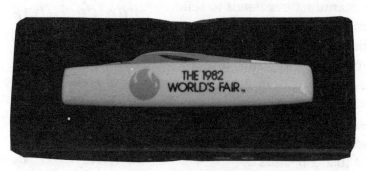

Case was one of several companies offering Worlds Fair commemoratives for the 1982 Knoxville Worlds Fair. What helps these knives is they are also actively sought after by Worlds Fair memorbilia collectors. Twice the chance of increasing value.

Investment

If all you want is the highest return possible on your cash investment—for the cash, not because you want to collect knives—my best advice is look into stocks, bonds, and CDs. There's so much more to knife collecting than simple return on investment, and if that "more" is not what you are looking for I recommend you look elsewhere.

There are commemorative knives that have gone up, just as there are other types of knives that have gone up. There are commemorative knives that have gone down at times, just as other knives have gone down.

Some top antique collectors like used Russell Barlows, but they do not bring any more (and maybe less) these days than they did ten years ago.

There are some name makers whose knives bring big money today – but their crude earlier work, that is simply not up to par, doesn't show any wild advance in price.

So just like anything else you may collect, in every branch of knife collecting you pay your money and you take your chances — and, if we are like most collectors, we have a good time along the way. Sometimes we may make a lot of money on a knife, and sometimes we may not. Some increase in value of your knives comes from wise investing, some from the seemingly annual price increases of similar knives in the manufacturer's regular line, and some from sheer luck.

The other stuff

But beyond investment there's the enjoyment of owning some extravagant, well-done examples of man's oldest tool.

There's the stimulation of history we can provoke in a young person with the gift of a commemorative knife. Ask him, "Son why do you think they would commemorate Pearl Harbor? Look it up in the encyclopedia and tell me about it". Commemorative knives can be a great stimulus to learning.

Commemoratives are safe. Because of the elaborate packaging, blade etchings, special patterns, etc., commemoratives are difficult to counterfeit, and as one collector told me, "I tried collecting Remingtons and Winchesters and purchased a lot of counterfeits. I don't want to spend the money and time it takes to become a proficient antique knife collector. But I want to collect knives—so I collect commemoratives. They're safer."

If you ever marveled at the tales of the old knife dealers and collectors who would spend their Saturdays driving through the country hunting for the old Case XX and the Case USA boards and wondered what it would be like, now is the time for you to go on that hunt too.

Prediction

Commemorative collecting is a profitable venture of knife collecting if you keep up with the market—simply because at this writing there are a lot of dealers and collectors who have kept up with the values of antique knives but who have little or no idea of the accurate value of commemoratives (that's one of the reasons for this book).

Therefore it is relatively easy to find modern commemorative knives undervalued on the tables of advanced knife collectors!

If you ever marveled at the tales of the old knife dealers and collectors who would spend their Saturdays driving through the country hunting for the old Case XX and the Case USA boards and wondered what it would be like, now is the time for you to go on that hunt too—but your hunt begins at the local knife club and at the larger knife shows. The potential is there as much as any time in the early 1970s.

The great treasure hunt of the 1990s will be commemoratives.

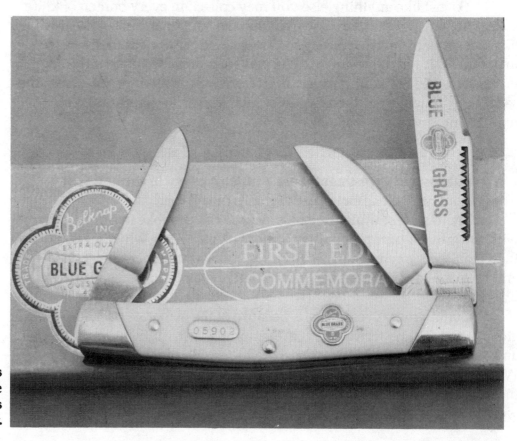

The first version of the Bluegrass commemoraative, prior to the putting of tool shields. Early '70's and hard to find today.

What to Look For In An Ideal Commemorative

The Choices

There are key things you can look for that will help you through the maze of what commemoratives are better than others. Commemorative knives are beginning to gain a history.

We can now step back and take a look back at what went right in commemoratives, what went wrong, and what the winners seem to have in their favor.

An ideal commemorative

Here's my checklist for an ideal commemorative. I know of very few, but the more commemoratives we collect that fit this profile the better our chance of realizing a positive return on our investment.

1. Commemorates something worth commemorating.

The "My Dog Spot" commemorative may sell well to the "My Dog Spot Memorial Committee," and Spot may appreciate it, but the real value in commemoratives comes years down the road, and most often when it is tied in with some historical event.

Old souvenirs from the 50th anniversary of the Civil War were in demand during the 125th anniversary of the war's end. Commemoratives tied into a national historic event—the Bicentennial, the Statue of Liberty 100th Birthday, etc.,—will be in demand in the future by those who are not yet knife collectors, increasing demand and giving you a better chance to see profit from your investment.

2. Uniqueness

The ideal commemorative is one that is not a regular production pattern: different pattern, blade configuration, and different handles than anything else on the market.

3. Well-Known Brand

Podunk Cutlery may enjoy seeing its name on the tang of a commemorative, but understand there are no Podunk Cutlery knife collectors. There are collectors who collect knives only with certain names on the tang. This gives a commemorative knife value from the subject

The "My Dog Spot" commemorative may sell well to the "My Dog Spot Memorial Committee," and Spot may appreciate it, but the real value in commemoratives comes years down the road, and most often when it is tied in with some historical event.

If we collect commemoratives by unknown knife companies, we have a knife with reduced appeal.

commemorated and also from the people who collect that brand. If we collect commemoratives by unknown knife companies, we have a knife with reduced appeal.

4. Good Pattern

A plus is if the pattern was a well-liked one that was long discontinued, revived just for one issue, and is popular among collectors. The commemorative based on the well-used trapper pattern is common today simply because there was a great demand in the late 1980s for any trapper pattern from trapper collectors. Increased demand increased the chances of seeing your investment increase.

5. Quality Construction

A poorly made knife is a poorly made knife, and worthy of few collections, no matter what the commemorated subject. If the price is not out of line you can sometimes go with a lesser commemorated subject if the knife is of extremely superior quality and still have a good investment opportunity.

6. Price in Relation to the Knife

A $20 knife with $10 worth of decoration is worth about $30. In a commemorative that cost should run about $40, adding costs to allow for advertising, promotion, and a bit of profit for the man spending his time putting it all together. However, the chance for the increase on your investment is not good if that knife is retailed at $1540 when in reality it is only a $40 value.

Some modern factories set all the prices of their knives on a seven-or-eight-time cost multiple. Etching, boxes, etc.,`` are often included on the cost side, causing a $3 etching to add $21 to the final price of the knife, when most knowledgeable knife collectors know it is a $3 etch.

If the company has taken a regular production knife and etched the blade, adding $21 to the price rather than $3, the knife is overpriced by $18. It takes many years for such a commemorative knife to appreciate on the collector market to cover this monetary distance.

7. Worst Case Scenario

In any case, any commemorative is worth the cost of that same knife in the manufacturer's regular production line. Keeping up with the current prices on regular production knives will enable us to by some commemoratives cheaper than dealer cost on newer, standard production knives!

Commemorative Knife Timeline

Pre-1969 : Most commemoratives and limited editions were novelty knives (such as World's Fair knives, etc.) These come under antique knife headings and as such are not listed in this book, but there were a few commemorative/limited editions at the time.

1969-1972: The forming period. Knife collecting became popular and a very few commemorative knives were tried. Boker made the first of their annual series in 1971. In 1972 the commemorative boom began with the issuance by A.G. Russell's Knife Collectors Club of the Kentucky Rifle Commemorative made by Schrade-Walden. Issue price $12. The knives debuted at a Louisville, Kentucky knife show. Buyers of the knives were buying from A.G., and turning around to the man behind them in line and selling the knife for $15-$18. Because of demand A.G. was unable to deliver dealer orders at the show, much to the consternation of those dealers wanting in on the boom that day.

1972-74: More limited editions, mostly from Boker and Schrade.

1974: James F. Parker begins the Eagle series, with each knife to be issued before the American Bicentennial. This was one of the first commemoratives to be issued with deep dealer and distributor discounts, and followed soon by the Service Series of three crimped bolster stock

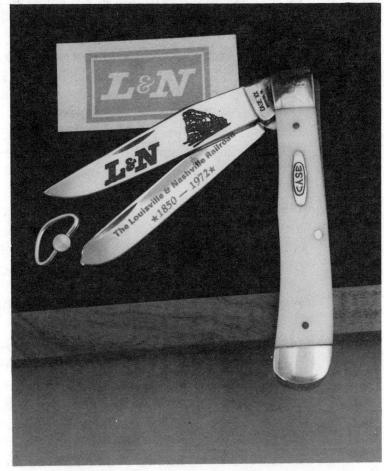

A good example of the customized commemorative: taking a standard production knife, etching the blade on a certain theme, housing it in a nice box, and in this instance making a nice package for either the knife enthusiast or the railroad collector.

knives, and the 14-knife "Thirteen Colonies" series. I was working on the first edition to the Official Price Guide to Knives at the time, and was asked by Parker to make a sales call or two near my home in Georgia. I made two calls before I was informed the Service Series was entirely sold out. I had two samples of the Thirteen Colonies knives, and I made one call before the entire run of 3,000 was also sold out. This is a good example of the frenzy to buy commemorative knives at the time.

1975: First pure club knife issued, the NKC&DA (National Knife Collectors and Dealers Association) whittler, a Robert Klass Kissing Crane cigar whittler. Cost to members was $12. Serial number 0001 was bid (and bought) for around $40 by Jim Koch. The knives didn't sell out and were re-offered to the members with a maximum of three per member. They sold out the second time around. In December of 1980 I purchased one for my father for Christmas. I paid $595. They were bringing $625 at the time.

1976: The American manufacturers wake up to the commemorative market and the flood begins, first with bicentennial knives, but once the manufacturers tasted the honey they began returning to the honey tree.

1977-1981: Boom times in knives. Everything everybody made seemed to sell, many dealers made big advances—at times fueled by their speculation in the silver boom of the same era.

1981-1985: Growing pains come to the knife collecting world. Dramatic increase in the number of shows, the number of knives, and the number of conflicts between various segments of the field. A large number of collectors decided it was more fun to collect coins or baseball cards.

1982: The Remington Bullet is reintroduced by Remington Firearms.

1984: Adrian Harris starts producing private-commemoratives on a grand scale. It soon becomes hard to tell the difference between a factory issued commemorative and an "Adrian special." Oversupply causes decline in the Case trapper commemorative market.

1989-90: Case sells to Jim Parker, who immediately begins producing several ambitious limited edition and commemorative series, all in an

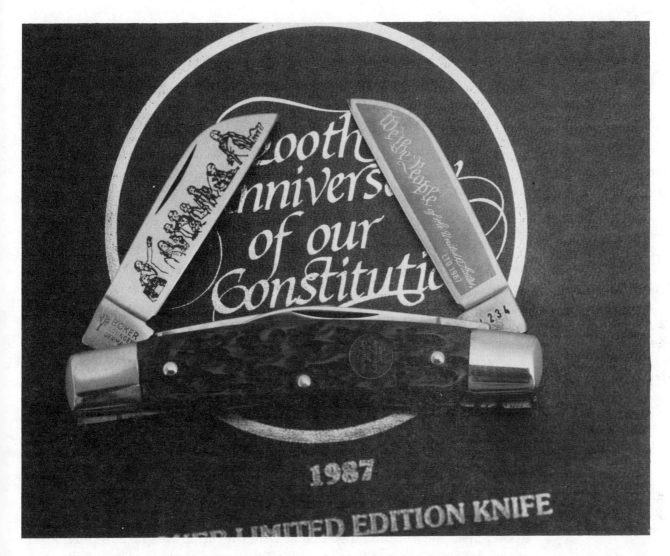

attempt to generate cash to pay the bills at Case and the Cutlery World store chain. Despite the quality and originality of many of the knives, the frequency with which the knives hit the market overwhelms some collectors.

1991: Commemoratives produced in the 1970s bottom out and start climbing in value. Many manufacturers realize that there is profit be made by nurturing the commemorative market rather than trying to loot it in a single stroke. Reduced number of issues led by companies like Case create a new interest in collecting current collectible knives.

1992-93: The commemorative market levels out, bottoms out in places and turns up across the board. The large accumulations of the 1970's era commemoratives are exhausted, and from there everything starts to build.

A key point in the escalation of price on this knife is the fact a four blade congress made in Germany is a rapidly appreciating knife whatever is on the blade.

How Many is Too Many for a Limited Edition?

We must remember that when commemorative knives started in the early '70s, the manufacturers were new to making commemorative knives, just as the collectors were new to buying them.

We were all stumbling around in the dark. No one really knew what the proper level was for quantity, price, or even the style of knife he should be buying. Manufacturers made a mistake when they made 10,000 and 12,000 runs of commemoratives and called them a limited edition, at a time when a 5,000 run was a year's supply of some of their slower moving regular production knives.

The manufacturer made a mistake, and the collector, hot to buy every available commemorative, bought the mistake—compounding the mistake as well, because the next run of the manufacturer was going to be just as large.

The commemorative market overburdened itself in the mid-1980s, and finally something had to give, and it did. Demand slowed. The manufacturer with a few thousand knives left over usually closed them out to a volume dealer, who sold them to the public at a price less than the price the collector paid who bought the knife from a retail shop immediately upon issue. The middle range dealer with unsold knives he had purchased at standard dealer price was caught, and no one involved was very happy about things.

There are few things sadder to knife collectors than seeing a knife we may have paid $45 for on sale in a discounter's catalog at $30. We feel we've been had, and our enthusiasm for buying commemoratives gets low.

In fact, I once had a factory contact tell me his company was making around 4,000 of a slow selling scout pattern as a regular production run—and that same year that company issued a 5,000 run "limited edition."

Any run over 5,000 quantity can hardly be considered a limited edition. I'm not saying it may not sell, I am saying don't call it a limited edition.

The true definition of a limited edition knife is a special knife (different from the similar pattern of the regular production line of the manufacturer) produced in a quantity less than the similar knife's regular production run.

The Story of a Commemorative Campaign That Failed

It was a historic event, for few cutlery manufacturers ever again dared to try anything like it for years.

That's how it should be—but there are times that it hasn't worked that way. For instance the Case Moby Dick. Suggested retail at issue $150. Dealer cost $75. A one blade folding hunter in a glass box, white undyed smooth bone handles scrimshawed with a whaling scene and with semi-engraved bolsters. Quantity 5000 of each prefix, Cxxxx, Axxx, Sxxx, Exxx. Total 20,000 knives. There were not a lot of knives made by Case that year that exceeded a production run of 20,000. And certainly not any single knife run that could generate $1.5 million at dealer price for the company.

Was it a commemorative? No—it did not commemorate anything. Was it a limited edition? No—not in that quantity. Did it do well on the market? It depends on who you talk to. Case sold out its supply to dealers—but every dealer who wanted one got one, and more.

It sold so slow that the follow-up Nantucket Sleigh Ride (same knife, slightly different whaling scene, but this box had a red background!) was delayed for almost a year before Case had the nerve to issue it to the collector market. Same quantity, same deal, only this time the Nantucket Sleigh Ride did not sell out to the dealers (and suggested retail was $200 now).

Those ill-fated knives are the premier examples of cutlery manufacturer greed—and the realization by collectors when they are being gouged. Were they being gouged? You bet. And in just a few short years the management who dreamed up this project were all replaced and moved into different fields of endeavor.

It was a historic event, for few cutlery manufacturers ever again dared to try anything like it.

How are those knives doing today? About $125 each—still nowhere near suggested retail. Let's just hope that the collector who bought these two at retail from the hardware store also bought the Randall 50th anniversary knife. If so, he's still far ahead.

Some Success Stories

Another successful commemorative is the Randall 50th anniversary knife, which sold in the $300 range upon issue in 1987. There were two at the New York Custom knife show in 1988 both priced in the $5,000 range, and they seem steady at that price today. Not a bad increase on an investment.

In 1975 the National Knife Collectors & Dealers Association issued a stag handled, three blade cigar whittler that sold to members for a price of $12. Today it sells for around $450 (and at one time brought $625). Even at $450 that is a good profit over the years.

In 1982 Remington Arms went to a U. S. cutlery manufacturer and contracted for a reproduction of the famed 1123 Bullet pattern as a promotion for the company's Model Four rifle. That Remington reproduction sold for $44. Today it brings around $500.

And there are other knives that have gone up too. A good friend who is an antique knife dealer was set up at a show when I stopped by to visit. He had a half-dozen commemoratives on his table. "I thought you didn't handle commemoratives," I commented.

"I don't, but the way I traded I don't have anything in those knives, they're all just junk anyway."

I spotted a Keen Kutter commemorative in the box. Pointing to it I told him, "I sold one just like that a few months ago for $45." He looked up, more interest showing on his face.

Two days later he called to tell me he too had sold the same knife for $45. He still doesn't like commemoratives, he says, except for Keen Kutter commemoratives, and he's actively looking for those!

Another successful commemorative is the Randall 50th anniversary knife, which sold in the $300 range upon issue in 1987. There were two at the New York Custom knife show in 1988 both priced in the $5,000 range, and they seem steady at that price today. Not a bad increase on an investment.

Of course I have cited the success stories—but keep in mind just two winning knives like a 1982 Remington or a Randall 50th Anniversary can cover up a lot of losing-money mistakes.

There is no way to know for sure—but that is one of the exciting aspects of knife collecting.

The revival of the Remington name is pure magic. There is a lot of loyalty even among antique dealers who would die before they would sell a commemorative or a limited edition knife but who are actively buying and trading Remington limited editions–because they respect the Remington name–and the knives are an in-demand product.

But how, when rumor has it Remington is producing above 5,000 runs? (Remington will not announce quantities—claiming the actual figures are proprietary information). Simply put, Remington has a great number of knives going into places that have never heard of knife collecting, that only know a Remington gun is a pretty good gun, so the knife must be pretty good as well. (Never mind that the Remington knives are made on contract by a well-known pocketknife manufacturer).

This increased demand helps, and the second factor is the massive amount of money Remington spends in promoting its limited edition knives. Posters, color advertising, window signs, nice packaging–it all adds up to the kind of push that is needed to stir the interest of the lukewarm collector–and this increased demand drives up the price. Even the posters themselves are bringing handsome prices on the collector market.

Of course we do have to realize that there are a great many antique knife collectors who have dreamed for years of owning a complete set of mint original Remington Bullets and couldn't afford the $35,000 or so an original set would bring. Instead they know they can own a complete set (if the current trend continues) for only a few hundred dollars.

But this is the only instance I know when a knife was made in a quantity over 5,000 within the past 10 years that has shown a steady acceleration in price. Just as you can make too many, a manufacturer can make too few as well. We've just seen in the case of Remington how an expansive advertising and promotional budget can have a positive influence on the price acceleration of a commemorative knife.

But this is the only instance I know when a knife was made in a quantity over 5,000 within the past 10 years that has shown steady acceleration in price.

The Price

Price structure on commemorative knives

If you are an advanced knife collector please keep in mind that the price structure for selling your commemoratives to dealers is much different than that of selling a fine old knife.

A fine old knife is always looked at, even if in the dealer's subconscious, he's thinking along the lines of, "if I don't buy this one where can I get another?" The declining supply of fine antique knives has brought this around. Antique knife collectors are now forced to accept knives with spots or even some use today when just a few years ago they would only accept spotless knives. It is more difficult than ever before to assemble a top collection of all mint antique knives at an economical price.

That means there is a higher demand for the good old knives, poor supply, and the discounts off of market price are very low (most dealers will usually go around 25-30% off current market value for old knives offered singly). Commemorative knives are different.

The Price versus VALUE

For the commemorative buyer this means that with all considerations involved you should always keep a close eye on the "value" of a knife. There are costs involved in etching the blade, boxing the knife and running the ads. The costs will increase the price of a knife—but the question you must ask is how much it increases the cost.

If the commemorative has standard handle materials, the usual box, and just standard etching, you know that the value of this knife is never going to be much more than the value of the standard knife with a little added in for the etching and box. These style knives are so easy to produce and knock off it is just not in the cards that they will equal the success stories of the other successful commemoratives. They aren't unique enough. They all look alike except for the blade etching and box color.

A standard production knife is a standard production knife, and at some point you have to look beyond the glitter and decoration and realize that—and not pay too much of a premium for the etching.

Much of your profit will come from advancing suggested retail from the manufacturers sometimes annual price increases.

And something else about the prices:

Suggested retail doesn't mean that was the market price of the knife at time the of issue!

A standard production knife is a standard production knife, and at some point you have to look beyond the glitter and decoration and realize that – and not pay too much of a premium for the etching.

And something else about the prices:
Suggested retail doesn't mean that was the market price of the knife at the time of issue!

In the early days (and sometimes even today) the suggested retail means absolutely nothing. There is instance after instance when the manufacturer will produce a knife, put a high retail on it, and retail the knife himself to consumers for up to 40 per cent off retail.

With that in mind please consider when reading this book that a knife that carried a suggested retail of say $200 might have been available on the show circuit or through mail order dealers as low as $120 individually or $100 each by the dozen. (The high volume boys had paid $75—and a few of them may have even been sold as low as $85!)

Today the value of that knife might be $175—and at first glance you may compare today's market price with the suggested retail and believe that the knife has gone down $25 in value—when in reality the suggested retail was always an artificial price and few if any knives were sold at that price. At $175 market value today for most of the people who bought it, it represents a $75 return on their investment.

Remember, the rules of commemoratives are different than other knives.

Unfortunately, the only standard reference we can rely upon is the suggested retail price—but as you use this book for pricing guidelines, please remember that the suggested retail does not always mean the price at which a commemorative knife was readily available on the collector market a few years ago.

Keep The Box!

There is only one way to collect commemoratives for investment: Mint in the original box. No exceptions.

You might buy one without a box for trading material, but if you are salting some knife away for a long-term investment, keep the box, etc., intact in as good a condition as possible, including all paperwork and the original sales receipt if you have it.

As for condition, there are no used commemoratives that are collectable beyond their use as a using knife. There is no tolerance for anything but mint.

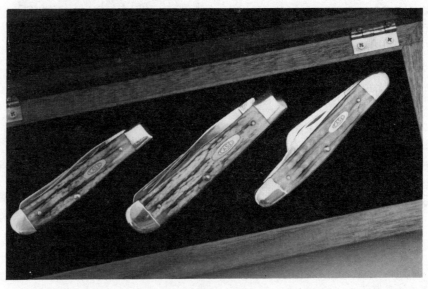

The checklist on this one just keeps going. Low quantity, exclusive handles and dating style (roman numerals) popular patterns, well known brand, and a set made by Case for Frost Cutlery that both can be excited about-- and the collectors will like it too!

Where to Get Commemoratives

One of the enjoyable aspects of commemoratives is by just getting into the field you can find dozens of dealers out there who buy collections of antique knives (which often contain some commemoratives as well). These antique knife dealers do not like or appreciate knives of such recent manufacture in boxes (since boxed knives do not roll up in a knife roll), and these dealers will often close out these commemoratives to the diligent commemorative collector at far below market price. But that is a trend that is changing fast as more and more antique knife collectors turn to commemoratives to make up for the declining supply of good old knives.

As we said earlier, the great treasure hunt of the 1990s is not going to be the hoards of old antique knives in the back storeroom of some ancient hardware store but the stashes of the 1970s-era commemoratives.

What the Future Holds for Commemorative Knives

Some ask why commemoratives should remain popular.

Why not? These are the only knives in history that have been actually designed for collectors. They have all the bells and whistles that turn collectors on, and the only thing lacking for commemoratives was scarcity and a steady, reliable appreciation in price.

As commemoratives get older, the scarcity is more than apparent—the attrition from rust and damage is already taking its toll—so we can expect a steady appreciation. There are instances of some of the celluloid-handled early commemoratives already shrinking and pulling away from the handles, and other instances where knives in the original wrappers that have never been unwrapped were improperly wrapped at the factory and have rusted inside the paper. All these tragedies to the owner still reduce the availability of the mint ones, and the knives properly taken care of will increase in value.

These are the only knives in history that have been actually designed for collectors. They have all the bells and whistles that turn collectors on, and the only thing lacking for commemoratives was scarcity and a steady, reliable appreciation in price. As commemoratives get older, the scarcity is more than apparent.

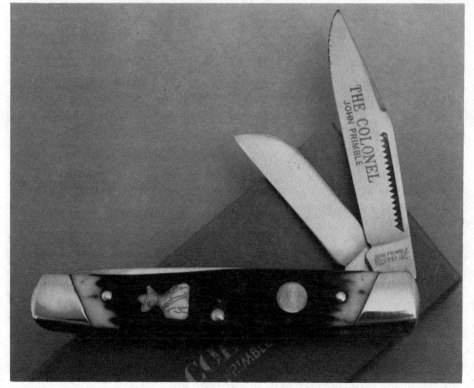

One of the oldest commemoratives is the legendary Kentucky Colonel. Suffice to say if you find one buy it while you can still find it. It predates organized knife collecting.

Commemoratives have what no other knife before has had: A clearly recorded history

The early 1970s commemoratives are already older knives now than the 10 dots and Case USAs were when many of the major dealers and collectors first got turned on to knives.

The manufacturers of commemoratives usually document the run somewhere in the packaging (or even on the blade etch itself) as to the date and the number produced. You usually know how many have been produced. Try to get those figures on 1940s-era Bullet Remingtons or Case Bulldogs.

The early 1970s commemoratives are already older knives now than the 10 dots and Case USAs were when many of the major dealers and collectors first got turned on to knives.

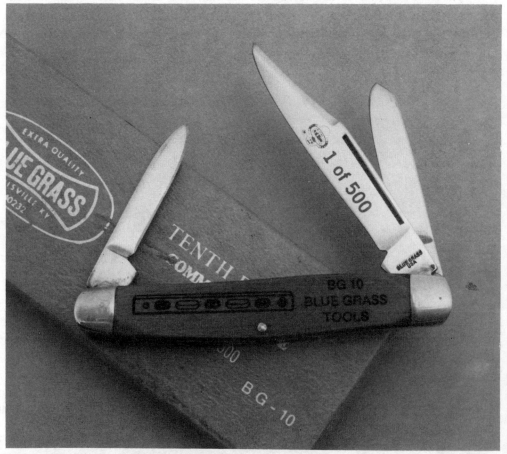

One of the last of the Bluegrass series (compare with the others pictured elsewhere in this section to note the change. Quantity 500, and essential to complete the set. However, the poor quality knife hurts this one.

Other Things to Know

Low Serial Numbers

Serial numbers are a standard accessory on most commemoratives, and while numbers under 100 are desirable, and matching serial numbered sets are important if you are trying to buy or sell a group of knives, numbers over 100 do not seem to have much effect on the value of a commemorative knife. However, an even number like 1000 or 500 does appear to make the knives sell a bit quicker over odd numbers.

How to store your commemoratives

If your commemorative knife is received with the blade open placing a stress on the backsprings, by all means close it.

Just because you have a factory sealed package, do not assume that the knife was packaged cleanly. Open the knife, wipe off the blade with a silicone cloth, being careful not to put fingerprints on the blade for the oil in your hands will cause the knives to rust.

Some people recommend that you store your knives outside the box but I've purchased too many collections when the heirs tossed the boxes and took a beating on the knives because they were stored separately and the heirs didn't know any better.

Club Knives: Why they are different

Club Knives are different.

Club knives are their own segment of collecting and are the subject of a separate chapter. Club knives and commemoratives are two different types of knives and different rules apply.

Why stop at 1990?

For serious collecting—and determining an accurate price—it is almost guessing in the dark for knives less than 10 years old. The quantities are still in flux, there are often large quantities on some dealer shelves, and they have not been rediscovered by collectors.

There is something about collectors forgetting about a knife, seeing it and wishing they had laid one back—and realizing they still can if they hurry—that stimulates collector interest. Then knives start seeking their own aftermarket price level.

For knives after 1990 we have included a representative shot-in-the-dark for the pages of *Edges* magazine, published by Krause Publications of Iola, Wisconsin (1-800-272-5233). This quarterly publication is absolutely vital to keep up with current market conditions, especially in the limited run production lines such as Fight'n' Rooster and Bulldog.

Just because you have a factory sealed package, do not assume that the knife was packaged cleanly. Open the knife, wipe off the blade with a silicone cloth, being careful not to put fingerprints on the blade for the oil in your hands will cause the knives to rust.

Alternatives and Club Knives

Fields to Collect.

When knife collecting first became popular and the commemorative knife first hit the market, there were a lot of collectors who actually set out to collect every commemorative that came down the line. Some even looked for specific serial numbers. And the dealers of the time knew who collected what: Conrad Allgood collected number one, Bobby Turner collected number two, Jim Parker number five, Warren Campbell number 11, etc. Gene Abernethy of the North Carolina Knife Club collected number 241 so diligently that he is known in some circles as "ole 241." But the number of knives finally overwhelmed nearly everyone trying to buy them all.

Club knives were the same way. In the first few years of club knives there were many collectors who started out to buy every club knife issued by every club—and the clubs found their membership rolls swelled by collectors joining from out-of-state just to buy the club knives. The only exception was the Sand Mountain (Alabama) Knife Club that refused to take out-of-state members—much to the dismay of more than one collector who wanted to join. When it became clear that there were too many knives to keep up with, the club memberships declined.

Therefore, like all collecting it is vital to specialize. G.T. Williams of Lexington, Kentucky, has a beautiful collection of Tennessee-Kentucky commemoratives. (And he fills two tables with a large upright, lighted display!)

If you want to start small with some knives you can enjoy searching for start with 1976 Bicentennial knives. Together they make a nice collection. Any 1970s-era commemorative is getting harder and harder to find, and even the poor appreciating knives of the time have bottomed out and started upward. If you play close attention to these knives (we called them "dogs" in those days) that have started up you can still find them at below market prices from less-than-attentive dealers.

Private Label Commemoratives

Here's the way it was explained to me when I first tried a private label commemorative.

"Why don't you start doing commemoratives? Here's what I'll do. I'll order the knives through my factory dealership and sell them to you at dealer cost (of course I'm making a little because I get a discount because of my large volume—but it is still as cheap as you would pay ordering direct).

"Then I'll take that knife, gold plate the blade, etch whatever you want on both blades, provide a vacuum-formed box and silk-screen whatever you want on the outside of the box. On the inside lid I'll etch a brass plate with type and a line drawing telling all about the knife and whatever you have etched on the blade."

Then the kicker: "And you only need to buy one! Use it for your advertising, I'll make you as many as you need within two weeks, and you only risk the cost of your advertising—you don't have to buy any knives that you can't sell."

That's the way Adrian Harris offered his Tennessee Knife Works services to many different knife dealers. Anyone could enter the commemorative market with an idea, the cost of an ad, and about $30 for the first knife.

The move created a tremendous influx of commemoratives on the market. Most were on a standard Case trapper, utilizing the same standard box, varied only by color and the blade etching.

It wasn't just a flood, it was a tidal wave. Adrian sold his entire operation to W. R. Case & Sons Cutlery in 1987, but others have continued what Adrian pioneered, although no one is currently gold plating blades on the scale that Tennessee Knife Works was.

During those hectic days a few of the more enterprising ordered different style boxes, and even ordered limited edition runs of handle materials so that their commemoratives would have a non-production handle material. A dealer could order 5,000 knives and split the exclusive handle around 20 different commemorative themes.

Some of the more enterprising homemade commemorative makers have even established exclusive arrangements with celebrities to use their images on commemoratives, and of the non-factory-produced commemoratives these exclusives are by far the best investments.

"Then I'll take that knife, gold plate the blade, etch whatever you want on both blades, provide a vacuum-formed box and silk-screen whatever you want on the outside of the box. On the inside lid I'll etch a brass plate with type and a line drawing telling all about the knife and whatever you have etched on the blade."

Then the kicker: "And you only need to buy one!"

The bottom line is these customized commemoratives seem to appreciate slower than factory produced commemoratives (primarily because the factory produced knives often vary quite a bit from the regular production knife, giving the collectors more trouble with perceived value).

These companies do provide a valuable service to the cutlery industry. For collecting they are a segment unto themselves, but for a short run for your small factory, the centennial of your town, were they not providing their service those kinds of special edition knives would not be available.

But that is not to say that these kinds of commemoratives can show reliable appreciation in comparison with some of the better known commemoratives.

The Difference between factory issue and private issue.

There is a difference between a knife produced from one of the "knife customizers" and the factory issued knife.

One disadvantage is that the customizer must start usually with a regular production knife, preventing any variation in patterns from the knives that can be bought in your local hardware store. This will affect the value.

If your Moose Lodge contracts for 50 or so customized commemoratives honoring your lodge then you might want to own one, but it would be nearly impossible for a Case trapper collector to make enough money to buy every Case trapper produced with a different etching on the blade.

The bottom line is these customized commemoratives seem to appreciate slower than factory produced commemoratives (primarily because the factory produced knives often vary quite a bit from the regular production knife, giving the collectors more trouble with perceived value).

In all collecting you must make choices, and if you choose to collect every variation of a pattern then you will want to add the customized commemoratives to your collection. You may even choose to collect only the customized commemoratives – or just the factory issues.

Of all the factory produced limited editions, only Case offers a method of telling the difference. All Case-issued factory commemoratives will be serial numbered inside a Long Tail C trademark. Contract issues and regular production knives will only have standard serial numbers.

Commemoratives Are Different

Buying and Selling: Commemoratives play by different rules

Perhaps that is the most important thing to always keep in mind when collecting commemorative knives is – they are different. They are not regular production knives with an endless supply always coming off the assembly line. They are not antique knives with a scarce supply. They are their own unique market and have their own unique set of rules. Abide by those rules and you can enjoy commemorative knife collecting, can make some money if you deal in them, and have the potential of seeing an increase in your investment over a period of time.

If you try to apply the rules of antique knives, or current production knives, or antique Bowie knives, or custom knives, to commemoratives you are headed for a fall.

Commemorative Supply: Limited after all

There are still hoards of commemoratives around, so the supply is still adequate to supply new collectors. This makes for an active, growing market. The knives now have a history, and some age to many of them. But few knife dealers are going to buy your knives at 20 per cent off market price when the next guy walking down the show aisle may have a backpack crammed with more of the same knife. Few businesses operate on 20 per cent gross profit.

What you can actually get is between you and the dealer, but don't be surprised if his initial offer is up to 40-50 per cent off market.

The reasons: he may not be keeping up. Commemoratives operate in that kind of high mark up, and you are fighting the fact that most dealers bought those knives originally (and in turn sold them) at less than 10 mark up over factory cost when the knives were new. If you bought them on that discount market you are in good shape – however, if you bought them at retail from a hardware store, you've already got problems, because you probably have too much money in them.

There are still hoards of commemoratives around, so the supply is still adequate to supply new collectors. This makes for an active, growing market. The knives now have a history, and some age on many of them.

Terminology

Etches
Standard knife terminology applies and an exploded view is enclosed for your reference. Since most commeoratives are etched on the master blade, there are several types of etches:

Surface etch: This is a light acid etch, usually gray in color, that appears on the surface of the knife.

Frosted etch: A surface etch over the entire blade, with the lettering or design the only part that is not etched.

Reverse Etch: The lettering or design is left untouched and the background is etched with a light frost etching. Same as frosted etch.

Deep etched: The etching is actually acid-etched deep into the blade. It is not uncommon to find this deep etch filled in with different color paints to give a colored etch effect.

Gold etched: Gold colored deep etching.

Serial numbers: Most commemoratives are numbered in sequential order beginning at number one and running through the end of the run. They are usually engraved on the bolsters, utilizing a pantagraph machine similar to the ones jewelry stores use to put initials on ID bracelets.

In the early days a few limited editions were serial numbred inside the liners before the knives were assembled.

What is not a serial number.
I know of no commemoratives that are etched via the etching on the master blades with the serial numbers, but some are pantagraphed, especially Fightn' Roosters.

The numbers on the back of the tang are usually the knife's factory pattern number. In Boker knives the pattern number is sometimes etched on the blade.

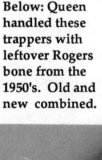

Below: Queen handled these trappers with leftover Rogers bone from the 1950's. Old and new combined.

Buying Commemoratives for Investment: Hard & Fast Rules

Rule No. 1. – Get In Early!
First of a series

As evidenced by the successes of such knives as the Remington 1123 reproduction, the Kentucky rifle, the NKC&DA 1975 whittler, the 1982 ABCA club knife and the first Blade Show "show knife," the first knife of a continuing series often does very well.

If you know of an annual series beginning it is a good idea to lay back a couple of the first year's issue. They stand to improve greatly percentage wise, but you will have to wait until the second or third year of the series to reap the benefits.

The first issue of a series is always the best for investment, from prints to coins, to commemorative knives. As time goes by more people start buying the latter knives, and then back up to obtain complete sets. If a first knife is a success it usually sells out and the manufacturer makes more knives for the second edition—which adds even more people looking to find the first one to fill out their complete set. Some of these first knives just never get back on the collector market again, so the demand increases the price. Both the Remington reproduction and the NKC&DA 1975 knife are prime examples.

Rule No. 2 – If you are dealing with commemoratives made in quantities of 5,000 or more, invest most of your money on knives that have been on the market for at least 10 years.

The 10-year rule was taught to me by an old coin collector. He said the idea is to let the hoarders and the speculators get out of their stocks, to let the volume dealers go through all the close-outs and the trades, and finally let the market price of the item find its own level.

Rule No. 3 – The amount of advertising and promotion that is spent on a knife will often have a direct effect on the value of the commemorative knife. If little or no promotion or advertising is spent on a knife, there is not enough demand to make a good market, or to stimulate value appreciation.

Let's compare two companies and how they might produce a

Rule No. 1. –
Get In Early!

Rule No. 2 –
If you are dealing with commemoratives made in quantities of 5,000 or more, invest most of your money on knives that have been on the market for at least 10 years.

Rule No. 3 –
The amount of advertising and promotion that is spent on a knife will often have a direct effect on the value of the commemorative knife.

commemorative. Company A decides to make a commemorative. It contracts with a factory for a run of 10,000 knives, which will cost Company A $15 per knife. Company A decides to sell the knife for $25.

But Company A has not included any money for advertising, so three dollars is added to the price. The knife now costs $28, which should have little effect on demand.

Now Company A has $30,000 to advertise and promote. That can mean color ads in the top publications, an incentive like a poster or fancy box, and even attendance at some of the better knife shows to introduce the knife first hand.

Company B wants to issue a commemorative too, but it wants one in an edition of 300. First, few manufacturers are interested in knife runs of 300. Company B finally finds a cooperative manufacturer, but in this small quantity, the same knife Company A has made will cost company B around $40 per knife.

To compete with the ad budget of Company A, company B must also add $100 per knife to the cost. So what you have is equal promotion (and demand) for the same knife, only Company A is selling one for $28, and Company B must sell the same knife for $140. Which one do you think will be the better investment?

With EQUAL demand and EQUAL promotion the lesser quantity should win out over the long haul.

Part of a new style of commemorative for Schrade. In addition to the knife a limited edition print is included. More bang for the buck—add to that something worth commemorating: Lady Liberty.

A

Ahead Of The Game, Ltd. Limited Edition / Buck Knife, Manufacturer - Buck, Pattern - 110 folder, solid pewter grips with hand sculpted detail and scene, quantity 5000, price $125, 1987, value $120.

Alabama Gun Collector's Association 25th Anniversary, Manufacturer - Case, Pattern - Trapper, Bone handles, special etching on blade, value $65.

Alabama Gun Collector's Association 26th Anniversary, Manufacturer - Case, Pattern - SR6254 Trapper, smooth bone handles, special etching on blade, quantity 125, 1981, value $65.

Alabama Gun Collector's Association 27th Anniversary, Manufacturer - Case, Pattern -Trapper, Green bone handles, special etching on blade, quantity 224, 1982, value $65.

Alabama Gun Collector's Association 28th Anniversary, Manufacturer - Case, Pattern - CCC6254 trapper, walnut handles, etched, light green collector box, quantity 265, 1983, value $65.

Alabama Gun Collector's Association 29th Anniversary, Manufacturer - Case, Pattern - 5254 trapper, stag handles, red box, quantity 281, 1984, value $85.

Alabama Gun Collector's Association 30th Anniversary, Manufacturer - Case, Pattern - I254 trapper, ivory handles, box, quantity 304, 1985, value $185.

American Blade Cutlery American Game Series, Manufacturer - American Blade Cutlery (trademark was licensed by American Blade Magazine from 1981-1984) Patterns - (1) Metal lockback, matching serial numbers were available, duck inlay, 1982, value $20. (2) Micarta lockback, buck inlay, 1982, value $20. (3) three blade stockman, doe inlay, 1982, value $30.

American Blade Magazine 150th Anniversary of the Vidalia Sandbar Fight, complete set value $2500, set produced by Beinfield Publishing in 1977. Following are individual prices for set components:

(1) Jimmy Lile, Double Edged fighter, quantity 200, price $1650, 1977, value $800.

(2) American Blade Magazine Vidalia Sandbar Fight, Manufacturer -W.R. Case, Pattern - '72 clasp knife with African Blackwood handles, quantity 200, value $600.

(3) American Blade Magazine Vidalia Sandbar Fight, Manufacturer - Schrade-Loveless, Pattern - 8" hunter, quantity 200, value $300.

(4) American Blade Magazine Vidalia Sandbar Fight,
Manufacturer - Crawford, Pattern - 13-1/2" Bowie, quantity 200,
value $500.

(5) American Blade Magazine Vidalia Sandbar Fight,
Manufacturer - A. G. Russell, Pattern - 6" hunter, quantity 200,
value $550.

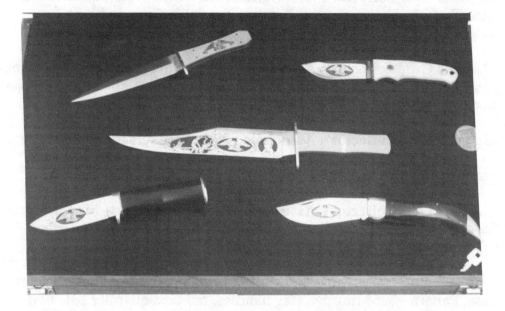

*American Blade Magazine 150th Anniversary of the Vidalia Sandbar
Fight complete set value $4,200.*

American Commemorative Institute, Ltd., Vietnam, Manufacturer - n/a,
Pattern - fighting knife, sterling-on-pewter, quantity 750, 1982, value $100.

The American Historical Foundation

*Based in Richmond, Virginia, The American Historical Foundation
specializes in selling limited edition commemorative firearms and knives via
space advertising in major magazines, as well as hosting in their restored ante-
bellum offices several museums related to military history. Following is a
representative selection of their knives. Collectors will find little price variation
between the same knife honoring two different branches of service, so even with
an incomplete listing you should be able to determine the value of your AHF
commemorative.*

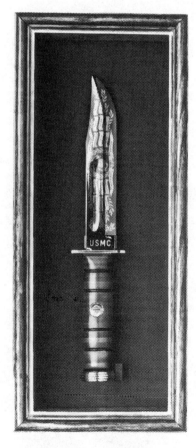

*American Historical
Foundation 45th
Anniversary*

American Historical Foundation 45th Anniversary, Marine Raider,
Manufacturer - Ka-Bar, Pattern - Bayonet, 24K gold plated with Raider
battle honors, motto, USMC symbol, serial numbered, certificate of
authenticity, display case $29, quantity 2,500, price $195, value $250.

American Historical Foundation Airborne Commemorative,
Manufacturer - Ek Commando, Pattern - model #4 commando knife, grips
are maroon rosewood, laminated, deep etched combat scene, 24k gold
plating, serial numbered, certificate of authenticity, quantity 2,500, price
$195, 1985, value $250.

American Historical Foundation The Battle of the Bulge, Manufacturer - Wilkenson Sword, Pattern - stiletto, 18K gold-on-brass hilt, bright "peacock" blue blade and luxurious blue velvet covered display case, quantity 2,500, price $295, 1982, value $350.

American Historical Foundation Boot Camp Ka-Bar Commemorative, Manufacturer - Ka-Bar, Pattern - USMC fighting/utility knife, two versions: (1) In honor of Parris Island Recruit Training, (2) In honor of San Diego Recruit Training, 24K gold on guard and butt, full blade etch with scrolls depicting each phase of training in Boot Camp, display case $29, Value $175 each.

American Historical Foundation Boot Camp Ka-Bar Commemorative

American Historical Foundation D-Day, Manufacturers - Wilkenson Sword Ltd., London, Pattern - stiletto, 18k gold-on-brass hilt, green velvet covered display case, quantity 2,500, price $295, 1981, value $350.

American Historical Foundation Fighting Knife, Pattern - model #4 Commando knife, grips are maroon rosewood, laminated, deep etched combat scene, 24k gold plating, serial numbered, certificate of authenticity, quantity 2,500, price $195, 1985, value $250.

American Historical Foundation Men of the U.S. Armed Forces in World War II, Manufacturer - n/a, Pattern - 4" stiletto, solid sterling silver miniature, complimentary display drawer, price $39, 1981, value $75.

American Historical Foundation Semper Fidelis Collection, Manufacturer - Ka-Bar, Pattern - Set of six presentation-grade fighting knives, honoring each of the six Marine Divisions, mirror polished, blue blade, USMC symbol and battle honors in 24K gold, display case $29, quantity 1,775, price $195, value $225.

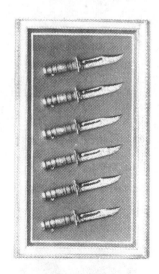

American Historical Foundation Semper Fidelis Collection

American Historical Foundation Six Marine Divisions Leatherneck Pocket Knife, Manufacturer - Ka-Bar, Pattern - 8-3/4" folding lockback, Marine Corps name and founding date etched, 6 knives, one for each division, quantity 1,775, price $89, 1988, value $110.

American Historical Foundation U. S. Army Tribute Collection, Manufacturer - n/a, Pattern - USMC trench knife, each division's battle honors in 24K gold on blade, shoulder patch, nickname and branch symbol, display case $24, quantity 1,943, price $195, value $225.

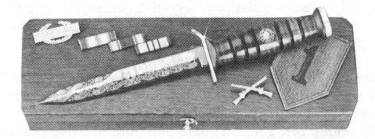

American Historical Foundation U. S. Army Tribute Collection

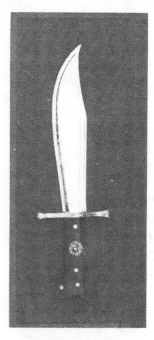

American Historical Foundation U. S. Marine Raider Commemorative Gung Ho

American Historical Foundation U. S. Navy Vietnam Fighting Knife

American Historical Foundation U. S. Army Vietnam Fighting Knife, Manufacturer - SOG Specialty Knives Inc., Pattern - Bowie, 24K gold etch, leather grip, full color cloisonne symbol, display case $29, quantity 2,500, price $195, value $225.

American Historical Foundation U. S. Marine Corps Commemorative, Manufacturer - H.G. Long & Co., Pattern - Stiletto, sterling silver plated hilt, full-color cloisonne enamel insignia, serial number, authorized by the U.S. Marine Raider Association, quantity 2,500, price $195, 1983, value $250.

American Historical Foundation U. S. Marine Raider Commemorative Gung Ho, Manufacturer- Collins & Co., Pattern - Bowie knife, mirror polished, deep etched dates and names of Raider battalions, 24K gold-plated crossguard, cloisonne enamel medallion, serial numbered, display case $39, quantity 2,500, price $245, value $275.

American Historical Foundation U. S. Marine Vietnam Fighting Knife, Manufacturer - SOG Specialty Knives Inc., Pattern - Bowie, 24K gold combat scene etched on blade, USMC symbol inlay in leather grip, 24K gold mounts, display case $29, quantity 2,500, price $195, value $225.

American Historical Foundation U. S. Navy Vietnam Fighting Knife, Manufacturer - SOG Specialty Knives Inc., Pattern - Bowie, 24K gold combat scene of Navy SEALS and vessels on blade, display case $29, quantity 2,500, price $195, value $225.

American Historical Foundation V-42 Stiletto, Manufacturer - Case, Pattern - 12-1/2" V-42 stiletto, serial numbered, skull crusher pommel, leather, crossguard handle, quantity 1,500, price $195, 1984, value $250.

American Historical Foundation Victory In Europe, Manufacturer - Sykes-Fairbain, Pattern - Stiletto, gold etched, presentation case, value $250.

American Historical Foundation Vietnam Bayonet of Honor U. S. Army, Manufacturer - n/a, Pattern - Bayonet, deep acid-etched, 24K gold gilt, black enamel infilled for contrast, black phenolic handle, full color inset cloisonne medallion, serial numbered, display case, quantity 2,500, price $189, 1985, value $235.

American Historical Foundation Vietnam Bayonet of Honor U. S. Marine Corps, Manufacturer - n\a, Pattern - Bayonet, deep acid- etched, 24K gold-gilt, black enamel infilled for contrast, black phenolic handle, full color inset cloisonne medallion, serial numbered, display case, quantity 2,500, price $189, 1985, value $235.

American Historical Foundation Vietnam Bayonet of Honor U. S. Navy, Manufacturer - n\a, Pattern - Bayonet, special heat treated blade, black phenolic black grip, 24K gold plated crossguard and parts, gold-gilt etched black blade, quantity 2,500, price $189, value $235.

American Historical Foundation Vietnam Tribute, U. S. Army, Manufacturer - Gerber, Pattern - Mark II combat knife, fatigue-colored handle, wasp body blade shape, U.S. Army insignia on grip, quantity 2,500, price $189, 1982, value $225.

American Historical Foundation Vietnam Tribute, U. S. Marine Corps, Manufacturer - Gerber, Pattern - Mark II combat knife, oak leaf camouflage hilt, combat scene etched on blade, display case $29, quantity 2,500, price $189, 1982, value $225.

American Historical Foundation Vietnam Tribute, U. S. Navy, Manufacturer - Gerber, Pattern - Mark II combat knife, U. S. Navy insignia on handle, 24K gold etched blade, display case $24, quantity 2,500, price $189, 1982, value $225.

American Historical Foundation Vietnam Bayonet of Honor U. S. Marine Corps

American Historical Foundation Vietnam Tribute, U. S. Marine Corps

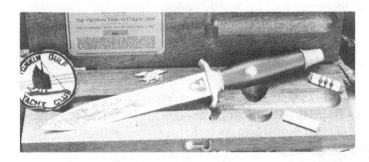

American Historical Foundation Vietnam Tribute, U. S. Navy

American Historical Foundation WWII Cloak & Dagger, Manufacturer - H.G. Long & Co. of Sheffield, Eng., Pattern - 7" sleeve dagger, exact recreation of the dagger originated by the OSS, British counterparts in SOE, 24k gold plated, quantity 1945, price $129, 1984, value $140.

American Historical Foundation World War II Tribute, Manufacturer - Dave Murphy, Pattern - 11-1/4" Murphy combat knives, set of four, commemorative aluminum handle, matching serial numbers, etchings of Army, Navy, Air Corps and Marines, velvet-lined American Oak case $29, quantity 2,500, price $195, value $225.

Aurum Etchings

Aurum is a company that specializes in etching knife blades, and occasionally they have ventured into the commemorative arena with knives made to their specifications by other companies.

Aurum Limited Edition, Manufacturer - Alcas, Pattern - Model 1123, two blade trapper, stag, price $185, value $150.

Aurum Limited Edition, Manufacturer Alcas, Pattern - Hunting knife, stag handles (Two styles all a part of a series), value $125 each.

Aurum Limited Edition, Manufacturer - Alcas, Pattern - Model 1306, one blade lockback, stag. Value $125.

Aurum Limited Edition, Manufacturer - Alcas, Pattern - Baby bullet, one blade lockback, stag handles, Value 100.

Autumn Wood, Inc. Alamo, Manufacturer - n/a, Pattern - 13-5/8" Bowie replica of Jim Bowie's famous Alamo knife, full leather presentation sheath, price, $85, 1986, value $150.

B

Battle Ax Knives

Battle Axe knives were made in Germany on contract for a group of American importers who specialized in quality commemoratives of short runs. The knives are not readily available and are showing increasing demand. Founders were Tommy Shouse, a regular on the knife show tour, and George Smith,who would later become involved with the reemergence of Winchester knives.

Battle Axe Bluegrass Beauty, Manufacturer - Battle Axe, Solingen, Germany, Pattern - 4-1/16" whittlers, set of three, bone handles, quantity 400, price $250, 1980, value $150.

Battle Axe Bonnie & Clyde, Manufacturer - Battle Axe, Solingen, Germany, Pattern - Set of two lockbacks, bone handles, quantity 300, price $225, 1979, value $100.

Battle Axe Congress Whittlers, Manufacturer - Battle Axe, Solingen, Germany, Pattern - Set of four congress, bone handles, quantity 400, Price $250, 1980, value $200.

Battle Axe Conqueror, Manufacturer - Battle Axe, Solingen, Germany, Pattern - Set of two folding hunters, bone handles, quantity 300, price $200, 1981, value $140.

Axe Courthouse Canoe, Manufacturer - Battle Axe, Solingen, Germany, Pattern - Two blade canoe, pearl handle, etched blade, serial numbered, quantity 300, price $50, 1979, value $60.

Battle Axe Folding Hunters, Manufacturer - Battle Axe, Solingen, Germany, Pattern - Set of six folding hunters, pearl insets, quantity 400, price $300, 1979, value $300.

Battle Axe The Gamblers, Manufacturer - Battle Axe, Solingen, Germany, Pattern - Set of three canoes, stag handle, bone handle, and pearl handle, master blade is etched on all three, quantity 400, price $200, 1980, value $170.

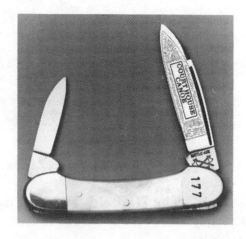

Battle Axe Courthouse Canoe

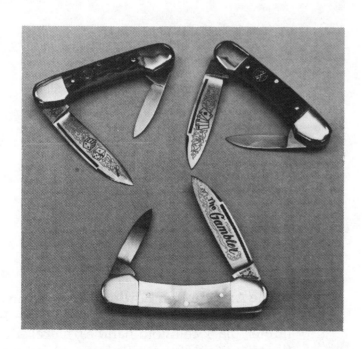

Battle Axe The Gamblers

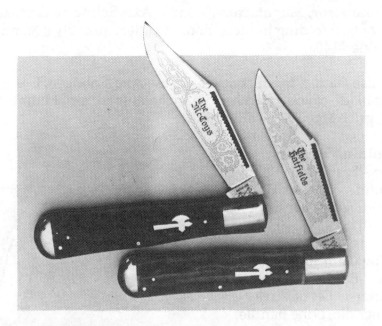

Battle Axe The Hatfields and McCoys

Battle Axe The Hatfields and McCoys, Manufacturer - Battle Axe, Pattern - Set of two lockback folders, quantity 1,000, price $60, value $60 each.

Battle Axe Indian Tribes, Manufacturer - Battle Axe, Solingen, Germany, Pattern - Set of three pearl canoes, quantity 600, price $120, 1979, value $180.

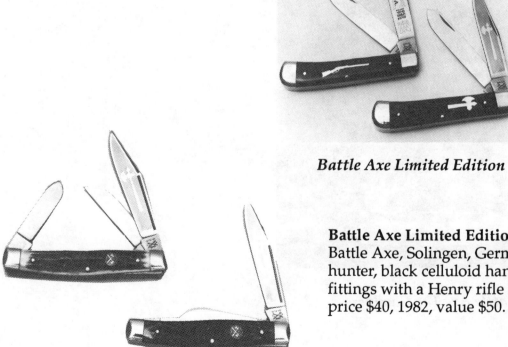

Battle Axe Limited Edition

Battle Axe Limited Edition, Manufacturer - Battle Axe, Solingen, Germany, Pattern - 4-1/8" hunter, black celluloid handles, nickel silver fittings with a Henry rifle inlay, quantity 600, price $40, 1982, value $50.

Battle Axe Limited Edition

Battle Axe Limited Edition, Manufacturer - Battle Axe, Solingen, Germany, Pattern -Three blade stockman, clip, spear, and sheepfoot blades, quantity 400, price $40, 1982, value $50.

Battle Axe Limited Edition, Manufacturer - Battle Axe, Solingen, Germany, Pattern -Two blade Barlow, sheep foot and pen blades, quantity 1,200, price $30, 1981, value $40.

Battle Axe Mountaineers Are Always Free, Manufacturer - Battle Axe, Solingen, Germany, Pattern - 3-5/8" stockman, set of three, Mother-of-Pearl, stag, & bone handles, quantity 400, price $300, 1980, value $175.

Battle Axe Piedmont Airlines 30th Anniversary, Manufacturer - Battle Axe, Solingen, Germany, Pattern - 3" canoe, blue symbols on fiery pearl, quantity 400, price $65, 1978, value $55.

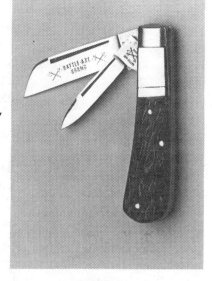

*Battle Axe
Limited Edition*

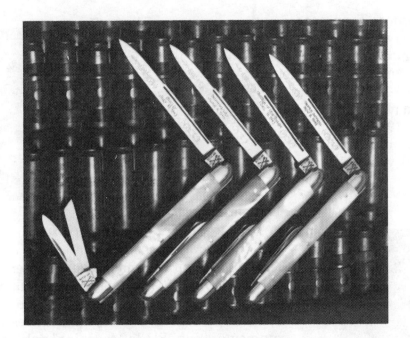

Battle Axe World War II

Battle Axe World War II, Manufacturer - Battle Axe, Solingen, Germany, Pattern - Set of four pearl whittlers, commemorates battles of Normandy, North Africa, Battle of the Bulge, and Sicily, quantity 300 sets, price $225, 1979, value $200

Battle Axe World War II, Manufacturer - Battle Axe, Solingen, Germany, Pattern - Two pair of pearl whittlers, commemorates battles of Okinawa, Iwo Jima, Pearl Harbor, and Guadalcanal, quantity 300 sets each, price $250 per pair, 1980, value $200 per pair.

Bear Creek Knives

Bear Creek Knives is a mark used by Taylor Cutlery of Kingsport, Tennessee.

Bear Creek - Stonewall Jackson and Robert E. Lee, Manufacturer- Taylor Cutlery, Pattern - 5-1/4" folding hunter, genuine stag handles, price $45, value $60.

Bear Creek - Tennessee, Kentucky and Virginia, Manufacturer - Taylor Cutlery, Pattern - sunfish, rosewood handle, quantity 1,000, price $60, 1977, value $65.

Bear Hunter - Tennessee Vols 100-Year Commemorative, Manufacturer - Bear Hunter, Pattern - 4-1/2" lockback, imitation ivory, color printing, 1990 football schedule on back side, gift box, 1990, value $15.

Bear MGC Shop at Home

Bear MGC Shop at Home, Manufacturer - Bear MGC, Pattern - 550 (Stag handle), 650 (Burnt bone handle), two blade folder, clip blade & razor blade, 4-1/8" closed, two separate knives commemorating "Blade Magazine" publisher Bruce Voyles's "The Knife Show" on Shop at Home television, etched blade, gift box, except for the handles both knives are identical, 1992, value $60 each. 100 of each made.

Bear MGC Talladega Superspeedway, Manufacturer - Bear MGC, Pattern - Model 554 two blade trapper, 4" closed, stag handle, 440 stainless steel, nickel-silver bolster, etched blade, serial numbered, quantity 1,000, price $69.99, 1992, value $69.99.

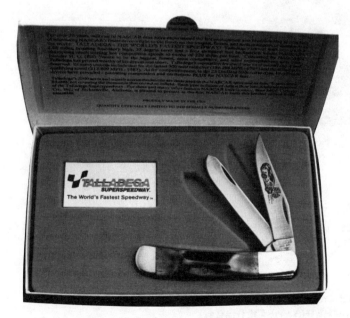

Bear MGC Talladega Superspeedway

Bear MGC Watkins Glen Commemorative

Bear MGC Watkins Glen Commemorative, Manufacturer - Bear MGC, Pattern - Model 554 two blade folding trapper, stag handle, etched blade, serial numbered, quantity 1,000, price $69.99, 1992, value $69.99.

Belknap Inc., The Colonel, Manufacturer - Belknap Inc., Pattern - Three blade stockman, Delrin handles, etched blade, "Primble" shield on handles, "Colonel" shield on handle, value $75. circia 1972.

Beretta Limited Edition, Manufacturer - Beretta, Pattern - 5-1/4" boot knife, serial numbered, comes with sheath and presentation case, quantity 500, price $94, 1984, value $100.

Beretta The Master Knifemaker's Series, Manufacturer - Beretta, Patterns:

(1) 7-1/8" folding lockback, 3 versions: engraved German silver, optional ebony or genuine ivory overlays, serialized, Gary Barnes designed, quantity 200, price $275, 1989, value $250.

(2) 15" Bowie, set of three, walnut handles, Jimmy Lile design, quantity 200, price $1,500, 1990, value $1,500.

(3) 11" skinning knife, set of three, walnut handles, Jimmy Lile design, quantity 200, price $1,500, 1990, value $1,500.

(4) 8-1/2" big 7 drop-point hunting knife, set of three, walnut handles, Jimmy Lile design, quantity 200, price $1,500, 1990, value $1,500.

(5) Lockback, bone handled, Jess Horn design, value $450.
(6) Jack Busfield interfram lockback, $550.00.

Blue Grass Series

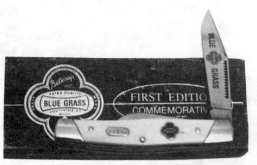
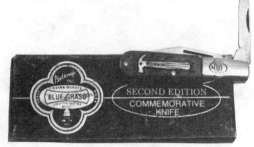

Forest Limited Edition, Manufacturer - Gutmann Cutlery, Pattern - One blade stockman, wooden display box, red bone handles, value $95.

Blue Grass Series, Manufacturer - Belknap Hardware Company, Patterns:
    (1) 3-1/2" two blade Stockman, antique finish, quantity 5,000, price $15, 1977, value $35.
    (2) 3-1/2" two blade Barlow, hammer shield, quantity 5,000, price $20, 1977, value $35.

    (3) 3-1/2" two blade Barlow, handsaw shield, quantity 5,000, price $20, 1977, value $35.
    (4) 3-1/2" two blade Stockman, axe shield, quantity 5,000, price $25, 1977, value $50.
    (6) 3-1/2" two blade Stockman, wood handles, screwdriver laser engraved on handle, quantity 750, price $25, value $25.

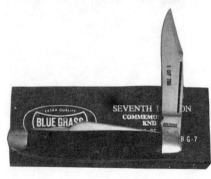

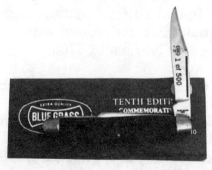

    (7) 3-1/2" two blade Stockman, wood handles, tape measure laser engraved on handle, quantity 750, price $25, value $25.
    (9) 3 1/2" two blade Stockman, wood handles, circular saw blade laser engraved on handle, quantity 500, price $25, value $25.
    (10) 3-1/2" two blade Stockman, wood handles, level laser engraved on handle, quantity 500, price $25, value $25.

Blue Grass Cutlery Limited Edition - The Scouts, Manufacturer - Winchester, Pattern - Two blade sleeveboard jack, Buffalo Bill Cody & Wild Bill Hickock etch, quantity 2,500, 1989, value $200.

Blue Ridge Knives Trophy Buck, Manufacturer - Buck, Pattern - 5" folding hunter, brown exotic wood handles, deep blade etch with 22K gold inlay, hardwood wall plaque, quantity 500, price $125, 1985, value $200.

Blue Ridge Knives Wild Turkey, Manufacturer - Buck, Pattern - 5" folding hunter, brown exotic wood handles, deep blade etch with 22K gold inlay, hardwood wall plaque, quantity 250, price $135, 1986, value $165.

Boker 1971 Year Knife, Manufacturer - Boker, Pattern - 7474 three blade stock, 2 shields, quantity 15,000, price $10.50, 1971, value $42.

Boker Wiss 1972 Commemorative, Manufacturer - Boker, Pattern - 3-1/2" round bolster equal end, black simulated handles, gold etched blade, two gold shields & "Tree Brand" emblem, quantity 12,000, price $11.95, 1972, value $55.

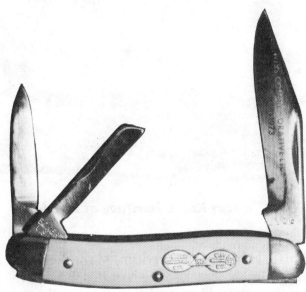

Boker 1972 Year Knife

Boker Wiss 1973 Commemorative, Manufacturer - Boker, Pattern - 5464 3-3/4" congress, black simulated handles with 2 red shields, four blades, quantity 18,000, price $16.95, 1973, value $44.

Boker 1974 Year Knife, Manufacturer - Boker, Pattern - 6063 4" stock, black simulated handles with 2 gold shields, three blades, quantity 18,000, price $19.95, 1974, value $40.

Boker 1975 Year Knife, Manufacturer - Boker, Pattern - 280 sternwheeler, three blade whittler, imitation pearl handle with shield, engraved sternwheeler illustration, serial numbered, etched master blade, quantity 20,000, price $21.95, 1975, value $30.

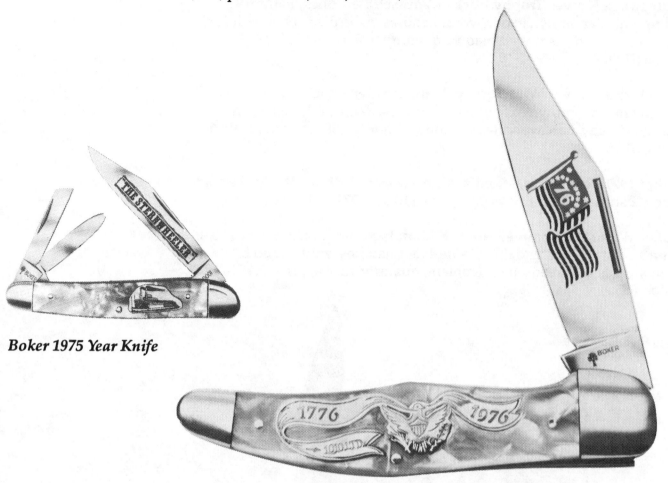

Boker 1975 Year Knife

Boker 1976 Year Knife, Heritage of Freedom

Boker 1976 Year Knife, Heritage of Freedom, Manufacturer - Boker, Pattern - 1010 folding hunter, cracked ice handles, boxed, (*Note: Beware of these because many of the celluloid handles have started pulling away from the handles in recent years, and sometimes the inlay in the handle falls off. This hurts the value.*) handles not warping $35, handles warping $15.

Boker 1977 Year Knife, Manufacturer - Boker, Pattern - American Indian 200 canoe, imitation pearl handle, etched blade, quantity 12,000, price $25, 1977, value $48.

Boker 1977 Year Knife

Boker 1978 Year Knife, The Hillbilly, Manufacturer - Boker, Pattern - 2525 hillbilly trapper, quantity 12,000, price $45, 1978, value $65.

Boker 1978 Year Knife, The Hillbilly

Boker 1979 Year Knife, Boker Hardware 1979 Commemorative, Manufacturer - Boker, Pattern - 5" folding 100 hunter lockback, wood handles and etched blades, quantity 20,000, price $52.95, 1979, Value $75.

Boker 1980 Year Knife, Boker Railroader 1980 Commemorative, Manufacturer - Boker, Pattern - 5" folding hunter, railroad etch, "Railroader" shield, quantity 8,000, price $40, 1980, value $100.

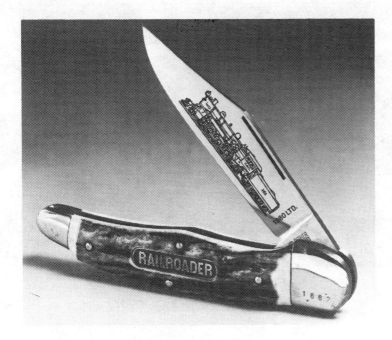

Boker 1980 Year Knife

Boker 1980 Year Knife, White Lightning, Manufacturer - Boker, Pattern - Bone trapper, quantity 10,00, price $40, 1980, value $55.

41

Boker 1981 Year Knife The Collector, Manufacturer - Boker, Pattern - 7474 4" long pull clip, etched "1869-1914", tang marked "Boker's-Cutlery Germany", boxed, 1981, quantity 10,000, price $45, 1981, value $50.

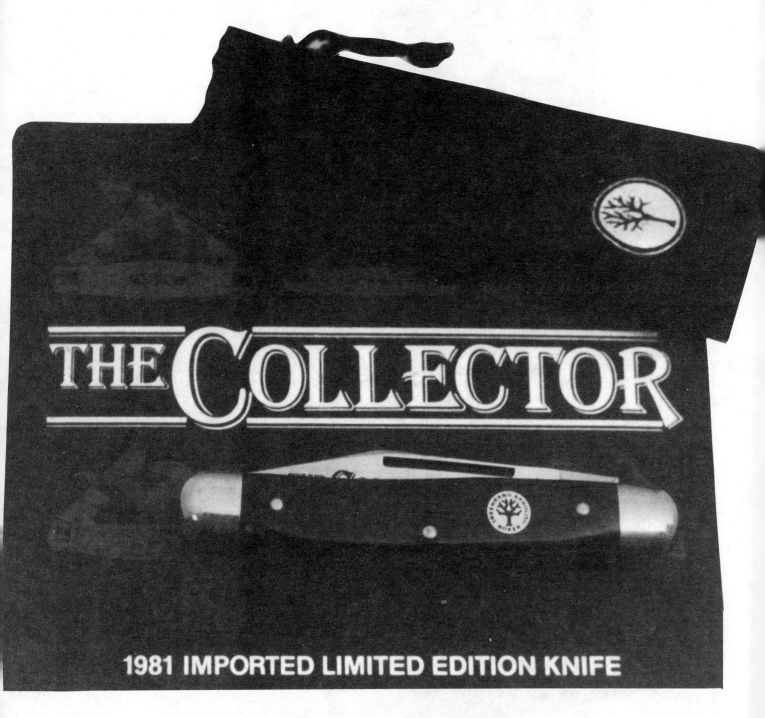

Boker 1981 Year Knife The Collector

Boker 1982 Year Knife, Boker Appalachian Trail 1982 Commemorative, Manufacturer - Boker, Pattern - 3-9/16" canoe, jigged rosewood handles, quantity 10,000, price $40, 1982, value $55.

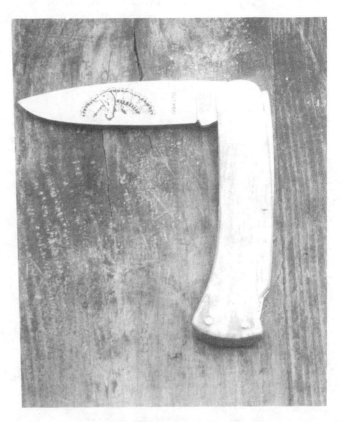

Boker 1983 Year Knife, The Farmboy

Boker 1984 Year Knife Old Tom

Boker 1983 Year Knife, The Farmboy, Manufacturer - Boker, Pattern - Two blade Barlow, etched blade, quantity 8,000, value $35.

Boker 1984 Year Knife Old Tom, Manufacturer - Boker, Pattern - 1000 one blade lockback, quantity 8,000, value $45.

Boker 1985 Year Knife, Boker Legend of Blackbeard, Manufacturer - Boker, Pattern - 2003 lockback hunter, white bone handles, inset "skull and crossbones" shield, treasure map etch on blade, quantity 4,100, price $110, 1985, value $150.

Boker 1985 Year Knife, Legend of Blackbeard

Boker 1986 Annual Knife, The Forty-Niner, Manufacturer - Boker, Pattern - 2525 trapper, two etched blades, brown bone handles, special shield, quantity 5,000, price $50, 1986, value $45.

Boker 1987 Year Knife, The Constitution, Manufacturer - Boker, Pattern - Four blade Congress, two sheepfoot blades, deep etched, quantity 8,000, price $60, 1987, value $35.

Boker 1988 Damascus Steel, Manufacturer - Boker, Pattern - custom boot knife, smooth bone handles, wood display box, 1988, value $250.

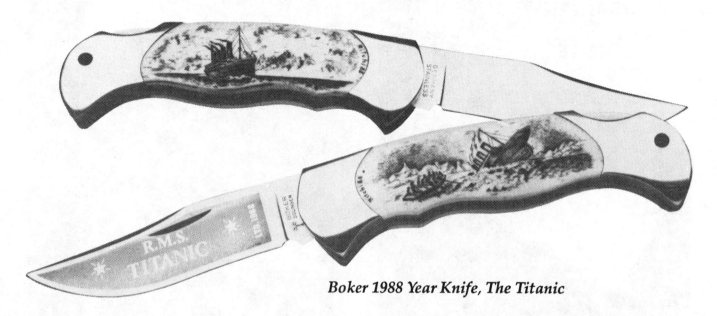

Boker 1988 Year Knife, The Titanic

Boker 1988 Year Knife, The Titanic, Manufacturer - Boker, Pattern - Lockback folding hunter, ivory composition handle, scrimshawed, wood display box, quantity 3,000, 1988, value $100.

Boker 1989 Year Knife, Spring Gobbler, Manufacturer - Boker, Pattern - Two blade trapper, laser engraved oak handles, quantity 3,000, 1989, value $45.

Boker 1989 Year Knife, The Graf Zeppelin, Manufacturer - Boker, Pattern - Two blade trapper, black composition handles, serial numbered, etched "Airship Graf Zeppelin", gift box with 1 Pfennig coin, quantity 3,000, 1989, value $42.

Boker American Truck Driver, Manufacturer - Boker, Pattern - Trapper, red pick bone handles, value $40.

Boker Bone Handled Set, Manufacturer - Boker, Pattern - Stockman, whittler, serpentine, and two congress, etched master blades, Boker shield, quantity 25,000, 1977, value $100 (set).

Boker Coal Miner Set, Manufacturer - Boker, Pattern - Three different patterns, medallions set into handles, quantity 8,000, price $125, value $150.

Boker Damascus Knife, Manufacturer - Boker, Pattern - Lockback, ivory handles, hand forged by Manford Sachse, 336 layer Damascus, quantity 300, 1980, value $390.

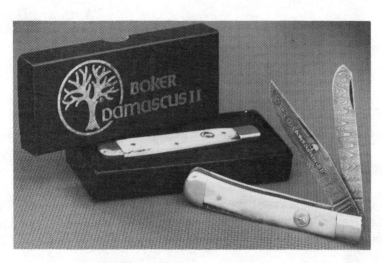

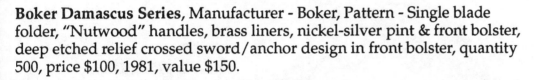

Boker Damascus Knife

Boker Damascus Series

Boker Damascus Series, Manufacturer - Boker, Pattern - Single blade folder, "Nutwood" handles, brass liners, nickel-silver pint & front bolster, deep etched relief crossed sword/anchor design in front bolster, quantity 500, price $100, 1981, value $150.

Boker East Meets West, Manufacturer - Boker, Pattern - Set of two stag trappers, gold plated blades, one is a one blade and one is a two blade, quantity 2,500, price $195, value $155.

Boker Great American Story Knives I: #1770, Sweet Land of Liberty, Manufacturer - Boker, Pattern - Large stock knife, Pilgrim and Map "Thirteen Colonies" etch, Great American Story Knives, quantity 10,000, price $11.95, 1974 , value $32.

Boker Great American Story Knives I: #1771, One Out of Many, Manufacturer -Boker, Pattern - Rounded bolster stock knife, "One out of Many" etch and shield showing the American eagle and the July 4, 1776 logo, Great American Story Knives, quantity 10,000, price $11.95, 1974, value $24.

Boker Great American Story Knives I: #1772, Manifest Destiny, Manufacturer - Boker, Pattern - Texas jack knife, Spanish Mission "The Alamo" etch, Great American Story Knives, quantity 10,000, price $11.95, 1974, value $19.95.

Boker Great American Story Knives I: #1773, Westward Ho!

Boker Great American Story Knives I: #1773, Westward Ho!, Manufacturer - Boker, Pattern - Large equal end jack knife, Conestoga Wagon "Prairie Schooner" etch, Great American Story Knives, quantity 10,000, price $11.95, 1974, value $19.95.

Boker Great American Story Knives I: #1774, The Melting Pot, Manufacturer - Boker, Pattern - Large stock knife, "Statue of Liberty" etch, Great American Story Knives, quantity 10,000, price $11.95, 1975, value $19.95.

Boker Great American Story Knives I: #1775, Dixie

Boker Great American Story Knives I: #1775, Dixie, Manufacturer - Boker, Pattern - Large congress, Confederate Soldier "Johnny Reb" etch, quantity 10,000, price $11.95, 1975, value $30.

Boker Great American Story Knives I: #1776, On to the Last Frontier, Manufacturer - Boker, Pattern - Large stock knife, Head-on Locomotives "The Golden Spike" etch, Great American Story Knives, quantity 10,000, price $11.95, 1975, value $19.95.

Boker Great American Story Knives I: #1777, Old Wild West, Manufacturer - Boker, Pattern - Large trapper's knife, set of two, Cowboy and Indian "Buffalo Bill & Sitting Bull" etch, Great American Story Knives, quantity 10,000, price $11.95, 1975, value $19.95.

Boker Great American Story Knives I: #1778, Rise to World Power, Manufacturer - Boker, Pattern - Large swell end jack knife, Sinking Battleship "Remember the Maine" etch, Great American Story Knives, quantity 10,000, price $11.95, 1975, value $20.

Boker Great American Story Knives I: #1778, Rise to World Power

Boker Great American Story Knives I: #1779, War to End All Wars, Manufacturer - Boker, Pattern - Large serpentine jack knife, Bi-Plane "Lafayette Escadrille" etch, Great American Story Knives, quantity 10,000, price $11.95, 1976, value $19.95.

Boker Great American Story Knives I: #1780, Dawn of the Atomic Age, Manufacturer - Boker, Pattern - Large stock knife, Atom "16 July 1945 – Alamagordo" etch, Great American Story Knives, quantity 10,000, price $11.95, 1976, value $19.95.

Boker Great American Story Knives I: #1781, 200 Years of Freedom

Boker Great American Story Knives I: #1781, 200 Years of Freedom Manufacturer - Boker, Pattern - Large stock knife, American Eagle "July 4, 1776" etch, Great American Stories, price $11.95,1974, value $18.

Boker Great American Story Knives II: #1782, Birth of Southern Industry, Manufacturer - Boker, Pattern - Congress, Cotton Gin "Cotton Gin" etch, Great American Stories, price $12.95, 1976, value $18.

Boker Great American Story Knives II: #1783, Westward Expansion, Manufacturer - Boker, Pattern - Trapper, map of Louisiana Purchase "Louisiana Purchase" etch, Great American Story Knives, quantity 6,000, price $14, 1976, value $18.

Boker Great American Story Knives II: #1783, Westward Expansion

Boker Great American Story Knives II: #1784, Blazing the Trail

Boker Great American Story Knives II: #1784, Blazing the Trail, Manufacturer - Boker, Pattern - Premium stock, Lewis & Clark "Lewis & Clark" etch, Great American Story Knives, quantity 6,000, price $14, 1976, value $18.

Boker Great American Story Knives II: #1785, American Proclamation, Manufacturer - Boker, Pattern - Texas jack, Monroe Doctrine Scroll "Monroe Doctrine" etch, Great American Story Knives, quantity 6,000, price $14, 1977, value $18.

Boker Great American Story Knives II: #1786, California Gold Rush, Manufacturer - Boker, Pattern - Premium stock, Panning for Gold at Sutters Mill "Sutters Mill" etch, Great American Story Knives, quantity 6,000, price $14, 1977, value $18.

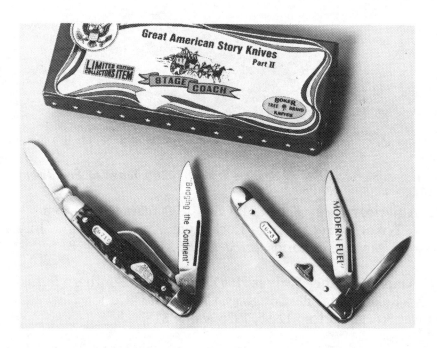

Boker Great American Story Knives II: #1787, Bridging the Continent

Boker Great American Story Knives II: #1788, Modern Fuel

Boker Great American Story Knives II: #1787, Bridging the Continent, Manufacturer -Boker, Pattern - Premium stock, Stage Coach "Stage Coach" etch, Great American Story Knives, quantity 6,000, price $18, 1977, value $18.

Boker Great American Story Knives II: #1788, Modern Fuel, Manufacturer - Boker, Pattern - Jack knife, Oil Derrick "Black Gold" etch, Great American Story Knives, quantity 6,000, price $14, 1977, value $18.

Boker Great American Story Knives II: #1789, Continental Mail Service

Boker Great American Story Knives II: #1789, Continental Mail Service, Manufacturer - Boker, Pattern - Congress, Pony Express Rider "Pony Express" etch, Great American Story Knives, quantity 6,000, price $18, 1977, value $28.

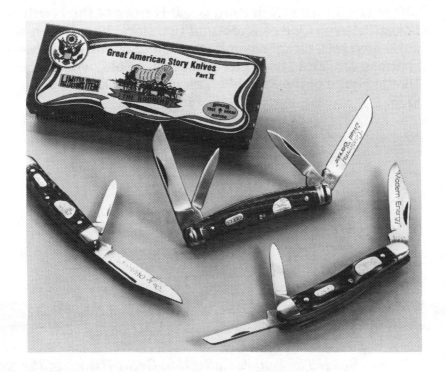

Boker Great American Story Knives II: Continental Mail Service, Modern Energy, On to Oklahoma

Boker Great American Story Knives II: #1790, Modern Energy, Manufacturer - Boker, Pattern - Whittler, First Hydro Electric Plant "Hydro Electricity" etch, Great American Story Knives, quantity 6,000, price $14, 1977, value $18.

Boker Great American Story Knives II: #1791, On to Oklahoma, Manufacturer - Boker, Pattern - Dogleg jack, Homesteaders "The Sooners" etch, Great American Story Knives, quantity 6,000, price $14, 1978, value $18.

Boker Great American Story Knives II: #1792, Revolution in Transportation, Manufacturer - Boker, Pattern - Premium stock, Henry Ford's Quadrocycle "Horseless Carriage" etch, Great American Story Knives, quantity 6,000, price $14, 1978, value $18.

Boker Great American Story Knives II: #1793, 200 Million Americans, Manufacturer - Boker, Pattern - Premium stock, map of Continental U.S.A. "One Nation" etch, Great American Story Knives, 1978, value $18.

Boker John Kennedy I, Manufacturer - Boker, Pattern - n\a, value $60.

Boker John Kennedy II, Manufacturer - Boker, Pattern - Congress, stag handles, quantity 1,200, value $60.

Boker Merrimac Famous Battles, Manufacturer - Boker, Pattern - Canoe, quantity 20,000, price $12, 1972, value $38.

Boker Storyteller Set, Manufacturer - Boker, Pattern - 3 knives: 4-1/8" two blade trapper, stag handle, etched "Jim Bridger", 3-11/16" three blade stock, smooth green bone handle, etched "Jesse Chisholm", 3-11/16" four blade congress, wood handle, etched "Davy Crockett", each has 3-1/8" shield, book shaped wood display, value $150.

Boker The Yankee Collection Great Heroes of the North, Manufacturer - Boker, Pattern - One congress and two stock, blue Delrin handles, serial numbered sets, nickel-silver bust emblem of one of the heroes—Lincoln, Sherman or Grant , deep etched, special shield, wood music box plays "Battle Hymn of the Republic", quantity 3,000, price $250, 1988, value $175.

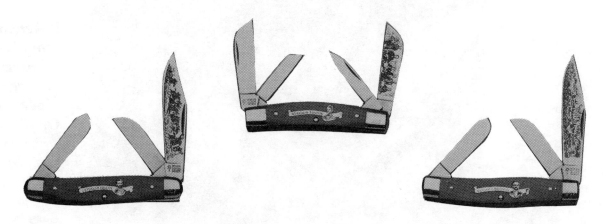

Boker The Yankee Collection Great Heroes of the North

Boker Wildlife Series, Bald Eagle, Manufacturer - Boker, Pattern - Stockman, laser-engraved oak handle, three blades-clip, spey, and sheepfoot, quantity 3,000, 1990, value $48.

Bowen Knife Co., The General - 1972 Commemorative, Manufacturer - Queen Cutlery, Pattern - 3-1/4" long blade stock, slant bolsters, hardwood handles, quantity 1,200, price $65, 1972, value $40.

Bowen Knife Co., The General

Brookfield Collector's Guild The American Eagle, Manufacturer - Gerber, Pattern - 5 1/4" hunter, etched eagle in flight, Cordia hardwood handles, quantity 3,000, price $195, 1982, value $200.

Browning USA Centennial 1878-1978

Browning USA Centennial 1878-1978, Manufacturer - Browning USA, Pattern - set of three: canoe, stockman, and lockback, all stag, etched, locking walnut display case, 1978, value $295.

Bryan, Skip Colorado Folding Hunter, Manufacturer - Skip Bryan, Pattern - Folding hunter, white bone handles, bullet shield, serial numbered, price $65, 1978, value $120.

Buck Commemoratives

Buck commemoratives are usually of good quality with top notch etchings, but are often priced at the upper end of the price range for comparative value and have not benefitted from the popularity enjoyed by Case and other more popular commemorative producers.

A notable exception to this is the elaborate David Yellowhorse knives produced by the Navajo artist of the same name, featuring inlaid handles and distinctive ornamentation.

If you follow Buck commemoratives, the easiest way is to obtain a Buck catalog each year since Buck rarely advertises their commemoratives in the knife media.

Buck Alaska's 25th (Black handles), Manufacturer - Buck, Pattern - Model 110 folding hunter, quantity 500, price$100, 1985, value $100.

Buck Alaska's 25th (Wine handles), Manufacturer - Buck, Pattern - Model 110 folding hunter, quantity 250, price $100, 1985, value $100.

Buck Al Buck's Signature, Manufacturer - Buck, Pattern - Model 110 folding hunter, Al's signature etched on blade, quantity 1,000, price $125, 1988, value $150. Autographed certificate included.

Buck America's Farmers, Manufacturer - Buck, Pattern - Model 110 folding hunter, quantity 500, price $125, 1987, value $120.

Buck Apple Blossom Festival, Manufacturer - Buck, Pattern - Model 103, quantity 25, price $225, 1988, value $200.

Buck Apple Blossom Festival, Manufacturer - Buck, Pattern - Model 110 folding hunter, quantity 100, price $100, 1984, value $85.

Buck Apple Blossom Festival, Manufacturer - Buck, Pattern - Model 119, quantity 20, price $225, 1986, value $200.

Buck Apple Blossom Festival, Manufacturer - Buck, Pattern - Model 501/503, quantity 50 sets, price $125, 1987, value $125.

Buck Arizona's 75th, Manufacturer - Buck, Pattern - Model 110 folding hunter, quantity 500, price $100, 1987, value $90.

Buck Bass, Large Mouth, Manufacturer - Buck, Pattern - Model 110 folding hunter, hardwood handles, gold filled blade etch, hardshell velveteen display box, quantity 250, value $100.

Buck Bear and Cubs, Manufacturer - Buck, Pattern - Model 110 folding hunter, quantity 1,500, price $100, 1985, value $100.

Buck Bicentennial, Manufacturer - Buck, Pattern - Cased sheath knife, etched blade and medallion, price $200, 1976, value $225.

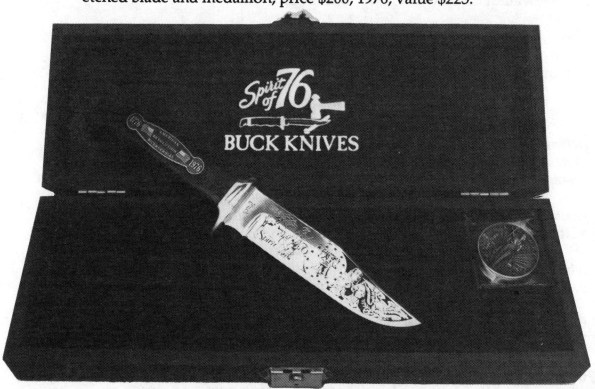

Buck Bicentennial

Buck Black Bear, Manufacturer - Buck, Pattern - Model 110 folding hunter, quantity 150, price $125, 1987, value $100.

Buck Brown Trout, Manufacturer - Buck, Pattern - Model 110 folding hunter, quantity 100, price $100, 1987, value $100.

Buck Bull Elk Bugling, Manufacturer - Buck, Pattern - Model 110 folding hunter, quantity 2,000, price $100, 1984, value $100.

Buck California Firefighters, Manufacturer - Buck, Pattern - Model 110 folding hunter, quantity 590+, price $100, 1983, value $90.

Buck California Highway Patrol, Manufacturer - Buck, Pattern - Model 110 folding hunter, quantity 900+, price $90, 1981, value $90.

Buck California State Knife, Manufacturer - Buck, Pattern - Custom model 112 Ranger designed by David Yellowhorse, handle inlaid with red coral, pearl, malachite, ironwood with brass bear inlay, engraved brass bolster, serial numbered, wood display box, value $265.

Buck Canadian Loon with Coin, Manufacturer - Buck, Pattern -Model 500, quantity 250, price $175, 1988, value $125.

Buck Colt, Manufacturer - Buck, Pattern - Clip blade stockman, quantity 5,500, price $65, 1978, value $80.

Buck Colt Firearms, Manufacturer - Buck, Pattern - Model 500, quantity 350, price $78, 1984, value $100.

Buck Colt Firearms Logo, Manufacturer - Buck, Pattern - Model 500, quantity 300, price $86, 1986, $100.

Buck Cowboy Scene, Manufacturer - Buck, Pattern - Model 110 folding hunter, quantity 25, price $150, 1986, value $100.

Buck Custom Series, Manufacturer - Buck, Pattern - Set of three standard Buck models, handmade by David Yellowhorse, turquoise and other native Southwest stones with brass and wood, 704 coyotes, 112 horses, 102 buffalos, 1987, value (704) $150, (102) $250, (112) $250.

Buck Dallas P.D. Badge, Manufacturer - Buck, Pattern - Model 110, folding hunter, quantity 290+, price $95, 1982, value $90.

Buck David Yellowhorse American Flag Knife, Manufacturer - Buck, Pattern - Custom model 112 Ranger, value $300.

Buck David Yellowhorse Confederate Flag Knife, Manufacturer - Buck, Pattern - Custom model 112 Ranger, value $300.

Buck David Yellowhorse "Cuthair", Manufacturer - Buck, Pattern - Custom model 112 Ranger designed by David Yellowhorse to honor his grandfather who made the historic long walk, brass guard and pommel, handle made of pearl, turquoise, ironwood and coral, brass inlay of "Cuthair", chipped flint steel blade designed by Bill Cheatham, ironwood with brass, serial numbered, wood display box , value $750.

Buck Deer Country, Manufacturer - Buck, Pattern - Deer scene in pewter for handles, quantity 1,500, price $125, 1983, value $100.

Buck Dog Pointing Quail, Manufacturer - Buck, Pattern - Model 110 folding hunter, quantity 250, price $125, 1987, value $100.

Buck Ducks in Flight I, Manufacturer - Buck, Pattern - Model 500, quantity 2,000, price $80, 1984, value $70.

Buck Ducks in Flight II, Manufacturer - Buck, Pattern - Model 500 Duke, wood handles, gold Aurum etch, leather sheath, gift box, quantity 1,500, price $90, 1984, value $85.

Buck Ducks Unlimited (Canada), Manufacturer - Buck, Pattern - Model 112, quantity 1,000+, price $125, 1988, value $120.

Buck Ducks Unlimited 50th Anniversary, Manufacturer - Buck, Pattern - Model 112, quantity 5,000+, price $125, 1987, value $115.

Buck Ducks Unlimited, Manufacturer - Buck, Pattern - Model 119, quantity 100, 1983, value $100.

Buck Ducks Unlimited Set of two, Manufacturer - Buck, Pattern - Model 110 folding hunter & model 505, quantity 4,000, price $150.85, 1985, value $135.

Buck Eagle with Fish, Manufacturer - Buck, Pattern - Model 110 folding hunter, quantity 2,000, price $125, 1988, value $100.

Buck Fisherman and Bass, Manufacturer - Buck, Pattern - Model 501, quantity 500, price $85, 1986, value $90.

Buck Flushing Quail, Manufacturer - Buck, Pattern - Model 110 folding hunter, quantity 750, price $100, 1988, value $95.

Buck Flying Eagle, Manufacturer - Buck, Pattern - Model 500, quantity 1,000, price $95, 1987, value $100.

Buck Flying Geese, Manufacturer - Buck, Pattern - Model 110 folding hunter, quantity 1,000, price $100, 1984, value $100.

Buck Four Generations, Manufacturer - Buck, Pattern - 10" Bowie, etched portraits of the four generations of the Buck family, quantity 1,500, price $519.98, 1989, value $400.

Buck Frontiersman (W. Va.), Manufacturer - Buck, Pattern - Model 110 folding hunter, quantity 250, price $100, 1987, value $90.

Buck Game Series Limited Edition, Manufacturer - Buck, Pattern - Model 110 folding hunter, price $60, 1978, value $65.

Buck Game Series Limited Edition, Manufacturer - Buck, Pattern - Model 112, price $50, 1978, value $60.

Buck Game Series Limited Edition, Manufacturer - Buck, Pattern - Model 501, quantity 200, price $45, 1978, value $40.

Buck Game Series Limited Edition, Manufacturer - Buck, Pattern - Model 402, quantity 50, price $110, 1979, value $125.

Buck Game Series Limited Edition, Manufacturer - Buck, Pattern - Model 401, quantity 100, price $125, 1979, value $145.

Buck Geronimo Presentation Dagger, Manufacturer - Buck, Pattern - Dagger, genuine stag handles, gold etched, nickel silver guard, shield, gift box, quantity 2,000, price $450, 1985, value $250.

Buck "Good Luck!", Manufacturer - Buck, Pattern - Model 535, "Good Luck" etched in gold, price $30, value $35.

Buck Grazing Deer, Manufacturer - Buck, Pattern - Model 110 folding hunter, quantity 100, 1988, value $90.

Buck Grazing Deer (Stag), Manufacturer - Buck, Pattern - Model 500 Duke, gold Aurum etch, quantity 1,000, price $125, 1988, value $100.

Buck Grazing Deer (Wood), Manufacturer - Buck, Pattern - Model 500 Duke, gold Aurum etch, wood handles, leather sheath, value $75.

Buck Grouse, Manufacturer - Buck, Pattern - Model 500 Duke, gold Aurum etch, leather sheath, quantity 150, price $100, 1987, value $75.

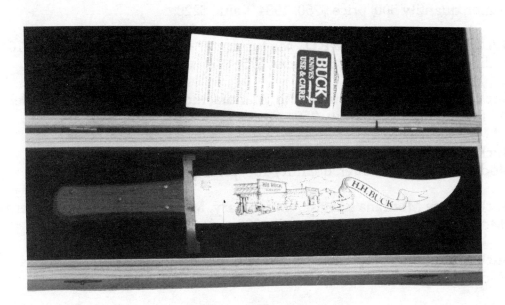

Buck H.H. Buck

Buck H.H. Buck, Manufacturer - n\a, Pattern - 15" Bowie, depicts H.H. Buck in his Kansas blacksmith shop around 1900, value $300.

Buck H.H. Buck's Smithy, Manufacturer - Buck, Pattern - Model 110 folding hunter, wood handles, gold filled etch, serial numbered, walnut wall plaque, quantity 1,500, price $125, 1989, value $120.

Buck Hastin Naat'aani Navajo Chief, Manufacturer - Buck, Pattern - Custom model 112 Ranger designed by David Yellowhorse, chipped flint steel blade, handle inlaid with onyx, pearl, turquoise, ironwood with brass, serial numbered, wood display box, value $400.

Buck Idaho's 100th, Manufacturer - Buck, Pattern - Model 110 folding hunter, quantity 500, price $125, 1988, value $90.

Buck Iditarod Race, Manufacturer - Buck, Pattern - Model 525, pewter handles, quantity 25,000, price $65, 1986, value $40.

Buck Iditarod Race, Manufacturer - Buck, Pattern - Model 110 folding hunter, quantity 3, price $125, 1987, value $90.

Buck Knives 25th Anniversary, Manufacturer - Buck, Pattern - Model 110 folding hunter, quantity 2,500, price $125, 1986, value $110.

Buck Loon On Nest, Manufacturer - Buck, Pattern - Folding hunter, gold filled Aurum blade etch, wood handles, oak display box, genuine marble lid picturing gamebird, quantity 500, value $110.

Buck Loon On The Water, Manufacturer - Buck, Pattern - Model 110 folding hunter, marbleized lid on wood box, quantity 500, price $160, 1989, value $110.

Buck Mastodon (Ivory), Manufacturer - Buck, Pattern - Model 110 folding hunter, quantity 500, price $250, 1984, value $220.

Buck Mission, San Diego P.D., Manufacturer - Buck, Pattern - Model 110 folding hunter, quantity 350+, price $75, 1981, value $60.

Buck Missouri Conservation 50th, Manufacturer - Buck, Pattern - Model 110 folding hunter, quantity 250+, price $125, 1987, value $90.

Buck Montana's 100th Anniversary, Manufacturer - Buck, Pattern - Model 110 folding hunter, quantity 100, price $125, 1989, value $90.

Buck Moose Montana's 100th Anniversary, Manufacturer - Buck, Pattern - Model 110 folding hunter, quantity 200, price $100, 1987, value $90.

Buck Mountain Sheep Grand Slam Set, Manufacturer - Buck, Pattern - Model 501, quantity 2,500, price $450, 1982, value $300.

Buck Mustang, Manufacturer - Buck, Pattern - Model 701, quantity 5,500, price $68, 1979, value $80.

Buck New Mexico's 75th Anniversary, Manufacturer - Buck, Pattern - Model 110 folding hunter, quantity 200, price $100, 1987, value $90.

Buck North Dakota's 100th Anniversary, Manufacturer - Buck, Pattern - Model 110 folding hunter, quantity 250+, price $100, 1988, value $90.

Buck Paul Revere "Old North Church", Manufacturer - Buck, Pattern - Model 500, quantity 350, price $275, 1988, value $200.

Buck Pewter Handle Deer, Manufacturer - Buck, Pattern - Model 110 folding hunter, quantity 1,500, price $100, 1984, value $100.

Buck Pewter Handle Eagle, Manufacturer - Buck, Pattern - Model 110 folding hunter, quantity 300, price $100, 1984, value $100.

Buck Phoenix Fire Department, Manufacturer - Buck, Pattern - Model 110 folding hunter, quantity 250+, price $75, 1986, value $75.

Buck Pony, Manufacturer - Buck, Pattern - Model 705, quantity 5,500, price $45, 1979, value $48.

Buck Quail and Dog, Manufacturer - Buck, Pattern - Model 110 folding hunter, quantity 250, price $100, 1986, value $100.

Buck Raccoon, Manufacturer - Buck, Pattern - Model 501, quantity 250, price $70, 1982, value $55.

Buck Redbone Set, Manufacturer - Buck, Pattern - Model 301 stockman, 303 cadet, 305 lancer, 309 companion, original "hammer, bolt and bolt" shield, red bone handles, serial numbered, deluxe knife pack, quantity 500, price $149.99, 1990, value $150.

Buck Red Fox, Manufacturer - Buck, Pattern - Model 110 folding hunter, quantity 150, price $125, 1987, value $110.

Buck Republic Studios, Manufacturer - Buck, Pattern - Model 110 folding hunter, quantity 100+, price $75, 1986, value $75.

Buck Red Tail Hawk, Manufacturer - Buck, Pattern - Model 110 folding hunter, quantity 750, price $125, 1988, value $100.

Buck Sabretooth, Manufacturer - Buck, Pattern - Model 501, ivory, quantity 500, price $250, 1984, value $200.

Buck San Francisco Cable Car, Manufacturer - Buck, Pattern - Model 505, quantity 250, price $65, 1985, value $48.

Buck Silver Anniversary of the Folding Hunter, Manufacturer - Buck, Pattern - Model 110 folding hunter, quantity 2,500, price $47.80, 1986, value $50.

Buck Silver Anniversary of the Ranger, Manufacturer - Buck, Pattern - Model 112 Ranger, quantity 2,500, price $45.40, 1986, value $48.

Buck South Dakota's 100th Anniversary, Manufacturer - Buck, Pattern - Model 110 folding hunter, quantity 200+, price $100, 1988, value $90.

Buck Sports Afield 100th Anniversary, Manufacturer - Buck, Pattern - Model 103, set of two, quantity 100, price $125, 1987, value $75.

Buck Sportsman's Paradise, Manufacturer - Buck, Pattern - Model 110 folding hunter, quantity 250, price $100, 1987, value $85.

Buck Statue of Liberty Commemoratives

Buck Statue of Liberty Commemoratives, Manufacturer - Buck, Pattern - (1) Model 500 folder, walnut handles, etched blade, Statue of Liberty shield & plaque, (2) Model 525 cast-pewter-handled, quantity (1) 2,500, (2) 15,000, 1986, value (1) $95, (2) $20.

Buck Stonewall Jackson, Manufacturer - Buck, Pattern - Model 110 folding hunter, quantity 250, price $100, 1988, value $100.

Buck Texas's 150th Anniversary, Manufacturer - Buck, Pattern - Model 110 folding hunter, quantity 500, price $110, 1987, value $100.

Buck Texas State Knife, Manufacturer - Buck, Pattern - Custom model 112 ranger design by David Yellowhorse, handle inlaid with red coral, pearl, turquoise, ironwood, brass state outline inlay, sculptured brass bolsters, serial numbered, wood display box, value $350.

Buck Trophy Buck, Manufacturer - Buck, Pattern - Brown wood handles, quantity 500, price $80, 1985, value $200.

Buck Trophy White Tail Deer, Manufacturer - Buck, Pattern - Model 110 folding hunter, quantity 500, price $125, 1986, value $100.

Buck Two Bucks Fighting, Manufacturer - Buck, Pattern - Model 110 folding hunter, quantity 700, price $100, 1985, value $100.

Buck Two Ducks On Pond, Manufacturer - Buck, Pattern - Model 110 folding hunter, quantity 250, price $125, 1988, value $100.

Buck Two Turkeys (W. Va.), Manufacturer - Buck, Pattern - Model 110 folding hunter, quantity 1,000, price $80, 1986, value $95.

Buck U.S.S. Constitution , Manufacturer - Buck, Pattern - Model 500 Duke, wood handles, gold Aurum etch, leather sheath, gift box, value $47.

Buck Vietnam Memorial, Manufacturer - Buck, Pattern - Model 110 folding hunter, quantity 100, price $100, 1986, value $100.

Buck Virginia's 200th Anniversary, Manufacturer - Buck, Pattern - Model 110 folding hunter, quantity 250, price $125, 1987, value $90.

Buck White House 200th Anniversary, Manufacturer - Buck, Pattern - Model 531 one blade folder, gold etched blade depicts White House as it looked in 1877, serial numbered in gift box, quantity 500, 1992, value $130.

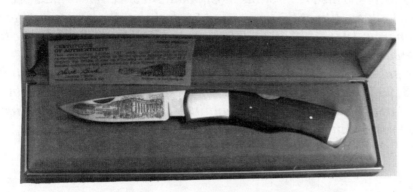

Buck White House 200th Anniversary

Buck White Water Canoeing, Manufacturer - Buck, Pattern - Model 112, quantity 2,500, price $90, 1986, value $90.

Buck Whitetail Deer Herd, Manufacturer - Buck, Pattern - Model 110 folding hunter, quantity 1,500, price $90, 1984, value $100.

Buck Wild Turkey, Manufacturer - Buck, Pattern - Model 110 folding hunter, 5" deep etched blade, 22k gold inlay of wild turkey in flight, serial numbered, certificate of authenticity, walnut case, quantity 500, price $79.95, 1985, value $100.

Buck Wildlife Series: Canadian Geese, Manufacturer - Buck, Pattern - Folding hunter, gold filled Aurum blade etch, wood handles, oak display box, marblized lid picturing gamebird, quantity 1,000, value $110.

Buck Wildlife Series: Mallard Ducks, Manufacturer - Buck, Pattern -110 Folding hunter, gold filled Aurum blade etch, wood handles, oak display box, marblied lid picturing gamebird, quantity 500, value $110.

Buck Wildlife Series: Pheasants , Manufacturer - Buck, Pattern - 110 folding hunter, gold filled Aurum blade etch, wood handles, oak display box, marblized lid picturing gamebird, quantity 500, value $150.

Buck Wildlife Series: Turkeys, Manufacturer - Buck, Pattern - Folding hunter, gold filled Aurum blade etch, wood handles, oak display marblized lid picturing gamebird, quantity 1,000, value $150.

Buck World Record Bass, Manufacturer - Buck, Pattern - Model 110 folding hunter, quantity 500, $95, 1988, value $90.

Buck Yearling, Manufacturer - Buck, Pattern - Model 709, quantity 5,500, price $47, 1979, value $52.

Bulldog Brand Knives

Bulldog knives are entirely limited edition knives but few are commemoratives. This is one of the most popular collectible brands because of both the high quality of the knives and the fact that the knives were out of production from 1986 until 1993. It is rare for a Bulldog run to be more than 300. An update on Bulldog prices is included regularly in the knife collectors publication Edges *(Krause Publications, 700 East State Street, Iola, WI 54990-001). The Bulldog trademark was purchased in 1993 by the James F. Parker Trust, which was planning to put Bulldog brand knives back into production.*

Bulldog Knife Co. Lumberjack, Manufacturer - Bulldog Knife Co., Pattern - Set of two stockman, blade etch "Lumberjack", diamond shield, value $90. *(A complete listing of Bulldog prices, values, and patterns can be found in the Appendix to this book.)*

Bulldog Knife Co. Oktoberfest, Manufacturer - Bulldog Knife Co., Pattern - Two 3-5/8" three blade stockmans, handles: red sparkley, celluloid, and antique marble, etched master blade, beer stein shield 300 each handle, price $64.95, 1984, value $80. *(See Appendix for further information)*

Bulldog Knife Co. Lumberjack and Peacocks

Bulldog Knife Co. Oktoberfest

Bulldog Knife Co. Pit Bulls, Manufacturer - Bulldog Knife Co., Pattern-n/a, Pearl handle, clip or spear blade, engraving on pearl, quantity 300 sets, 1983, value $300 set. (*See Appendix for further information*)

Bulldog Knife Co. Saddle Tramp, Manufacturer - Bulldog Knife Co., Pattern - 3-3/4" gunstock stockman, stag handles, 3 blade, square bolsters, heart design on shield, "Saddle Tramp" etched on blade, quantity 300, price $23.50, 1982, value $100. (*See Appendix for further information*)

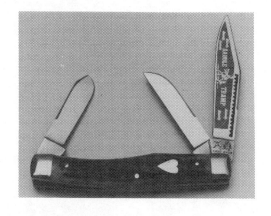

Bulldog Knife Co. Saddle Tramp

Bulldog Knife Co. The Henry Repeater Series, Manufacturer - Bulldog Knife Co., Pattern-n/a, set of two, quantity 600, price $140, value $200. (*See Appendix for further information*)

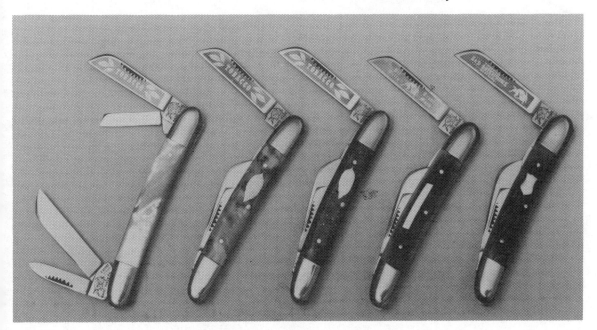

Bulldog Knife Co. Tobacco Congress

Bulldog Knife Co. Tobacco Congress, Manufacturer - Bulldog Knife Co., *See Appendix for further information*

Byars, Lawrence & Associates Captain Jack Hays, Manufacturer - Jack W. Crain, Pattern - 15-3/4" Bowie, history of Hays etched, quantity 20, price $2,000, 1984, value $2,000.

C

Camillus 115th Year Anniversary, Manufacturer - Camillus, Pattern - 4-1/2" double lockback trapper, stag handle, anniversary etching and etch of Camillus factory, Value $20.

Camillus American Wildlife Series 1st Edition, Manufacturer - Camillus,

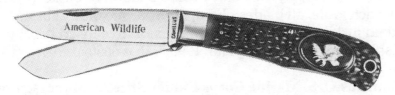

Camillus American Wildlife Series 1st Edition

Pattern - 4-1/2" folding knives, four knife set, Delrin handles (#10 A,B,C,D), 1976, value $50.

Camillus American Wildlife Series 2nd Edition, Manufacturer - Camillus, Pattern - 4-1/2" folding knives, four knife set, Delrin handles (#10 E,F,G,H), 1977, value $50.

Camillus American Wildlife Series 3rd Edition, Manufacturer - Camillus, Pattern - 3-7/8" muskrat with guthook, four knife set, Turkish clip blade, Delrin handles (#17 A,B,C,D), 1978, value $32.

Camillus American Wildlife Series 4th Edition, Manufacturer - Camillus, Pattern - 11" fillet and 5" folding knife, two knife set, Delrin handles (#1006, #32), 1979, value $50.

Camillus American Wildlife Series 5th Edition, Manufacturer - Camillus, Pattern - 4-3/4" lockbacks, four knife set, recessed thumb-lock, Delrin handles (#11AP, BP, CP, DP), 1980, value $40.

Camillus Buford Pusser (#1450), Manufacturer - Camillus, Pattern - 1123, blade etch, special shield, special packaging, quantity 5,000, price $50, 1976, value $100.

Camillus CCC1 30-30 Limited edition knife, based on a two blade bone handled pattern Remington bullet style muskrat. $75.00. $100.

Camillus CCC2 1992 $75.00.

Camillus CCC3 1993 Texas toothpick, cartdridge shield $75.00.

Camillus Centennial, Manufacturer - Camillus, Pattern - No. 100, 3" pen, Delrin handles contain an engraved jewelers "gold" shield, price $22.50, 1976, value $24.

Camillus "Remember Pearl Harbor", Manufacturer - Camillus, Pattern - U.S. Navy Mark 2 Combat Knife, high luster blued finish with 18k gold inlay of the USS Arizona, appropriate legend and listing of Pear Harbor Ships, value $55.

Camillus Rimfire classic series. Two blade pen knife with a .22 rifle style shield. delrin handles. 3" pen knife. 1992 Limited edition. Retail $26.95. Value $19.95.

Camillus Rimfire classic series II. .22 Bullet shield, delrin handles, trapper pattern. Limited edition. Retail $26.00 Value $19.95

Camillus U.S. Armed Forces, Manufacturer - Camillus, Pattern - Set of 4: (1) U.S. Air Force Pilot survival knife, 5" blade, (2) U. S. Marines fighting knife, 5" blade, (3) U.S. Navy Mark 2 knife, 7" blade, (4) U.S. Army Mark 3 trench knife, all blades blued, appropriate official branch of service seal inlaid in 18k gold on blade, commemorative insert brochure, wooden display case with brass plate, 1990, value $650.

Camillus U. S. Marine Corps Raider Stiletto, Manufacturer - Camillus, Pattern - 12-1/8" stiletto, gun blued double edge blade, 18K gold etch, pewter handle, oak and glass display case, quantity 2,000, 1990, value $200.

Cargill Limited Edition, Manufacturer - Cripple Creek, Pattern - Two blade canoe, 3-1/2" closed, stag handles, buckeye shield, quantity 100, price $125, value $150.

Case

Case is probably the king of commemorative/limited edition knives. They were among the first and always the most popular. For the commemorative collector there is a constant supply and ready demand when it comes time to sell Case commemoratives.

Case is one of the few brands you can find commonly traded among antique knife collectors.

The disadvantage to commemorative collectors is that, while sometimes you can find a commemorative underpriced on the table of an antique knife dealer who has taken it in on trade or received one when purchasing an entire collection, if he has a Case commemorative the odds are he will know well what it is worth.

Case commemoratives flooded the market when the company came into financial difficulties in 1989-1990 (and changed ownership—at this writing, Zippo of Bradford, Pa. has issued a letter of intent to purchase Case). In 1991 assets of Case were purchased by a new company and the leftover inventories were closed out at a greatly discounted price. This was an opportunity for commemorative collectors to buy certain Case commemoratives at below wholesale distributor cost, and while this had dampened the appreciation of knives made in that era, it is likely that in the future they have the potential to reclaim some of their lost glory in the eyes of collectors.

In addition to the regularly issued Case commemoratives, Case has also granted a license to Parkers Knife Collectors Service to produce knives under the Case classic series, featuring antique patterns with adaptations of the old tang marks, including an extensive line imported from Germany with many old Case tang marks. See the appendix at the back of this book for information on Case Stag Sets.

Knives commemorating race car figures, especially those of NASCAR drivers and themes, have been a new segment of collecting that showed some of the most aggressive growth values in the 1980s. See the appendix for more information.

Case 5th Anniversary of Quail Unlimited Grand Slam, Manufacturer - Case, Pattern - Trapper, "The Bob White" etched on blade, quantity 500, 1986, value $50.

Case 35th Anniversary of Dixie Gun Works, Inc., Manufacturer - Case, Pattern - Two blade lockback, "Dixie Gun Works, Inc. 35 years 1954-1989" etched on blades, 1989, value $40.

Case 50th Anniversary Great Smoky Mtn. National Park, Manufacturer - Case, Pattern - Single blade mini-trapper, handled with imitation smoked pearl, price $30, value $45.

Case 50th Anniversary of Pearl Harbor, Manufacturer - Case, Pattern - 9294 gunboat canoe, imitation pearl handles, surgical steel blades, etched blade, display box, quantity 2,000, 1991, value $185.

Case 5th Anniversary of Quail Unlimited Grand Slam

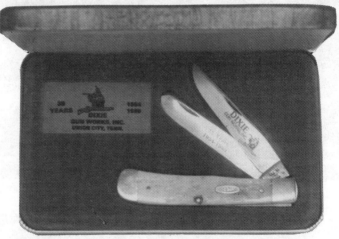

Case 35th Anniversary of Dixie Gun Works, Inc.

Case 50th Anniversary of Pearl Harbor

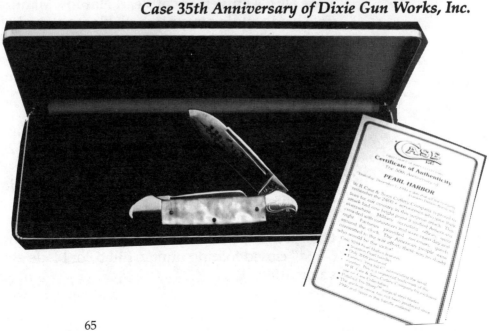

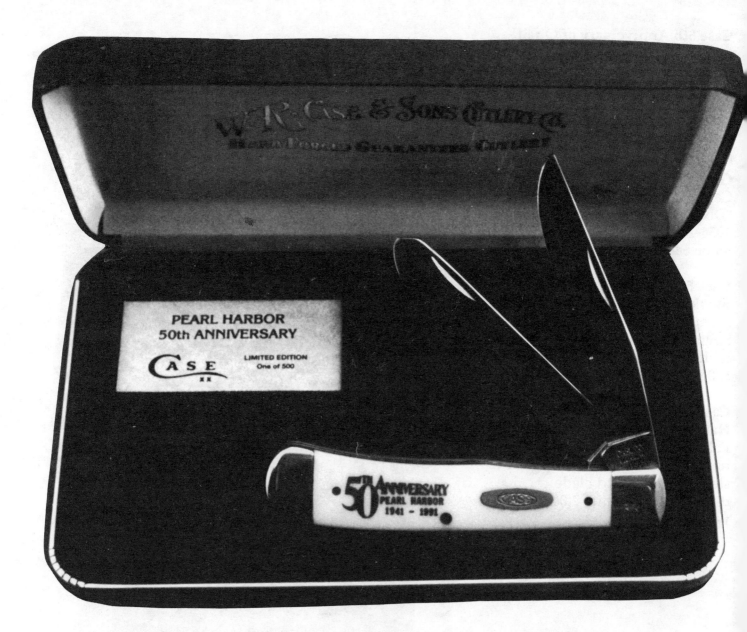

Case 50th Anniversary of Pearl Harbor

Case 50th Anniversary of Pearl Harbor, Manufacturer - Case, Pattern - Two blade folding trapper, both blades etched with commemorative designs, 50th anniversary logo on handle, quantity 500, 1991, $75.

Case 60 years of Ace Hardware1924-1984, Manufacturer - Case, Pattern - Stag handle, price $85, 1984, value $75.

Case 75th Anniversary Canoe Set, Manufacturer - Case, Pattern - Stag canoes, set of three, 52131, 53131, 5394, price $265, 1980, value $400.

Case 80th Anniversary, Manufacturer - Case, Pattern - Stag Bowie, low serial numbers, price $165, value $250.

Case 80th Anniversary Folding Hunter, Manufacturer - Case, Pattern - 5-1/4" closed folding hunter, full color blade etch, glass shadow box, value $100.

Case 150th Anniversary of the Battle of the Alamo, Manufacturer - Case, Pattern - Western style Bowie, wood handle, etched blade, quantity 3,000, 1988, value $200.

Case 200th Anniversary of Nation's First President, Manufacturer - Case, Pattern - 21050 foldling hunter, wood handles, photo etch of George Washington on blade, quantity 3,000, 1989, value $80.

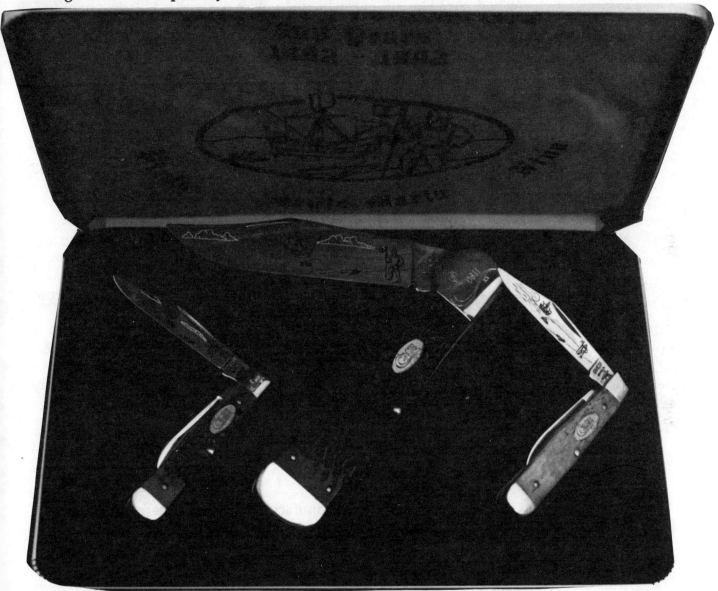

Case 500th Anniversary of Discovery of America, Manufacturer - Case, Pattern - (1) DR6 1050 large single blade coke bottle, (2) Two 6225 1/2 smaller coke bottle, Jigged bone handles, surgical steel blades, etched blade, comes in a deluxe jewelry box with a certificate of authenticity, quantity 2,000, 1992, value $225.

Case 1982 World's Fair, Manufacturer - Case, Pattern - 82079, quantity 5,000, price $45, 1982, value $56.

Case 1989 SEC Champs University of Alabama, Manufacturer - Case, Pattern - 6240 dogleg trapper, red pick bone handles, color etched, serial numbered, display box, 1989, value $100.

Case 1990 Presidential Set, Manufacturer - Case, Pattern - Set of three, BL06263, WS6220, R6333, blue pick bone, red pick bone, white smoothbone handles, etched individually: "Eisenhower", "Roosevelt", and "Washington", serial numbered, display box 1990, value $120.(*Priced individually under separate listings*)

Case Ace Fastener, Manufacturer - Case, Pattern - (1) 31048 SH R SSP, etched "Ace Florist", sheep blade in place of standard blade, quantity 500 each, 1979.value $50, (2) 61011 etched "Ace Pruner", value $25, (3) 12031 LHR etched "Ace Pruner-Lock", value $25.

Case African Safari Set, Manufacturer - Case, Pattern -Two fixed blade stag handled knives, Etched with gold & green inks, small knife depicts prowling lion and large knife portrays elephant, quantity 500, price $149.99, 1986, value $250. (*This is a Case set made for Remington Shavers*)

Case Alabama Cutlery Company, Manufacturer - Case, Pattern - 6205R, light brown jigged bone handles, quantity 5,000, 1981, value $40.

Case Alaska Commemorative Sodbuster - Alaska Pipeline, Manufacturer - Case, Pattern - P138LSS, quantity 500, price $135, value $150.

Case All Seasons, Inc. (The Acorn Shop, Gatlinburg, TN, Manufacturer - Case, Pattern - 3244, quantity 1,500, 1976, value $20.

Case American Blade Magazine, Manufacturer - Case, Pattern - P172, ebony handles, "Hand Made USA" stamped on pile side, P172 stamp omitted, original order 500 but handle material not obtainable, quantity 50, 1977, value $600.

Case American Brands Executives, Manufacturer - Case, Pattern - 82033 with letter opener, genuine mother of pearl handles, quantity 60, 1980, value $85.

Case American Spirit Set, Manufacturer - Case , Pattern - Bowie hunter and 5165 folding hunter, price $145, Bicentennial set, 1976, value $550.

Case American Trucker, Manufacturer - Case, Pattern - 3240 dogleg trapper, yellow handles, color engraved, etched, serial numbered, hardshell display case, value $40.

Case Apollo II 20th Anniversary, Manufacturer - Case, Pattern - Astronaut's knife, white space age handles, etched, serial numbered, deluxe gray moonscape wall plaque, value $200.

Case Appaloosa Peanut, Manufacturer - Case, Pattern - A6220, price $20, 1978, value $38.

Case Appaloosa Set, Manufacturer - Case, Pattern - Set of five: A62009 1/2 Barlow, A6235 1/2, A6208, A62042, A62033, quantity 250, 1980, value $125.

Case Astronaut Knife, First Model, Manufacturer - Case, Pattern - 11"
Bowie, wood display, quantity 2,494, 1965, value $350.

**Case Astronaut's Knife 25th
Anniversary,** Manufacturer -
Case, Pattern -11-1/2", etched
on blade, quantity 1,000, price
$250, value $150.

Case Atocha Commemorative,
Manufacturer - Case, Pattern -
Coke bottle with clip blade,
buffalo horn handles, serial
numbered, #BHC1050SS, etch of
Nuestra Senora de Atocha, 1 oz.
commemorative coin made of
silver salvaged from the sunken
vessel, quantity 960, 1989, value
$200.

Case Avellino for Knives,
Manufacturer - Case, Pattern -
P172, serial number on bolster,
quantity 1,000, 1981, value $100.

**Case B & H Hardware San
Angelo, Texas,** Manufacturer -
Case, Pattern - 2137 (green
handles), 150 engraved
"Clayton Cattle Feeders", 100
engraved "Bill Shaw", quantity 250, 1980, value $35.

Case Atocha Commemorative

Case Babe Ruth, Manufacturer - Case, Pattern - 4" closed trapper,
finished in music box that plays "Take Me Out to the Ballgame", red
jigged bone stag handles, quantity 1,000, price $176.47, 1987, value $140.

Case Babe Ruth, Manufacturer - Case, Pattern - 3240 dogleg trapper,
yellow handles, engraved signature, etched, serial numbered, hardshell
display case, value $48.

Case Babe Ruth, Manufacturer - Case, Pattern - 6240 dogleg trapper, red
pick bone handles, engraved signature, etched, serial numbered, wood
box plays "Take Me Out To The Ball Game", value $140.

Case Bill Boatman & Company

*Bill Boatman knives were never available through Case dealers but instead only
through the Bill Boatman Company of Bainbridge, Ohio, a mail order firm
dealing in hunting equipment. These limited editions are very scarce and are
quite popular with all types of knife collectors.*

Case Bill Boatman & Company, Manufacturer - Case, Pattern - Case XX USA 1973, 7-dot skinner, serrated blade, etched "Miracle-Edge Skinner - Bill Boatman & Company - Bainbridge, Ohio", quantity 150, 1973, value $150.

Case Bill Boatman & Company, Manufacturer - Case, Pattern - 6265 SAB DR, skinner blade, etched "Miracle-Edge Skinner - Bill Boatman & Company - Bainbridge, Ohio", quantity 506, 1974, value $110.

Case Bill Boatman & Company, Manufacturer - Case, Pattern - 6265 SAB DR, Miracle-Edge skinner blade, etched with company name, quantity 144, 1975, value $100.

Case Bill Boatman & Company, Manufacturer - Case, Pattern - 6265 SAB XX with company etch, bone handles, quantity 3,000, 1976, value $165-$225.

Case Bill Boatman & Company, Manufacturer - Case, Pattern - 6265 SAB DR, skinner blade, Miracle-Edge, etched "Miracle-Edge Skinner, Bill Boatman & Co., Bainbridge, Ohio", quantity 300, 1977, value $90.

Case Bill Boatman & Company, Manufacturer - Case, Pattern - 6265 SAB DR, skinner blade, Miracle-Edge, etched "Miracle-Edge Skinner, Bill Boatman & Co., Bainbridge, Ohio", quantity 300, 1978, value $90.

Case Bill Boatman & Company, Manufacturer - Case, Pattern - 6265 SAB DR, skinner blade Miracle-Edged, etched with company name, quantity 144, 1979, value $95.

Case Bowie and Kodiak

Case Black Diamond Miner, Manufacturer - Case, Pattern - One blade folding hunter, black plastic handles, etched, serialized, coal miner display case, value $50.

Case Blue Grass Sportsman's League, Manufacturer - Case, Pattern - 5265 SAB DR, genuine stag handles with shield, pattern stamp 6265 SAB DR , silk screened master blade, serial numbered, quantity 250, 1982, value $75.

Case Blue Grass Sportsman's League, Manufacturer - Case, Pattern - 5207 SS, genuine stag handles with shield, both blades etched, serial numbered, pattern stamp normal, quantity 250, 1983, value $50.

Case Bowie and Kodiak, Manufacturer - Case, Pattern - Damascus stag kodiak and stag horn Bowie, quantity 500, 1989, value Kodiak $250, value Bowie $250.

Case Buckeye Special, Manufacturer - Case, Pattern - 4-1/8" tears shaped jack, quantity 200, value $50.

Case Buford Pusser, Manufacturer - Case, Pattern - 6254, white smooth bone handles, etched blade, serial numbered, display box, value $50.

Case C. M. Hobbs & Sons, Inc., Manufacturer - Case, Pattern - 11055, wood handles, no shield, quantity 50, 1975, value $60.

Case Cale Yarborough, Manufacturer - Case, Pattern - 6254 trapper, white pick bone handles, etched, serial numbered, display box, value $90.

Case California Gold Rush of 1849, Manufacturer Case, Pattern - Clip blade knife, golden-yellow jigged bone handle, gold color case shield, quantity 3,000, 1988, value $100.

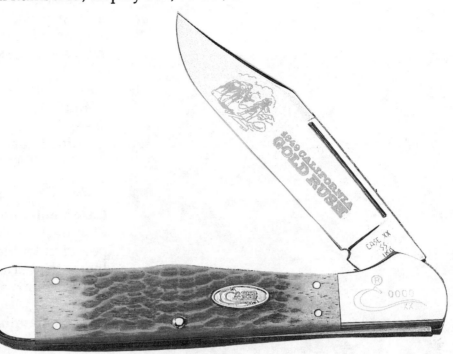

Case California Gold Rush of 1849

Case Case/Winchester Classic, Manufacturer - Case, Pattern - 4-5/8" two blade sleeveboard, Rogers bone handles, tang stamped "Winchester" on front, "Case" on back, gift box with Winchester knife opener, 1989, value $120.

Case Centennial Series - 100th Anniversary, Manufacturer - Case, Pattern - 52042SS, spear and pen blades, 3" closed, genuine India stag horn handles, quantity 3,000 ind., 500 as a mint set, price $48.99, 1990, value $36.

Case Centennial Series – 100th Anniversary, Manufacturer - Case, Pattern - 5111 1/2SS, clip blade, 4-3/8" closed, genuine India stag horn handles, quantity 3,000 ind., 500 as a mint set, price $79.99, 1990, value $55.

Case Centennial Series – 100th Anniversary, Manufacturer - Case, Pattern - 5143 one blade daddy Barlow, 5-1/2" closed, genuine stag handles and etched blade, quantity 10,000, price $85, 1990, value $58.

Case Centennial Series – 100th Anniversary, Manufacturer - Case, Pattern - 5165SS, clip blade, flat ground, 5-1/4" closed, genuine India stag horn handles, quantity 3,000 ind., 500 as a mint set, price $89.99, 1990, value $75.

Case Centennial Series – 100th Anniversary, Manufacturer - Case, Pattern - 5220SS, peanut, clip and pen blades, 2-3/4" closed, genuine India stag horn handles, quantity 3,000 ind., 500 as a mint set, price $48.99, 1990, value $40.

Case Centennial Series – 100th Anniversary, Manufacturer - Case, Pattern - 5240SPSS, clip and spey blades, 4-3/8" closed, genuine India stag horn handles, quantity 3,000 ind., 500 as a mint set, price $79.99, 1990, value $60.

Case Centennial Series – 100th Anniversary, Manufacturer - Case, Pattern - 5318SS, clip, sheep foot, and spey blades, 3-1/2" closed, genuine India stag horn handles, quantity 3,000 ind., 500 as a mint set, price $61.99, 1990, value $52.

Case Centennial Series – 100th Anniversary, Manufacturer - Case, Pattern - 51059SS, drop point hunter blade, 3-1/8" closed, genuine India stag horn handles, quantity 3,000 ind., 500 as a mint set, price $48.99, 1990, value $36.

Case Centennial Series – 100th Anniversary, Manufacturer - Case, Pattern - 52005SS, razor and spear blades, 3-3/4" closed, genuine India stag horn handles, quantity 3,000 ind., 500 as a mint set, price $61.99, 1990, value $48.

Case Centennial Series – 100th Anniversary, Manufacturer - Case, Pattern - 511098SS, razor blade, 3" closed, genuine India stag horn handles, quantity 3,000 ind., 500 as a mint set, price $41.99, 1990, value $32.

Case Centennial Series – 100th Anniversary, Manufacturer - Case, Pattern - GS200SS, clip and spey blades, 3-7/8" closed, goldstone handles, quantity 3,000 ind., 500 as a mint set, price $44.99, 1990, value $40.

Case Centennial Series – 100th Anniversary, Manufacturer - Case, Pattern - GS207SS, clip and spey blades, 3-1/2" closed, goldstone handles, quantity 3,000 ind., 500 as a mint set, value $30.

Case Centennial Series – 100th Anniversary, Manufacturer - Case, Pattern - GS225 1/2SS, clip and pen blades, 3" closed, goldstone handles, quantity 3,000 ind., 500 as a mint set, price $44.99, 1990, value $28.

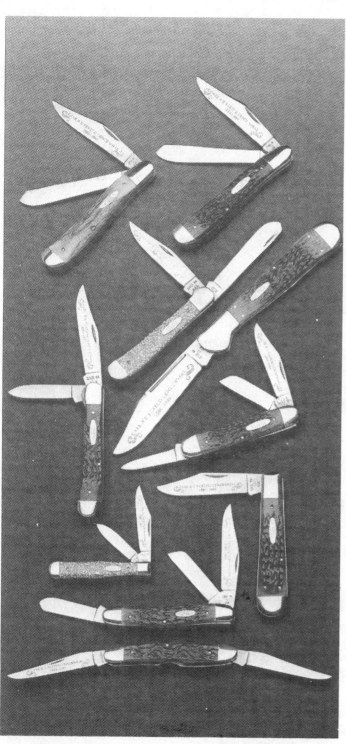

Case Centennial Series - 100th Anniversary

Case Centennial Series – 100th Anniversary, Manufacturer - Case, Pattern - GS227SS, clip and pen blades, 2-3/4" closed, goldstone handles, quantity 3,000 ind., 500 as a mint set, price $39.99, 1990, value $28.

Case Centennial Series – 100th Anniversary, Manufacturer - Case, Pattern - GS2042SS, spear and pen blades, 3" closed, goldstone handles, quantity 3,000 ind., 500 as a mint set, price $39.99, 1990, value $28.

Case Centennial Series – 100th Anniversary, Manufacturer - Case, Pattern - R6111 1/2LSS, clip blade, 3-3/4" closed, genuine red bone stag handles, quantity 3,000 ind., 500 as a mint set, price $54.99, 1990, value $48.

Case Centennial Series – 100th Anniversary, Manufacturer - Case, Pattern - R6199 1/2SS, clip blade, 4-1/8" closed, genuine redbone stag handles, quantity 3,000 ind., 500 as a mint set, price $44.99, 1990, value $38.

Case Centennial Series – 100th Anniversary, Manufacturer - Case, Pattern - R6201SS, spear and pen blades, 2-5/8" closed, genuine red bone stag handle, quantity 3,000 ind., 500 as a mint set, price $36.99, 1990, value $30.

Case Centennial Series – 100th Anniversary, Manufacturer - Case, Pattern - R6211 1/2SS, spear and pen blades, 4-3/8" closed, genuine red bone stag handles, quantity 3,000 ind., 500 as a mint set, price $59.99, 1990, value $50.

Case Centennial Series – 100th Anniversary, Manufacturer - Case, Pattern - R6215SS, gunstock, spear and pen blades, 3" closed, genuine red bone stag handles, quantity 3,000 ind., 500 as a mint set, price $36.99, 1990, value $32.

Case Centennial Series – 100th Anniversary, Manufacturer - Case, Pattern - R6220SS, peanut and pen blades, 2-3/4" closed, genuine red bone stag handles, quantity 3,000 ind., 500 as a mint set, price $36.99, 1990, value $34.

Case Centennial Series – 100th Anniversary, Manufacturer - Case, Pattern - R6227SS, clip and pen blades, 2-3/4" closed, genuine red bone stag handles, quantity 3,000 ind., 500 as a mint set, price $36.99, 1990, value $30.

Case Centennial Series – 100th Anniversary, Manufacturer - Case, Pattern - R6240SS, clip and spey blades, 4-3/8" closed, genuine red bone stag handles, quantity 3,000 ind., 500 as a mint set, price $52.99, 1990, value $44.

Case Centennial Series – 100th Anniversary, Manufacturer - Case, Pattern - R6243SS, clip and spear blades, 5" closed, genuine red bone stag handles, quantity 3,000 ind., 500 as a mint set, price $59.99, 1990, value $48.

Case Centennial Series – 100th Anniversary, Manufacturer - Case, Pattern - R6265SS, clip and skinner blades, 5-1/4" closed, genuine red bone stag handles, quantity 3,000 ind., 500 as a mint set, price $69.99, 1990, value $60.

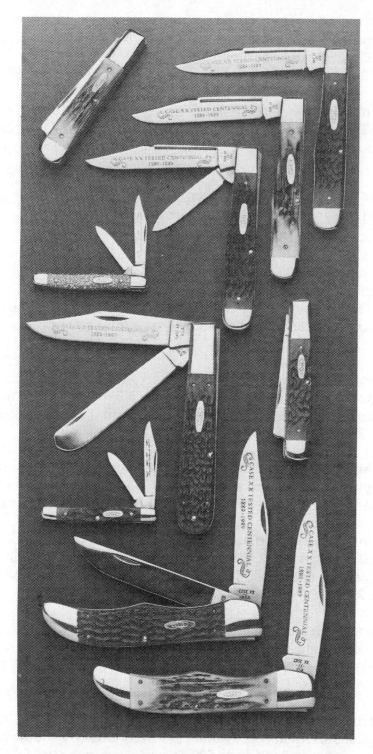

Case Centennial Series – 100th Anniversary

Case Centennial Series – 100th Anniversary, Manufacturer - Case, Pattern - R6275SS, clip and spey blades, 4-1/4" closed, genuine red bone stag handles, quantity 3,000 ind., 500 as a mint set, price $46.99, 1990, value $40.

Case Centennial Series – 100th Anniversary, Manufacturer - Case, Pattern - R6318SS, clip, sheepfoot, and spey blades, 3-1/2" closed, genuine red bone stag handles, quantity 3,000 ind., 500 as a mint set, price $43.99, 1990, value $38.

Case Centennial Series – 100th Anniversary, Manufacturer - Case, Pattern - R6345 1/2SS, clip, sheepfoot and, spear blades, 3-1/8" closed, genuine red bone stag handles, quantity 3,000 ind., 500 as a mint set, price $47.99, 1990, value $40.

Case Centennial Series – 100th Anniversary, Manufacturer - Case, Pattern - R6347SS, clip, sheepfoot, and spey blades, 3-7/8" closed, genuine red bone stag handles, quantity 3,000 ind., 500 as a mint set, price $45.99, 1990, value $40.

Case Centennial Series – 100th Anniversary, Manufacturer - Case, Pattern - R6375SS, clip, sheepfoot, spey blades, 3" closed, genuine red bone stag handles, quantity 3,000 ind., 500 as a mint set, price $49.99, 1990, value $40.

Case Centennial Series – 100th Anniversary, Manufacturer - Case, Pattern - R61048SS, clip blade, 4-1/8" closed, genuine red bone stag handle, quantity 3,000 ind., 500 as a mint set, price $36.99, 1990, value $32.

Case Centennial Series – 100th Anniversary, Manufacturer - Case, Pattern - R61059SS, drop point hunter blade, 3-1/8" closed, genuine red bone stag handles, quantity 3,000 ind., 500 as a mint set, price $36.99, 1990, value $28.

Case Centennial Series – 100th Anniversary, Manufacturer - Case, Pattern - R61066SS, clip blade, 5-1/2" closed, genuine red bone stag handles, quantity 3,000 ind., 500 as a mint set, price $41.99, 1990, value $34.

Case Centennial Series – 100th Anniversary, Manufacturer - Case, Pattern - R62005SS, razor and spear blades, 3-3/4" closed, genuine red bone stag handles, quantity 3,000 ind., 500 as a mint set, price $44.99, 1990, value $40.

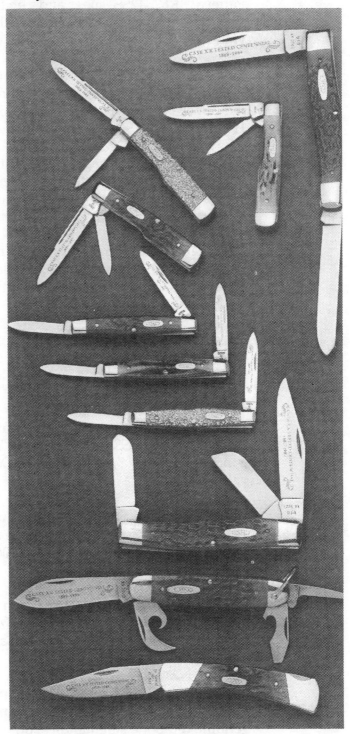

Case Centennial Series – 100th Anniversary

Case Centennial Series – 100th Anniversary, Manufacturer - Case, Pattern - R62019SS, spear and pen blades, 4-1/16" closed, genuine red bone stag handles, quantity 3,000 ind., 500 as a mint set, price $54.99, 1990, value $48.

Case Centennial Series – 100th Anniversary, Manufacturer - Case, Pattern - R62042SS, spear and pen blades, 3" closed, genuine red bone stag handle, quantity 3,000 ind., 500 as a mint set, price $36.99, 1990, value $30.

Case Centennial Series – 100th Anniversary, Manufacturer - Case, Pattern - R62048SS, trapper, clip and spey blades, 4-1/8" closed, genuine red bone stag handles, quantity 3,000 ind., 500 as a mint set, price $41.99, 1990, value $38.

Case Centennial Series – 100th Anniversary, Manufacturer - Case, Pattern - R62052SS, sheepfoot and pen blades, 3-1/2" closed, genuine red bone stag handles, quantity 3,000 ind., 500 as a mint set, price $44.99, 1990, value $38.

Case Centennial Series – 100th Anniversary, Manufacturer - Case, Pattern - R62495SS, clip and spey blades, 3-15/16" closed, genuine red bone stag handles, quantity 3,000 ind., 500 as a mint set, price $44.99, 1990, value $40.

Case Centennial Series – 100th Anniversary, Manufacturer - Case, Pattern - R64052SS, sheepfoot, pen, spear, and coping blades, 3-1/2" closed, genuine red bone stag handles, quantity 3,000 ind., 500 as a mint set, price $54.99, 1990, value $50.

Case Centennial Series – 100th Anniversary, Manufacturer - Case, Pattern - R611098SS, razor blade, 3 " closed, genuine red bone stag handles, quantity 3,000 ind., 500 as a mint set, price $29.99, 1990, value $26.

Case Centennial Series – 100th Anniversary, Manufacturer - Case, Pattern - R640045SS, multi-purpose utility knife, 3-3/4" closed, genuine red bone stag handles, quantity 3,000 ind., 500 as a mint set, price $44.99, 1990, value $42.

Case Centennial Series – 100th Anniversary, Manufacturer - Case, Pattern - RC61050SS, clip blade, 5-3/8" closed, genuine red bone stag handles, quantity 3,000 ind., 500 as a mint set, price $41.99, 1990, value $34.

Case Centennial Series – 100th Anniversary, Manufacturer - Case, Pattern - R Muskrat SS, identical clip blades, equal end, 3-7/8" closed, genuine red bone stag handles, quantity 3,000 ind., 500 as a mint set, price $44.99, 1990, value $40.

Case Centennial Series - 100th Anniversary, Manufacturer - Case, Pattern - GS201SS, spear and pen blades, 2-3/4" closed, goldstone handles, quantity 3,000 ind., 500 as a mint set, price $39.00, 1990, value $28.

Case Centennial Series – 100th Anniversary, Manufacturer - Case, Pattern - GS215SS, gunstock, spear and pen blades, 2-3/4" closed, goldstone handles, quantity 3,000 ind., 500 as a mint set, value $30.

Case Centennial Series – 100th Anniversary, Manufacturer - Case, Pattern - M1059LSS, all surgical steel, 3-1/8" closed, all surgical steel handles, quantity 3,000 ind., 500 as a mint set, value $15.

Case Centennial Series – 100th Anniversary, Manufacturer - Case, Pattern - R6207SS, mini trapper, clip and spey blades, 3-1/2" closed, red bone handles, quantity 3,000 ind., 500 as a mint set, value $35.

Case Centennial Series – 100th Anniversary, Manufacturer - Case, Pattern - R61405SS, clip blade, 3-3/4" closed, genuine red bone stag handles, quantity 3,000 ind., 500 as a mint set, value $35.

Case Centennial Series – 100th Anniversary, Manufacturer - Case, Pattern - 52155SS, gunstock, spear and pen blades, 3" closed, genuine red bone stag handles, quantity 3,000 ind., 500 as a mint set, value $45.

Case Central Knife Exchange, Manufacturer - Case, Pattern - 61051 L SSP, eleven different etchings of 100 each, special shield engraved on handle, each 100 serial numbered 1-99, quantity 1,100, 1980, value $25 each.

Case Chatham Manufacturing, Manufacturer - Case, Pattern - W107 SS, smooth white bone handles with shield, blade etched, serial numbered, no pattern stamp, quantity 250, 1983, value $40.

Case Chatham Manufacturing, Manufacturer - Case, Pattern - W154, smooth white bone handles with shield, blade etched, serial numbered, no pattern stamp, quantity 250, 1983, value $60.

Case Chief Crazy Horse, Manufacturer - Case, Pattern - Kodiak sheath knife, stag companion to Winchester commemorative of same name, quantity 5,000, price $225, 1983, value $400. (*Made for Davidsons Sporting Goods Distributors.*)

Case Cherokee Council Reunion, Manufacturer - Case, Pattern - Set of three canoes, one blade, two blade, and three blade, each knife describes either "Raven," "Nancy Ward," or "Five Killer", quantity 1,500 sets, price $300, 1984, value $400.

Case Chevrolet, Manufacturer - Case, Pattern - 3240CH, yellow handles, gold inlay shield, color enamel Chevrolet logo, value $45.

Case Clemson, Manufacturer - Case, Pattern - 3240C, yellow handles, gold inlay shield, color enamel Clemson logo, value $45.

The Case classics are a licensed project of Parker Knife Collectors Service, which produces replicas of antique Case patterns in limited quantities. Prices listed are based on information provided by Parker's Knife Collector's Service at press time.

Case Classic Series, Manufacturer - Case, Pattern - 6391, three blade whittler, Rogers bone handles, bowtie style shield, Case, value $120.

Case Classics Case Brothers Tang Stamp, Manufacturer - Case, Pattern - 51050 SAB, authentic reproduction of 1800's knife, one blade coke bottle, genuine stag handles, bowtie shield, Case Brothers tang stamp, old style gift box, quantity 3,000, price $150, 1989, value $120.

Case Classic Series, Manufacturer - Case, Pattern - 50275, two blade moose, Rogers bone handles, bowtie shield, Case Brothers tang, old style Case box, 1990, value $120.

Case Classic Series, Manufacturer - Case, Pattern - 53091, three blade whittler, genuine stag handles, bowtie shield, Case value $120.

Case Classic Series, Manufacturer - Case, Pattern - 60275, two blade moose, Rogers bone handles, bowtie shield, Case Brothers tang, old style Case box, 1990, value $100.

Case Classic Series, Manufacturer - Case, Pattern - 61050, one blade coke bottle, green bone handles, bombshell shield, Brothers tang stamp, old style gift box, 1990, value $100.

Case Classic Series, Manufacturer - Case, Pattern - G61050, one blade coke bottle, green bone handles, bombshell shield, W. R. Case & Sons tang stamp, old style gift box, 1990, value $100.

Case Classic Series, Manufacturer - Case, Pattern - G63091, three blade whittler, green pick bone handles, bombshell shield, Case tang stamp, old style gift box, 1990, value $100.

Case Classic Series, Manufacturer - Case, Pattern - ROG 61072 Bulldog, one blade clasp knife, green bone handles, bowtie shield, Case Tested Circle "C" tang stamp, old style gift box, exclusive for Blue Ridge Knives, quantity 3,000, 1990, value $150.

Case Coal Miner, Manufacturer - Case, Pattern - Lockback, "Coal Hauler" etch, price $29.99, value $22.

Case Coal Miner, Manufacturer - Case, Pattern - Lockback, "We Dig Coal" etch, price $29.99, value $24.

Case Coal Miner, Manufacturer - Case, Pattern - Lockback, "Work Safely" etch, price $29.99, value $20.

Case Coal Miner, Manufacturer - Case, Pattern - Small lockback, price $22, value $18.

Case Coca-Cola, Manufacturer - Case, Pattern - 2226 1/2 (modified 6225 1/2), smooth black handles, artwork, flat bolsters, resembles a Coke bottle, blade etched one thru 5,000, quantity 5,000, 1979, value $60.

Case Coca-Cola, Manufacturer - Case, Pattern - 2226 1/2 (modified 6225 1/2), smooth black handles with flat bolsters, resembles a Coke bottle, Coke bottle artwork on mark side, Coke truck on pile side, quantity 2,500, 1981, value $60.

Case Coke Bottle Knives, Manufacturer - Case, Pattern - SR6225-1/2 1 dot, blade etched "Pilot Run", serial numbered, quantity 1,500, price $60, value $40.

Case Curly Maple Centennial Set, Manufacturer - Case, Pattern - Set of twelve different knives, 1990, value $300.

Case Dale Earnhardt 5 Time Winston Cup Champion, Manufacturer - Case, Pattern - 6265, two blade folding hunter, red pick bone handles, etched, serial numbered, display box , value $175.

Case Dale Earnhardt 1991 Winston Cup Champion , Manufacturer - Case, Pattern - 6254RSB 4-1/8" Trapper, red smooth bone handle, nickel silver bolsters, surgical steel blades, etched blades, certificate of authenticity, laser etched display box, quantity 2,000, 1991, value $210.

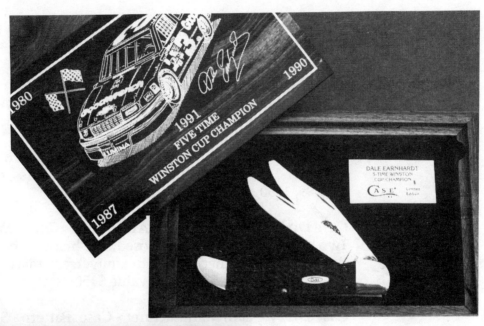

Case Dale Earnhardt 5 Time Winston Cup Champion

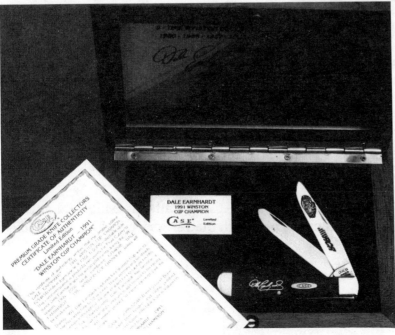

Case Dale Earnhardt 1991 Winston Cup Champion

Case Davey Allison – NASCAR's 1987 Rookie of Year, Manufacturer - Case, Pattern - 6254 trapper, red pick bone handles, etched, serial numbered, hardshell display box, certificate of authenticity, quantity 2,000, 1987, value $100. (*See"Knives of Thunder" article in the Appendix for further information*)

Case David Pearson– Stock Car Legend, Manufacturer - Case, Pattern - 6240 dogleg trapper, smooth blue bone handles, engraved signature, etched, serial numbered, hardshell box, value $100. (*See "Knives of Thunder" article in the Appendix for further information*)

Case Dewees Fertilizer Company, Manufacturer - Case, Pattern - 6254SSP, yellow Delrin covers, engraved blade, quantity 50, 1976, value $30.

Case Dillingham Graphics, Manufacturer - Case, Pattern - 6165, deep etched blade and engraved bolsters, quantity 750, value $50.

Case Display Knife, Manufacturer - Case, Pattern - Giant one blade coke bottle, 11-1/4" closed, brown wood handles, engraved Case logo, Case Brothers tang stamp, serial numbered, old style gift box, 1989, value $400.

Case Display Knife, Manufacturer - Case, Pattern - Coffin bolstered folder, 11-1/4" closed, black pakkawood handles, quantity 1,000, price $449.99, 1990, value $400.

Case Dixie Gun Works 35th Anniversary, Manufacturer - Case, Pattern - Two blade trapper, 2" long closed, one blade etched with Dixie Gun Works logo, the other with 35th anniversary mark, comes in gift box, quantity 250, price $75, 1989, value $150.

Case Dizzy Dean, Manufacturer - Case, Pattern - 3240 dogleg trapper, yellow handles, engraved with signature, etched, serial numbered, display box, value $50.

Case Dizzy Dean, Manufacturer - Case, Pattern - 6240 dogleg trapper, green pick bone handles, engraved signature, etched, serial numbered, wood box plays "Take Me Out To The Ball Game", value $100.

Case Doctor Knife Set, Manufacturer - Case, Pattern - Three knives, SR6185, 5185, and 6185, display box, serialized, quantity 500 sets, price $135, value $200.

Case Drake's Oil Well, Manufacturer - Case, Pattern - M5FINN and FINN hunting knife, stag handles, 2-color etch blades, price $145, value $160.

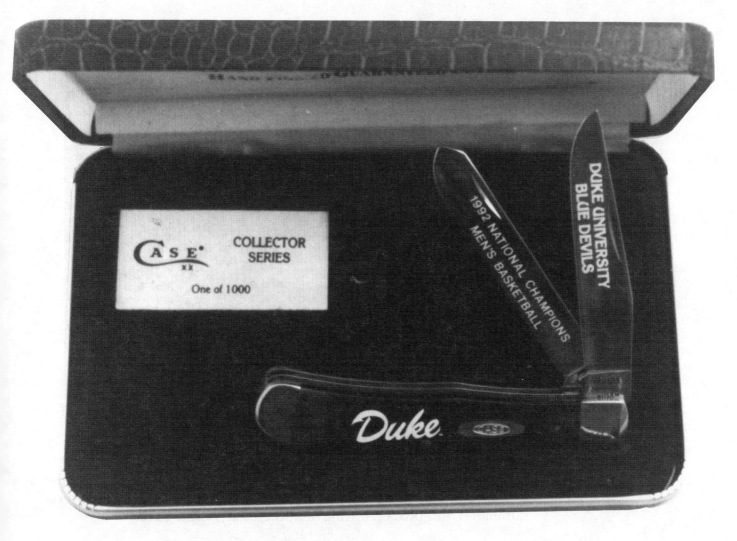

Case Duke National Champions

Case Duke National Champions, Manufacturer - Case, Pattern - Two blade folding trapper, Duke logo on handle, etched blades commemorating 1992 National Championship basketball team, display box, quantity 1,000, value $75.

Case Dwight D. Eisenhower, Manufacturer - Case, Pattern - R6333, red pick bone handles, gold shield, etched "Eisenhower", serial numbered, display box 1990, value $40.

Case Elite Fighting Troops of WWII, Manufacturer - Case, Pattern - U.S.M.C. Corps fighting knife, pinned butt, leather handles & grooves, 1990, value $52.

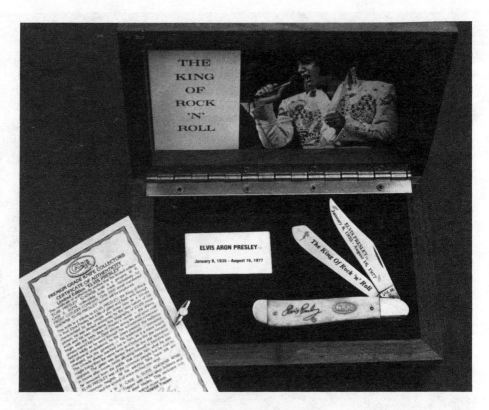

Case Elvis Presley

Case Elvis Presley, Manufacturer - Case, Pattern - 6240 dogleg trapper, 4-1/2" two blade, blue pick bone handles, gold tone shield, etched, serial numbered, gift box, certificate of authenticity, value $125.

Case Evel Knievel, Manufacturer - Case, Pattern - 6240 dogleg trapper, red pick bone handles, color etched, serial numbered, display box, value $75.

Case Family Tree Set, Manufacturer - Case, Pattern - Set of six, green bone, hardshell display box, 1990, value $300.

Case Fire Department, Manufacturer - Case, Pattern - 3240FD, yellow handles, gold inlay shield, color enamel fire department logo shield, value $60.

Case First Edition, Manufacturer - Case, Pattern - 62046J moose stockman, sabre ground clip & spear blades, 3-5/8" closed, quantity 1,000, price $120, value $100.

Case First Flight of the Wright Brothers, Manufacturer - Case, Pattern - Two blades, clip & skinner, Tru-shop surgical steel blades, photo etched with illustration of the Wright Brothers, quantity 3,000, price $199, 1988, value $175.

Case Ford, Manufacturer - Case, Pattern - 3240F, yellow handles, gold inlay shield, color enamel Ford logo, value $45.

Case Ford Mustang, Manufacturer - Case, Pattern - 3240MU, yellow handles, gold inlay shield, color enamel Ford Mustang logo shield, value $45.

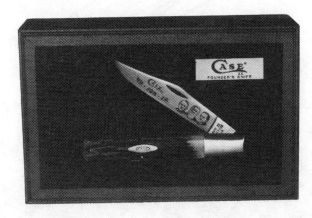

Case Founders Knife

Case Founders Knife, Manufacturer - Case, Pattern - 5143SS daddy Barlow, etched with "W. R.", "Job", and "J. R. Case", price $65, value $80.

Case Franklin D. Roosevelt, Manufacturer - Case, Pattern - B06263 pen knife, blue pick bone handles, gold shield, etched "Roosevelt", serial numbered, display box, 1990, value $40.

Case Freemasonry, Manufacturer - Case, Pattern - 6207 mini-trapper, blue smooth bone handles, color enamel Masonic emblem inlay shield, etched, serial numbered, 1990, value $45.

Case for Frost Cutlery, Manufacturer - Case, Pattern - G6254, jigged green bone handles with shield, pattern stamp normal, spey blade is Miracle-Edge, quantity 1,200, 1982, value $60.

Case for Frost Cutlery, Manufacturer - Case, Pattern - G61093 SSP, jigged green bone handles with shield, pattern stamp normal, quantity 1,250, 1982, value $50.

Case for Frost Cutlery, Manufacturer - Case, Pattern - R6254, jigged red bone handles with shield, pattern stamp normal, spey blade Miracle-Edged, quantity 1,200, 1982, value $60.

Case for Frost Cutlery, Manufacturer - Case, Pattern - R61093 SSP, jigged red bone handles with shield, pattern stamp normal, quantity 1,250, 1982, value $50.

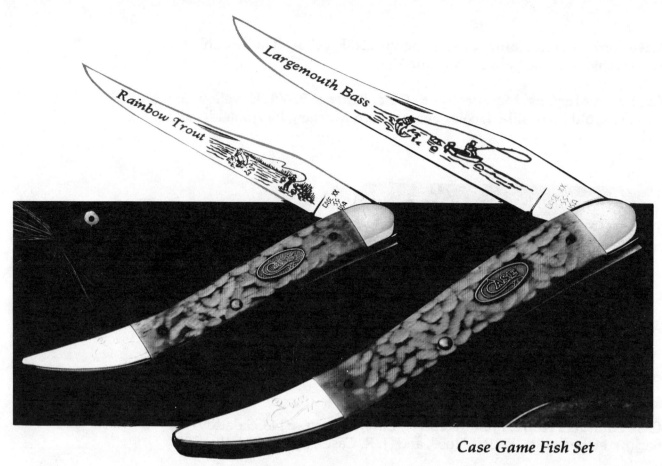

Case Game Fish Set

Case Game Fish Set, Manufacturer - Case, Pattern - Set of two fishing knives, photo etch illustrating a fisherman landing his favorite fish – rainbow trout or large mouth bass, burnt bone handles, serial numbered, hardshell display box, quantity 2,000, 1989, value $150.

Case George Washington, Manufacturer - Case, Pattern - W6220 peanut, white smooth bone handles, gold shield, etched "Washington", serial numbered, display box, 1990, value $40.

Case George Washington – First U. S. President, Manufacturer - Case, Pattern - One blade big coke bottle, cherry wood handles, etched, serial numbered, hardshell display box, 1989, value $65.

Case Glen "Fireball" Roberts Early Racing Legend, Manufacturer - Case, Pattern - 6254 trapper, genuine stag handles, color etch, serial numbered, hardshell display box, value $10. (*See "Knives of Thunder" article in Appendix for further listing*)

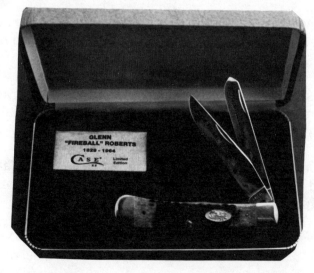

Case Glen "Fireball" Roberts Early Racing Legend

Case Grandpa/Grandson Set, Manufacturer - Case, Pattern - 6220 peanuts, red pick bone and bone stag handles, etched, serial numbered, display box, quantity 1,100, price $95, 1989, value $80.

Case Great Smoky Mountains National Park 50th Anniversary Bowie, Manufacturer - Case, Pattern - Stag handle Bowie, 3-color blade etch, quantity 1,000, price $165, 1984, value $180.

Case Green's Cutlery Sales Jackson, Tennessee, Manufacturer - Case, Pattern - 2254, smooth black Delrin handle with shield, correct pattern stamp, quantity 2,500, 1981, value $40.

Case Green's Cutlery Sales Jackson, Tennessee, Manufacturer - Case, Pattern - 4254 smooth white Delrin handle with CASE shield, correct pattern stamp, quantity 2,500, 1981, value $40.

Case Gunboat Canoe 75th Anniversary Canoe Set, Manufacturer - Case, Pattern - Set of three, 52131, 53131, and 5394 canoes, engraved gold slated bolsters, quantity 5,000, price $200, value $400.

Case Guns That Tamed The Wild West, The, Manufacturer - Case, Pattern - Set of two, 5215SS and 5230SS gunstocks, commemorating lever-action and peacemaker guns, name etched on blade, genuine stag handles, etched, serial numbered hardshell display box, quantity 3,000, 1989, value $125.

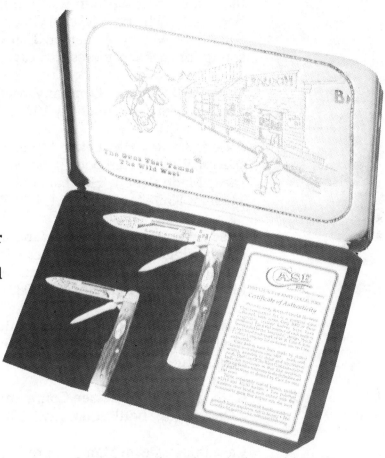

Case Guns That Tamed The Wild West

Case Handsome Harry Gant, Great NASCAR Competitor, Manufacturer - Case, Pattern - 6254 trapper, Rogers bone handles, color etch, serial numbered, hardshell display case, value $100. (*See "Knives of Thunder" article in Appendix for further information*)

Case Indian Head Penny, Manufacturer - Case, Pattern - 6200 copperhead, red pick bone handles, deep etched, Case logo and Indian head penny inlay shields, serial numbered, hardshell display case with genuine Indian head insert, value $60.

Case Indian Head Penny– Knife & Coin Set, Manufacturer - Case, Pattern - Bone handle copperhead, Indian head penny shield, etched color filled stainless blades, quantity 1,500, price $80, 1990, value $60.

Case J. C. Penney Co. #1, Manufacturer - Case, Pattern - 2138SS, series sold by Carolina-based Case salesman, etched blade for following: South Carolina Battleground of Freedom, Siege of Charleston, Battle of Hobkirks Hill, Battle of King's Mountain, Battle of Cedar Springs, Greenville County, Florence County, Battle of Cowpens, Battle of Camden, Battle of Eutaw Springs, Battle of Musgrave's Mill, Battle of Fort Moultrie, Charleston County, 1 thru 199, value $40.

Case J. C. Penney Co. #2, Manufacturer - Case, Pattern - 2138SS, etched blade for following counties: Orangeburg, Oconee, Chester, Abbeville, Barnwell, Richland, Pickens, Greenwood, Bamberg, Beaufort, Edgefield, Saluda, Newberry, Anderson, Laurens, 1 thru 199 engraved above pattern stamp for each 200 pieces, 200 each. 3,000 total, 1976, value $30 each.

Case for J. F. Parker Company, Manufacturer - Case, Pattern - W165 SSP, slick undyed bone, quantity 100, 1978, value $150.

Case J. Stanley Hawbaker, Manufacturer - Case, Pattern - Muskrat special, jigged green bone handles with shield, pattern stamp G Muskrat, sheep blade etched "Hawbaker Special", clip blade etched "Improved Muskrat Knife", quantity 1,114, 1982, value $60.

Case J. Stanley Hawbaker, Manufacturer - Case, Pattern - Muskrat special, jigged red bone handles with shield, pattern stamp R Muskrat, sheep blade etched "Hawbaker Special", clip blade etched "Improved Muskrat Knife", quantity 681, 1982, value $60.

Case Jack Daniels Set, Manufacturer - Case, Pattern - Set of three whittlers, display plaque shaped like the bottom of a liquor barrel, price $160, value $250.

Case Jackson, Tennessee Commemorative, Manufacturer - Case, Pattern - 2226-1/2 coke bottle, quantity 5,000, price $45, value $60.

Case James Dean, Manufacturer - Case, Pattern - 6254, white pick bone handles, etched blades, serial numbered, display box, value $60.

Case Jedediah Smith, Manufacturer - Case, Pattern - 6254 trapper, bone handles, etched, wood box, value $50.

Case Jerry Clower, Manufacturer - Case, Pattern - Razor trapper, Rogers bone handle, value $60.

Case Jim Bowie 200th Anniversary Special, Manufacturer - Case, Pattern - Bowie, same as V-44 military issue used in WW II survival kits, black handle with brass guard, etched, leather sheath, gift box, value $100.

Case Jim Bridger and Jedediah Smith, Manufacturer - Case, Pattern - Set of two 6254 trappers, etched, wood box, value $100 set.

Job Case/Jim Parker – Ivory Trapper, Manufacturer - Case, Pattern - IV254SSD, 512 layer Damascus spey blade, illustration of Job Case and Jim Parker, quantity 500, value $500.

Case John F. Kennedy, Manufacturer - Case, Pattern - 6254 trapper, white smooth bone handles, color engraving, etched, serial numbered, display box, value $50.

Case John Wayne, Manufacturer - Case, Pattern - 3254 yellow trapper, clip and spey blades with deep, two-color etch, serial numbered, display box, value $50.

Case John Wayne, Manufacturer - Case, Pattern - Trapper, scrimshawed white smooth bone handles, value $60.

Case Johnny Cash, Manufacturer - Case, Pattern - Muskrat, 3-7/8" closed, genuine honeycomb bone handles, Johnny Cash signature, wood and glass display box, glass etched with train, quantity 1,000, price $69.99, 1990, value $100.

Case Johnny Rutherford, Three Time Indy 500 Winner, Manufacturer - Case, Pattern - 6240 dogleg trapper, blue pick bone handles, gold shield, etched, serial numbered, hardshell display case, value $85.

Case Journeyman Wireman, Manufacturer - Case, Pattern - 6347, gold on blue, hard display, value $40.

Case Junior Johnson, Manufacturer - Case, Pattern - 5254 trapper, genuine stag handles, color etch, serial numbered, hardshell display value $100. (*See "Knives of Thunder" article in Appendix for further information*)

Case Junior Johnson/Bill Elliott Legendary Owner Set, Manufacturer - Case, Pattern - Set of two one-blade folding hunters, "Junior Johnson - Master of the Machine" and "Bill Elliott - Master of the Track" etched on respective blades, comes in gift box with autographed photo and plaques, 1992, value $400. (*See "Knives of Thunder" article in Appendix for further information*)

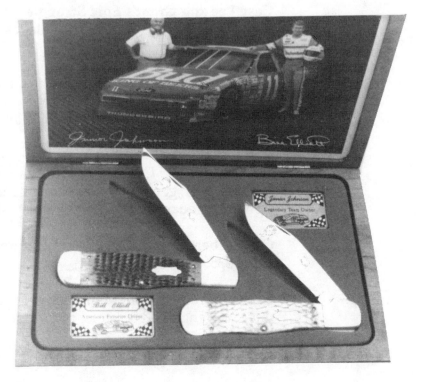

Case Junior Johnson/Bill Elliott Legendary Owner Set

Case Kentucky Bicentennial, Manufacturer - Case, Pattern - G137, commemorates the opening of the Case South Bradford Plant on September 24, 1975, quantity 100, 1975, value $85.

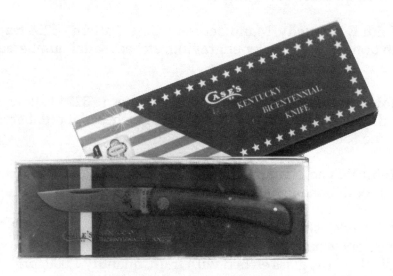

Case Kentucky Bicentennial

Case Kentucky Sodbusters Bicentennial, Manufacturer - Case, Pattern - Sodbuster Jr,. 4-5/8" blades, 1975.

Case Kentucky Thoroughbreds, Manufacturer - Case, Pattern - P172 buffalo, set of three knives honoring Man O War, Native Dancer, and Citation, deep acid etched with a black background, quantity 10 each, value $150.

Case Kentucky Wildcats, Manufacturer - Case, Pattern - 6249, bone handled, lettered on hard dark blue display, value $50.

Case Lee and Grant's Epic Struggle, Manufacturer - Case, Pattern - mirror polished 3" surgical steel blades, Confederate gray & Union blue jigged bone handles, quantity 3,000, 1987, value $130.

Case Lee Petty, Manufacturer - Case, Pattern - 6254 trapper, white smooth bone handles, engraved signature, etched, serial numbered, display box, value $90. (*See the "Knives of Thunder article in Appendix for further information*)

Case Legends of Country Music, Manufacturer - Case, Pattern - 4-1/8" razor trapper, genuine Rogers bone handles appliqued with the stars' signatures, quantity 1,250, price $39.99, 1990, value $40.

Case Liberty Bowl - 1982, Manufacturer - Case, Pattern - 3254, 1982, value $35.

Case Limited Edition, Manufacturer - Case, Pattern - 5233 three dot, engraved bolsters, prototype, price $80, value $90.

Case Limited Edition, Manufacturer - Case, Pattern - 3254 three dot Tennessee & Kentucky trappers, serial #7, nice walnut display box, quantity 500, price $95, value $125.

Case Limited Edition, Manufacturer - Case, Pattern - 52033 three dot, blue scroll, price $45, value $60. (Part of Case Stag Set)

Case Limited Edition, Manufacturer - Case, Pattern - G63047, without serial number or etch, quantity 5,500, 1980, value $45.

Case Limited Edition, Manufacturer - Case, Pattern - SR6225 1/2 one dot, engraved, quantity 1,500, value $40.

Case Limited Edition, Manufacturer - Case, Pattern - SR61093, smooth red toothpick NKCA, quantity 3,000, price $55, value $60.

Case Limited Edition, Manufacturer - Case, Pattern - W64052 congress, white stag, price $36.99, 1984, value $60.

Case Limited Edition, Manufacturer - Case, Pattern - #7 mini-trapper, gold blade etching and "TN Riverboat Trapper" engraving, value $75.

Case Limited Edition Barlow Set, Manufacturer - Case, Pattern - Set of three, 52009SSP, 52009 RAZ SSP, and 52009-1/2 SSP Barlows, satin finish, stainless steel blades, brass liners, quantity 5,000, value $200.

Case Lou Gehrig, Manufacturer - Case, Pattern - 6240 dogleg trapper, red smooth bone handles, engraved signature, etched, serial numbered, wood music box play "Take Me Out To The Ball Game", value $100.

Case Lou Gehrig "The Iron Horse", Manufacturer - Case, Pattern - 6240 dogleg trapper, green pick bone handles, etched, serial numbered, gift box with commemorative U.S. postage stamp, value $100.

Case Lou Gehrig "The Iron Horse", Customized by Frost, Manufacturer - Case, Pattern - 6240 dogleg trapper, 4-1/2" closed, green pickbone handles, quantity 1,200, price $150, value $125

Case Louisiana Game Warden

Case Louisiana Game Warden , Manufacturer - Case, Pattern - Clip lockback, 1987 Louisiana Game Warden # of 500 etch, state of Louisiana on bolster, quantity 500, 1987, value $50.

Case M. C. Matthews Cutlery, Manufacturer - Case, Pattern - Set of 3 patterns: 6185SSP, bone stag, SR 6185, jigged red bone, and 5185 SSP, genuine stag, quantity 5,000, 1980, value $140 set.

Case M. C. Matthews Cutlery, Manufacturer - Case, Pattern - Set of 4 patterns: SR 6205 R SSP, smooth red bone, A 6205 R SSP, Appaloosa, G6205 R SSP, jigged green bone, SG 6205 R SSP, smooth green bone, quantity 1,250, 1981, value $160 set.

Case Mario Andretti– Great Indy Racer, Manufacturer - Case, Pattern - 6240 dogleg trapper, white smooth bone handles, engraved signature, etched, serial numbered, hardshell display box, value $80.

Case Mark Martin – NASCAR's Rising Star, Manufacturer - Case, Pattern - 6200 copperhead, blue pick bone handles, color etch, serial numbered, hardshell display case, value $100. (*See "Knives of Thunder" article in Appendix for further information*)

Case Mason - Dixon Series, Manufacturer - Case, Pattern - Bowie, three color blade etch of General Lee and Confederate forces, value $200.

Case Masonic, Manufacturer - Case, Pattern - 3240M, yellow handles, gold inlay shield, color enamel Masonic logo, value $45.

Case Mid South Knife Collector's Association, Manufacturer - Case, Pattern - 6254 SSP, jigged green bone handles with shield, blade etched, double "C" stamped on blade, quantity 150, 1981, value $60.

Case Missouri - Mississippi River Expedition 1987, Manufacturers - Grizzly Knife and Works, Pattern - Canoe lockback, U.S. with river running etched on blade, quantity 500, value $65.

Case Moby Dick

Case Moby Dick, Manufacturer -Case, Pattern - Folding hunter, scrimshawed on slick undyed bone, richly engraved bolsters, quantity 10,000, value $175. (*See article about this knife and its history in the introduction section of this book*).

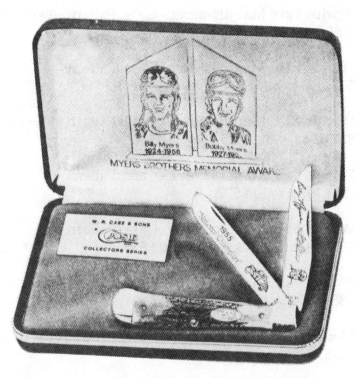

Case Myers Brothers Memorial Set

Case Myers Brothers Memorial Set, Manufacturer - Case, Pattern - Set of two, 5254SS stag trapper, ROG06200SS Rogers bone copperhead, both knives deeply etched and color filled, quantity 500 sets, price $240, value $200. (*See "Knives of Thunder" article in Appendix for further information*)

Case Myers Brothers Racing Set– Billy and Bobby Myers, Manufacturer - Case, Pattern - Set of two, 5254 stag trapper and ROG6200 Rogers bone with spey blade, color etch, matching serial numbers, separate hardshell display cases, value $175 set. (*See "Knives of Thunder " article in Appendix for further information*)

W.R. Case & Sons Nantucket Sleigh Ride, Manufacturer –Case, Pattern - Folding hunters, scrimshawed on slick undyed bone, richly engraved bolsters, quantity 10,000, value $170. (*See article about this knife and its history in the introduction section of this book*).

Case National Cutting Horse Association, Manufacturer - Case, Pattern - B6254 trapper, grey bone, NCHA shield and raised Case shield, etched with cowboy cutting cow, commemorative box with NCHA logo, quantity 1,000, value $50.

Case New Orleans Worlds Fair, Manufacturer - Case, Pattern - #2159LSSP, quantity 5,000, price $28, 1984, value $50.

Case New Orleans Worlds Fair, Manufacturer - Case, Pattern - LWE84SS, price $5, 1984, value $10.

Case New Orleans Worlds Fair, Manufacturer - Case, Pattern - LWE278, price $20, 1984, value $26.

Case New Orleans Worlds Fair, Manufacturer - Case, Pattern - LWE2254, price $18, 1984, value $36.

Case New Orleans Worlds Fair, Manufacturer - Case, Pattern - LWE2318SSp, price $18, 1984, value $30.

Case New Orleans Worlds Fair, Manufacturer - Case, Pattern - LWE21048SS, price $12, 1984, value $25.

Case New Orleans Worlds Fair, Manufacturer - Case, Pattern - LWE22087SSP, price $15,1984, value $22.

Case New Orleans Worlds Fair, Manufacturer - Case, Pattern - LWE82079, quantity 10,000, price $40, 1984, value $55.

Case New Orleans Worlds Fair, Manufacturer - Case, Pattern - LWEB254 (blue handle), price $35, 1984, value $42.

Case New Orleans Worlds Fair, Manufacturer - Case, Pattern - LWE2254 (black handle), price $35, 1984.

Case Nolan Ryan 5,000th Career Strike Out, Manufacturer - Case, Pattern - B61405 lockback, blue pick bone handles, etched signature, serial numbered, display box, 1990, value $85.

Case North Carolina State, Manufacturer - Case, Pattern - 3240NC, yellow handles, gold inlay shield, color enamel North Carolina state outline shield, value $45.

Case North Carolina Tarheels, Manufacturer - Case, Pattern - 6240 dogleg trapper, blue pick bone handles, color etch, serial numbered, hardshell display case, value $85.

Case North Carolina Tarheels, Manufacturer - Case, Pattern - 6240 dogleg trapper, blue smooth bone handles, color etch, serial numbered, hardshell display case, value $85.

*Case North
Carolina Wild
Turkey
Federation*

Case North Carolina Wild Turkey Federation, Manufacturer - Case, Pattern - Two blade trapper, jigged bone handle, Knife number and Federation seal etched on blade, quantity 300, value $50.

Case O'Dell Hardware Company, Manufacturer - Case, Pattern - P158LSSP special, regular P158LSSP except without Mako etch, special etch on blade, engraved on M.S. bolster, serial numbered, gift boxed, quantity 2,000, 1983, value $50.

Case Owens Illinois, Inc., Manufacturer - Case, Pattern - M279 ME SS, Miracle-Edged, engraved "Owens Illinois, Inc., Chicago, Illinois," quantity 77, 1976, value $15.

Case Owens Illinois, Inc., Manufacturer - Case, Pattern - M279 SS, Miracle-Edge blade, blade etched with company name, quantity 60, 1977, value $15.

Case Owens Illinois, Inc., Manufacturer - Case, Pattern - M279 SS, pen blade Miracle-Edged, quantity 50, 1982, value $15.

Case/Parker Trapper, Manufacturer - Case , Pattern - ROG6254SSD, 512 layer Damascus steel blade, quantity 3,000, 1989, value $120.

Case Paul "Bear" Bryant, Manufacturer - Case, Pattern - 6254 dogleg trapper, red pick bone handles, color engraving, etched, serial numbered, display box, value $50.

Case Paul "Bear" Bryant, Manufacturer - Case, Pattern - 6254, white smooth bone handles, color engraving, etched, serial numbered, display box, value $50.

Case Pennsylvania Game Commission, Manufacturer - Case, Pattern - P158L SSP special, regular P158L SSP without Mako etch, engraved M.S. bolster, special serial number, quantity 375, 1983, value $45.

Case Pennsylvania Tricentennial 1681-1981, Manufacturer - Case, Pattern - M1051LSSP, 14k gold high relief handle, quantity 300, 1981, value $160.

Case Pennsylvania Tricentennial Proof Set, Manufacturer - Case, Pattern - M1051LSSP, set of five, one knife in gold, one in sterling silver, pewter, sterling with gold plating and pewter with gold relief painting, 1981, value $400.

Case Peterbilt, Manufacturer - Case, Pattern - 3240PB, yellow handles, gold inlay shield, color enamel Peterbilt logo, value $45.

Case Petty Legend Set, Manufacturer Case, Pattern - Set of three, BW61050, BW6125 1/2, BW6225 1/2, coke bottles, commemorating Richard, Kyle, and Lee, burnt white bone handles, gold shield, engraved with images matched with signatures, serial numbered, cherry display case with laser engraved lid, includes silver numbers medallion, certificate of authenticity, quantity 1,500 sets, price $380, value $380.

Case Pony Express, Ivory 1058 Msko. $150. Made for Cutlery World Stores.

Case for R. J. Werner Company, Manufacturer - Case, Pattern - 6205 R, jigged bone handles (light), 500 serial numbered 1 thru 500, quantity 5,000, 1981, value $45.

Case Rainbow Set, Manufacturer - Case & Sons, Pattern - Set of five single blade trappers, five different colored handles, 1988, value $400.

Case Rainbow Damascus Set, Manufacturer - Case, Pattern - Set of five single blade trappers, five different colored handles, Damascus blades, 1989, value $600.

Case Red Scroll Set, Manufacturer - Case, Pattern - Set of seven pocketknives, stag handled, stainless steel blades, etched blades, quantity 25,000, 1979, value $325 set.

Case Relic Room & Knife Shop, Manufacturer - Case, Pattern - R Muskrat, jigged red bone handles with shield, pile side blade Miracle-Edged, pattern stamp "R Muskrat", quantity 1,200, 1981, value $55.

Case Relic Room & Knife Shop, Manufacturer - Case, Pattern - G Muskrat, jigged green bone handles with shield, pile side blade Miracle-Edged, pattern stamp "G Muskrat", quantity 1,200, 1981, value $55.

Case Return of the Lady, Manufacturer - Case, Pattern - Trapper with clip & spey blades, one has "Half U.S. Dollar In God We Trust 1916-1947" etched in blade, one has "U.S. Dollar In God We Trust 1986-1987" etched in blade, 1987, value $65.

Case Return of the Lady

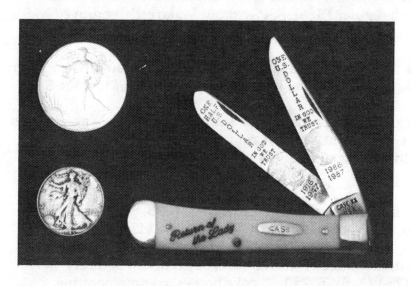

Case Richard Petty, Manufacturer - Case, Pattern - Big coke, clip blade, red or blue handle, quantity 1,500, value red handle $600, blue handle $450. (*See "Knives of Thunder" article in Appendix for further information*)

Case Rick Mears– 3 Time Indy 500 Winner, Manufacturer - Case, Pattern - 6240 dogleg trapper, blue pick bone handles, gold shield, etched, serial numbered, hardshell display case, value $80.

Case Rio Grande Camp Knife, Manufacturer - Case, Pattern - English style Bowie, knife made notorious by John Wilkes Boothe after killing Lincoln, India stag horn handle and buffalo handles, quantity 1,000 each handle, 1990, value $135 each.

Case Roy Acuff King of Country Music, Manufacturer - Case, Pattern - Gunstock, genuine stag handles, music box plays "Wabash Cannonball", quantity 100, price $170, 1985, value $200.

Case Roy Acuff Signature Knife, Manufacturer - Case, Pattern - Photo etch of "King of Country Music", nickel silver bolsters, stag handle, pen blade, serial numbered, quantity 5,000, 1985, value $100.

Case S. Stanley Hawbaker, Manufacturer - Case, Pattern - G muskrat, jigged green bone handles with shield, pattern stamp "G Muskrat", sheep blade etched "Hawbaker Special", also "Improved Special", quantity 1,000, 1981, value $60.

Case S. Stanley Hawbaker Special Muskrat, Manufacturer - Case, Pattern - Muskrat, clip blade etched "Improved Muskrat Knife", sheep blade etched "Hawbaker Special!", Delrin handles, quantity 60, 1973, value $55.

Case S. Stanley Hawbaker & Son, Manufacturer - Case, Pattern - Muskrat special, jigged red bone handles with shield, pattern stamp "R Muskrat", etched on sheep blade "Hawbaker Special", etched on clip blade "Improved Muskrat Knife", quantity 1,000, 1981, value $60.

Case S. Stanley Hawbaker & Son, Manufacturer - Case, Pattern - Muskrat, 9 dot-3 dot transition piece, quantity 600, value $65.

Case S. Stanley Hawbaker & Son Special Muskrat, Manufacturer - Case, Pattern - Special muskrat, clip blade etched "Improved Muskrat Knife", sheep blade etched "Hawbaker Special", quantity 1,000, 1978, value $65.

Case Statue of Liberty, Manufacturer - Case, Pattern - Set of two limited edition trappers, etched blades, one with yellow Micarta handle, one with jigged bone handle, display boxed, bone handled knife also comes with a one troy ounce .999 fine silver medallion, quantity 1,000 each, value $40 (Yellow handle), $55 (Jigged bone handle).

Case Scottish Rite Knife, Manufacturer - Case, Pattern - Three blade serpentine, 3-1/2" long, price $20, 1981, value $30.

Case Shaw Leibowitz, Manufacturer - Case, Pattern - P172, without etching, quantity 200, 1974, value $200.

Case Shaw Leibowitz, Manufacturer - Case, Pattern - 5275, genuine stag handles, quantity 300, 1975, value $200.

Case Shaw Leibowitz, Manufacturer - Case, Pattern - 6235 1/2, bone stag, quantity 300, 1975, value $200.

Case Shaw Leibowitz, Manufacturer - Case, Pattern - 6250, without etching, quantity 200, 1975, value $200.

Case Shaw Leibowitz, Manufacturer - Case, Pattern - 6380, bone stag handles, quantity 300, 1975, value $200.

Case Shaw Leibowitz, Manufacturer - Case, Pattern - 62131, without etching, quantity 300, 1975, value $200.

Case Signature Set, Manufacturer Case, Pattern - G64088, green bone, signatures of Russell Case and W. R. Case, price $85, 1989, value $100.

Case Smoky Mountain Knife Works, Manufacturer - Case, Pattern - G6154, jigged green bone handles with shield, pattern stamp G6154, quantity 2,500, 1982, value $55.

Case Smoky Mountain Knife Works, Manufacturer - Case, Pattern - R6154, jigged red bone handles with shield, pattern stamp R6154, quantity 2,500, 1982, value $55.

Case Smoky Mountain Knife Works, Manufacturer - Case, Pattern - 3250, yellow Delrin handles with shield, pattern stamp 3250, quantity 600, 1983, value $90.

Case Smoky Mountain Knife Works, Manufacturer - Case, Pattern - B6254, 300 with jigged blue bone handles with pattern stamp B6254, 300 with smooth blue bone handles with pattern stamp SB6254, CASE shield on both knives, quantity 600, 1983, value $45.

Case Smoky Mountain Copperheads, Manufacturer - Case, Pattern - Set of two, 62109X and 6249, quantity 600 sets, price $65, value $135.

Case Sorghum Festival, Manufacturer - Case, Pattern - R6249 SP SS copperhead, red bone, 1988, value $40.

Case Star-Spangled Banner Commemorative, Manufacturer - Case, Pattern - Bowie, etched artwork showing portion of song "The Star-Spangled Banner", Fort McHenry with National Emblem waving in wind, quantity 500 gold etch, 1,500 black etch, price $250, 1989, value $275 gold etch, $230 black etch.

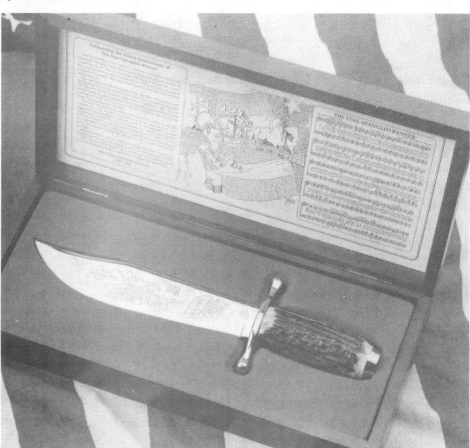

Case Star-Spangled Banner Commemorative

Case Stark Brothers, Manufacturer - Case, Pattern - 11055, wood handles, no shield, 92 spey blade, quantity 144, 1976, value $50.

Case Stark Brothers, Manufacturer - Case, Pattern - 11055, wood handle, no shield, 92 spey blade, quantity 288, 1977, value $50.

Case Starter Set, Manufacturer - Case, Pattern - Set of seven 1 dot: SR6325 1/2, 6250, 2138, 63027, 6344, 6165SAB, 06247 pen, serialized, quantity 1,500, 1979, value $200.

Case Sterling Silver Edition, Manufacturer - Case, Pattern - Handles by Shaw Leibowitz, 1980 Lake Placid Olympic Knife, 1980, value $200.

Case Swingline Executives, Manufacturer - Case, Pattern - 8179 LO, special run, quantity 60, 1980, value $65.

Case Swinston Company, Manufacturer - Case, Pattern - 13031 LR, National Mines Service logo etched on blade, no serial number, quantity 3,000, 1977, value $25.

Case Texas Special

Case Texas Special, Manufacturer - Case, Pattern - Texas special, 4165SSP, white composition handles, blade etch, plaque in shape of Texas with logo, quantity 5,000, price $65, 1977, value $100.

Case "The Gators" for Time Tested Products, Manufacturer - Case, Pattern - Set of two: 51093 and 61093, serial numbered 1 thru 2,750, quantity 2,750, price $99, 1978, value $200.

Case Titanic, Manufacturer - Case, Pattern - 6254 trapper, white smooth bone handles, color engraving, etched, serial numbered, display box, value $45.

Case Tom T. Hall, Manufacturer - Case, Pattern - Razor trapper, Rogers bone handle, value $50.

Case Transition Canoe Set, Manufacturer - Case, Pattern - Set of five 62131 canoes, corn cob jigged bone handles in red, green, yellow, blue, honey bone, 1 dot stamp on master blades and new 1990 stamp on small blades, serial numbered, canoe shaped wall plaque, quantity 1,200, price $300, 1990, value $300.

Case Transition Canoe Set

Case Ty Cobb – The Georgia Peach, Manufacturer - Case, Pattern - 3240 dogleg trapper, yellow handles, engraved signature, etched, serial numbered, hardshell display case, value $60.

Case Ty Cobb– The Georgia Peach, Manufacturer - Case, Pattern - 6240 dogleg trapper, blue pick bone handles, engraved signature, etched, serial numbered, wood box plays "Take Me Out To The Ball Game", value $125.

Case U.S. Constitution, Manufacturer - Case, Pattern - 6254 trapper, white smooth bone handles with color engraving, etched, serial numbered, display box, quantity 3,000, 1987, value $50.

Case U. S. Marine Corps, Manufacturer - Case, Pattern - 3240US, yellow handles, gold inlay shield, color enamel U.S. Marine Corps shield, value $45.

Case U. S. Orbital Space Flight by John Glenn, Manufacturer - Case, Pattern - Trapper, spear & clip blades, gold-plated artwork showing Friendship Seven circling Earth, quantity 2,000, 1987, value $85.

Case Ulysses S. Grant, Manufacturer - Case, Pattern - 6254 trapper, white smooth bone handles, color engraved, etched, serial numbered, display box, price $35, value $50.

Case Vietnam Commemorative, Manufacturer - Case, Pattern - 3254 trapper, yellow handles, etched, serial numbered, display box, value $40.

Case Vietnam War Commemorative, Manufacturer - Case, Pattern - Cast metal boot knife, blade etched "Those Who Served", value $100.

Case Vince Dooley, Manufacturer - Case, Pattern - 3254 trapper, yellow handles, engraved signature, etched, serial numbered, Georgia Bulldogs logo, display box, value $60.

Case Vince Lombardi, Manufacturer - Case, Pattern - 6240 dogleg trapper, green pick bone handles, etched, serial numbered, value $75.

Case Von Senden Company, Manufacturer - Case, Pattern - 4247 FK, quantity 1,300, 1973, value $200.

Case Wall Drug 50th Anniversary, Manufacturer - Case, Pattern - 5120R, 2 dot with shield, quantity 350, price $31, 1981, value $30.

Case Wall Drug 50th Anniversary, Manufacturer - Case, Pattern - SR6220, smooth red bone handles, no shield, "1931 Wall Drug 1981" etched in blade, quantity 350, price $22.95, 1980, value $30.

Case Wall Drug 50th Anniversary, Manufacturer - Case, Pattern - 5120R, 10 dot, no shield, quantity 350, price $31, 1981, value $28.

Case West Virginia Deerhunters Association , Manufacturer - Case, Pattern - Two blade folding trapper, bone handle, etched blade, quantity 500, 1986, value $65.

Case West Virginia Grouse, Manufacturer - Case, Pattern - 5165 folding hunter, etched, serial numbered, gift box, value $65.

Case West Virginia Miner, Manufacturer - Case, Pattern - 5-1/4" one blade folding hunter, deep etch of coal miner, black plastic handles, value $150.

Case West Virginia Wildlife, Manufacturer - Case, Pattern - 5165 folding hunter, etched, serial numbered, gift box, value $65.

Case West Virginia Deerhunters Association

Case Western Reserve Cutlery Association, Manufacturer - Case, Pattern - 5254 SS, genuine stag handles with shield, Pattern stamp 6254 SSP "©", etched clip blade, serial numbered, quantity 150, 1982, value $65.

Case Williams Jewelry & Manufacturing Company, Manufacturer - Case, Pattern - 6279 SS, pocket blade etched "Maramec Mining Company", Green Cross Safety emblem on mark side of handle, quantity 60, 1976, value $22.

Case Williams Jewelry & Manufacturing Company, Manufacturer - Case, Pattern - 6279 SS, blade etched on mark side "UNHP - MINES - GENERAL", on pile side "1 Million Hour Award", Green Cross Safety emblem embedded in mark side of handle, quantity 165, 1977, value $22.

Case Winchester, Manufacturer - Case, Pattern - P158L SSP, regular P158L SSP except with Winchester photo etch on blade, quantity 500, 1983, value $70.

Charlton Ltd. Damascus Ronald Reagan, Manufacturer - Damascus USA, Pattern - Bowie, Damascus steel, 1989, value $1,500

Charlton, Ltd. Limited Edition – "A Rajahs Dagger of State", Manufacturer - n\a, Pattern - 14" dagger, engraved with intricate 24 kt. damascene, forged Damascus, serial numbered, velvet-lined presentation case, quantity 40, price $895, 1985, value $1,000.

Charlton, Ltd W.T. "Bill" Moran 45th Anniversary, Manufacturer - Bill Moran, Pattern - 14-1/2" ST-23 combat , Damascus steel encased in hand fitted presentation case, price $895, 1985, value $1000.

Charlton, Ltd. Limited Edition – "A Rajahs Dagger of State"

Coleman-Western Joining of Coleman and Western Cutlery,
Manufacturer - Coleman-Western, Pattern - Model 701, double tangs, brass guards, certificate of authenticity, first 250 knives have both sides of blade etched, quantity 2,000, price $299, 1985, value $175.

Colonel Coon Knives

Colonel Coon knives was the house brand of Adrian Harris's Tennessee Knife works, one of the pioneers of private label commemoratives. He sold the trademark and left the business in the late 1980's, selling much of his equipment to W. R. Case & Sons.

Colonel Coon Limited Edition

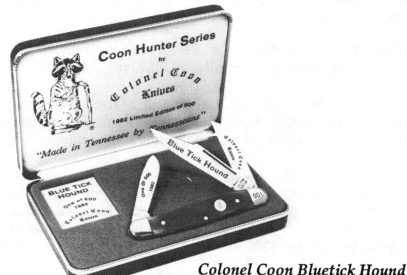

Colonel Coon Bluetick Hound

Colonel Coon Limited Edition

Colonel Coon Bluetick Hound, Manufacturer - Colonel Coon, Pattern - 4" stock, blue bone handle, serial numbered, presentation box, quantity 500, price $80, 1983, value $60.

Colonel Coon Limited Edition, Manufacturer - Colonel Coon, Pattern - Set of two Barlows, value $120.

Colonel Coon Limited Edition, Manufacturer - Colonel Coon, Pattern - Set of two stockmans , value $120.

Colonel Coon Redbone Hound, Manufacturer - Colonel Coon, Pattern - 4" stock, red bone handles, quantity 500, price $80, 1983, value $60.

Colonial 500th Anniversary of Discovery of America, Manufacturer - Colonial, Pattern - One blade lockback folder, etched handle with "500 Years Discovery of America", quantity $1,000, price $30, 1992, value $30.

Colonial Chattanooga Knife Collecting Capital of the World, Manufacturer - Colonial, Pattern - Two blade shadow '78 pattern in imitation tortoise, " Chattanooga, Tennessee, Knife Collecting Capital of the World" etch, less than 100 made, value $60.

Cripple Creek Knives

Cripple Creek knives are produced by National Knife Collectors Association President Bob Cargill from Old Fort, Tennessee. A former Case repairman as well, he lived for many years in Lockport, Ill. before moving south around 1990. Naturally his Illinois marked knives are getting harder and harder to find.

Colonial 500th Anniversary of Discovery of America

Cripple Creek Famous American Indians – Jim Thorpe All-American Athlete, Manufacturer - Cripple Creek, Pattern - Barlow, spear blade, value $130.

Cripple Creek Green River Rendezvous, Manufacturer - Cripple Creek, Pattern - Three blade serpentine, blade etch, value $150.

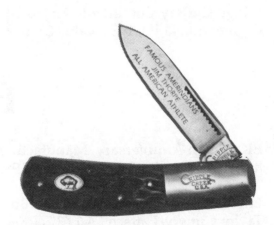

Cripple Creek Famous American Indians – Jim Thorpe All-American Athlete

Cripple Creek Green River Rendezvous

Cripple Creek Limited Edition – Half Breed, Manufacturer - Cripple Creek, Pattern - Trapper, "Half Breed" etched on clip, clip and spey blades, value $150.

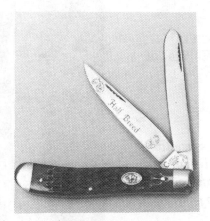

Cripple Creek Limited Edition – Half Breed

Cutlery World Of America Limited Edition, Manufacturer - Case, Pattern - IV254SSD, ivory trapper, Damascus clip blade, quantity 200, price $250, 1989, value $500.

Cutlery World Of America The Pony Express (125th Anniversary), Manufacturer - Case, Pattern - Clip knife, brass bolsters, 440C stainless steel blades, an Express rider scene scrimshawed on an ivory handle, quantity 500, price $120, 1986, value $180.

D

Dingo Cutlery Commando Knife, Manufacturer - n\a, Pattern - Commando knife, 1982, value $100.

E

EKA 100th Anniversary, Manufacturer - EKA, Pattern - 3-3/8" metal handled, quantity 500, price $100, 1982, value $40.

Elk Horn Cowboy Series I "The Bucking Bronco", Manufacturer - Taylor Cutlery, Pattern - 4-1/2" closed folding lockback, genuine pearl handles, customized backspring and blade, price $32, value $40.

Elk Horn Great American Indian Set, Manufacturer - Taylor Cutlery, Pattern - Set of two stag handled canoes, Indian chiefs Geronimo and Sitting Bull etch 450 sets, 1980, value $40.

Elk Horn Great American Ship Set, Manufacturer - Taylor Cutlery, Pattern - Set of two sunfish, commemorates the USS Constitution and the USS Raleigh, quantity 1,000, 1980, value $35.

Eye Brand Limited Edition - "Trapper", Manufacturer - Eye Brand, Pattern - 5" closed trapper, genuine stag scales, quantity 1,800, price $79.95, 1980, value $60.

Eye Brand Texas Rangers, Manufacturer - Eye Brand, Pattern - yellow composition trapper, value $40.

F

Ferguson, Mrs. Dewey Limited Edition, Manufacturer - Alcas, Pattern - M1051L trailpacker, covered bridge picture stamp, two versions-one in black stamping, one in red, value $55.

Franklin Mint 150th Anniversary of the Battle of the Alamo, Manufacturer - Bart Moore Bowie Replica, Pattern - 13-3/4" Bowie, J. Bowie etched in blade. Quantity 20,000, price $295, 1987, value $275.

Frank Buster Fight'n' Rooster Knives

Fight'n' Rooster knives, originated by Frank Buster of Lebanon, TN, are entirely limited edition knives, but few are commemoratives. They are one of the most popular collectible brands because of both the high quality of the knives and the fact that the knives are no longer in production. It is rare for a Fight'n' Rooster run to be more than 300. The following listings of Frank Buster knives are meant to be a representative sample. They are not intended to be a complete listing.

Frank Buster Cutlery The Alabama, Manufacturer - Fight'n Rooster, Pattern - Lockback canoe, red and black handles, silver inlays, fancy bolster, quantity 300, price $42.50, 1980, value $45.

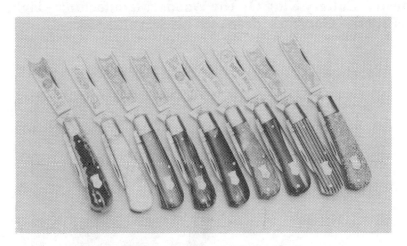

Frank Buster Cutlery Barlow Razors

Frank Buster Cutlery Barlow Razors, Manufacturer - Fight'n Rooster, Pattern - Barlow, set of nine, full blade etches, quantity 400 sets, value $30 each.

Frank Buster Cutlery Diamond Jim, Manufacturer - Fight'n Rooster, Pattern - Two blade swell center jack, pearl handle, etched, quantity 100, value $85.

Franklin Mint 150th Anniversary of the Battle of the Alamo

*Frank Buster
Cutlery Fire
Fighters of
America*

*Frank Buster
Cutlery "In God
We Trust:"*

Frank Buster Cutlery Fire Fighters of America, Manufacturer - Fight'n Rooster, Pattern - Barlow, tortoise shell, etched, boxed, quantity 100, 1987, value $50.

Frank Buster Cutlery "In God We Trust:", Manufacturer - Fight'n Rooster, Pattern - Barlow, pearl, blade etched, boxed, quantity 150, 1987, value $75.

Frank Buster Cutlery Kentucky/ Tennessee/ Southern Belle, Manufacturer - Fight'n Rooster, Pattern - 3-3/4" jack knives, three knife set, gold flake handles, gold etched, price $175, value $135.

Frank Buster Cutlery King Of The Woods, Manufacturer - Fight'n Rooster, Pattern - Gunstock, deep etch blade, value $50.

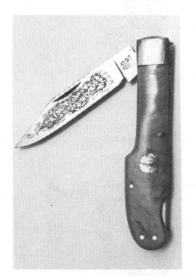

*Frank Buster
Cutlery King
Of The Woods*

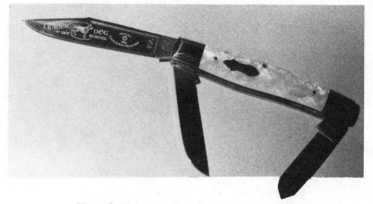

Frank Buster Cutlery Leader Dog

Frank Buster Cutlery Leader Dog , Manufacturer - Fight'n Rooster, Pattern - Three blade stockman, pick bone handle, etched blade, made for Lavergne, TN Lions Club, quantity 500, value $45.

Frank Buster Cutlery The Indian, Manufacturer - Fight'n Rooster, Pattern - Lockback canoe, silver inlays, fancy celluloid handles, engine turned bolster, quantity 300, price $42.50, 1980, value $45.

Frank Buster Cutlery The Texan, Manufacturer - Fight'n Rooster, Pattern - 4 1/2" lockback, shell celluloid handles, gold etch, quantity 300, price $46.50, 1980, value $45.

Frank Buster Cutlery Wharncliffe , Manufacturer - Fight'n Rooster, Pattern - Set of seven two blade serpentine wharncliffe, each with a different blade etch, each with a different handle material, large crest Fight'n Rooster shield, quantity 400, price $280, 1987, value $280.

Frank Buster Cutlery Wharncliffe

Frost Cutlery "4 Wheelin", Manufacturer - Frost, Pattern - One blade lockback, smooth bone handles, color print of jeeps, gift box, value $18.

Frost Cutlery 15th Anniversary, Manufacturer - Frost, Pattern - 11-1/2" Bowie, genuine stag handles, blade etch, serial numbered, belt sheath, deluxe wood display case, value $100.

Frost Cutlery 82nd Airborne Division, Manufacturer - Frost, Pattern - 3-3/4" lockback, white smooth bone The All Americans handles, color engraved logo, gift box, value $20.

Frost Cutlery 101st Airborne Division Screaming Eagles, Manufacturer - Frost, Pattern - 3-3/4" lockback, white smooth bone handles, color engraved logo, gift box, value $20.

Frost Cutlery 1989 Alabama Reunion, Manufacturer - Frost, Pattern - 3-5/8" one blade lockback, white smooth bone handles, color engraved, serial numbered, gift box, value $20.

Frost Cutlery 1989 SEC Champions Alabama, Manufacturer - Frost, Pattern - 3-7/8" lockback, white smooth bone handles, color print, serial numbered, gift box, value $70.

Frost Cutlery American Civil War Set, Manufacturer - Frost, Pattern - 4-1/2" folding hunters, bone handles and an image of a general on the handles, quantity 2,400 sets, price $70, value $70.

Frost Cutlery Archie Campbell, Manufacturer - Frost, Pattern - 3-5/8" lockback, smooth bone handles, color print, gift box, value $22.

Frost Cutlery Arkansas Razorbacks, Manufacturer - Frost, Pattern - 3-5/8" lockback, white smooth bone handles, color print, gift box, value $20.

Frost Cutlery Bear Bryant, Manufacturer - Frost, Pattern - 4" two blade razor folder, red pick bone handles, etched, serial numbered, gift box, value $24.

Frost Cutlery Billy the Kid and Pat Garrett Set, Manufacturer - Frost, Pattern - 3-3/4" closed, quantity 2,400, price $70, 1989, value $50.

Frost Cutlery Buddy Baker, Manufacturer - Frost, Pattern - 3-5/8" lockback, smooth bone handles, color print, serial numbered, gift box, value $24. (*See "Knives of Thunder" article in Appendix for further information*)

Frost Cutlery Buford Pusser, Manufacturer - Frost, Pattern - 3-5/8" one blade lockback, smooth bone handles, color print, gift box, value $20.

Frost Cutlery Cale Yarborough, Manufacturer - Frost, Pattern - 3-5/8" lockback, smooth bone handles, color print, serial numbered, gift box, value $24. (*See "Knives of Thunder" article in Appendix for further information*)

Frost Cutlery Clemson Tigers, Manufacturer - Frost, Pattern - 3-5/8" lockback, smooth bone handles, color print, gift box, value $20.

Frost Cutlery Coal Miners of America, Manufacturer - Frost, Pattern - Two 4-1/2" closed folding hunters, handled in smooth bone, etched, box pictures a coal miner, quantity 2,400, price $70, 1987, value $60.

Frost Cutlery David Pearson, Manufacturer - Frost, Pattern - 3-5/8" lockback, smooth bone handles, color print, serial numbered, gift box, value $22. (*See "Knives of Thunder" article in Appendix for further information*)

Frost Cutlery "Dirt Rider", Manufacturer - Frost, Pattern - One blade lockback, smooth bone handles, color print of motorcycle, gift box, value $18.

Frost Cutlery Dizzy Dean, Manufacturer - Frost, Pattern - 3-5/8" lockback, white smooth bone handles, color print, serial numbered, gift box, value $20.

Frost Cutlery Elvis Presley "The King", Manufacturer - Case, Pattern - 6240BPB, 4-1/2" closed stockman, blue pick bone (EP-1) and 6240WZB with bone stag (EP-2), box plays "Love Me Tender", quantity 3,000, price (EP-1) $150, (EP-2) $200, 1989, value (EP-1) $235, (EP-2) $235.

Frost Cutlery Evel Knievel, Manufacturer - Frost, Pattern - 3-5/8" lockback, smooth bone handles, color etch, serial numbered, gift box, value $20.

Frost Cutlery Frank & Jesse James Set, Manufacturer - Frost, Pattern - 3-3/4" closed, quantity 2,400, price $70, 1989, value $50.

Frost Cutlery Georgia Bulldogs, Manufacturer - Frost, Pattern - 3-5/8" lockback, smooth bone handles, color print, gift box, value $20.

Frost Cutlery Johnny Majors, Coach University of Tennessee, Manufacturer - Frost, Pattern - 3-5/8" lockback, smooth bone handles, color print, serial numbered, gift box, value $20.

Frost Cutlery Kentucky Wildcats, Manufacturer - Frost, Pattern - 3-7/8" lockback, white smooth bone handles, color print, gift box, value $20.

Frost Cutlery Lee Petty, Manufacturer - Frost, Pattern - 3-5/8" lockback, smooth bone handles, color print, serial numbered, gift box, value $30. (*See "Knives of Thunder" article in Appendix for further information*)

Frost Cutlery Little Claw Set, Manufacturer - Frost, Pattern - set of four 2" mini lockbacks, handles of green pick bone, smooth bone, candy stripe, Frostwood, serial numbered, hardshell gift box, value $50.

Frost Cutlery Lou Gehrig, Manufacturer - Frost, Pattern - 3-5/8" lockback, smooth bone handles, color print, serial numbered, gift box, value $22.

Frost Cutlery Mini Eagle-Eye Set, Manufacturer - Frost, Pattern - set of four 2-1/8" mini folders, thumb slots, green pick bone, red pick bone, Frostwood, candy stripe, serial numbered, hardshell gift box, value $50.

Frost Cutlery North Carolina Tarheels, Manufacturer - Frost, Pattern - 3-5/8" lockback, smooth bone handles, color print, serial numbered, gift box, value $20.

Frost Cutlery Oliver North, Manufacturer - Frost, Pattern - 3-5/8" lockback, smooth bone handles, color print, school mascot, gift box, value $20.

Frost Cutlery "Our Colors Don't Run Or Burn", Manufacturer - Frost, Pattern - 4" custom lockback, white smooth bone handles, color engraved, gift box, value $25.

Frost Cutlery Paul "Bear" Bryant, Coach University of Alabama, Manufacturer - Frost, Pattern - 3-3/4" lockback, peacemaker pattern, red smooth bone handles, engraved signature, etched, serial numbered, gift box, value $24.

Frost Cutlery POW-MIA Commemorative, Manufacturer - Frost, Pattern - 3-5/8" one blade lockback, smooth bone handles, black engraving, serial numbered, gift box, value $20.

Frost Cutlery Rick Honeycutt Baseball Series, Manufacturer - Frost, Pattern - 3-5/8" lockback, white smooth bone handles, color print, serial numbered, gift box, value $25.

Frost Cutlery "Slinging Dirt", Manufacturer - Frost, Pattern - one blade lockback, smooth bone handles, color print of 4 x 4 truck, gift box, value $18.

Frost Cutlery Stock Car Legends – Cale Yarborough Manufacturer - Hen & Rooster, Pattern - 4-1/8" trapper, white smoothbone handles & scrimshaw work on handle, quantity 2,000, price $112, 1990, value $99. (*See "Knives of Thunder" article in Appendix for further information*)

Frost Cutlery Stock Car Legends– Cale Yarborough, Manufacturer - Case, Pattern - 4-1/8" trapper, white pickbone handles, quantity 2,000, price $150, 1990, value $90. (*See "Knives of Thunder" article in Appendix for further information*)

Frost Cutlery Stock Car Legends – Dale Earnhardt, Manufacturer - Case, Pattern - 4-1/8" trapper, white pickbone handles, quantity 2,000, price $150, 1990, value$180. (*See "Knives of Thunder" article in Appendix for further information*)

Frost Cutlery Stock Car Legends - Lee Petty, Manufacturer - Case, Pattern - 4-1/8" trapper, white pickbone handles, quantity 2,000, price $150, 1990, value $90. (*See "Knives of Thunder" article in Appendix for futher information*)

Frost Cutlery Tennessee - Kentucky Trapper Set, Manufacturer - Frost, Pattern - Two 2-blade bullet pattern trappers, etched, hardwood hinged display case, value $70.

Frost Cutlery Tennessee Vols, Manufacturer - Frost, Pattern - 3-5/8" lockback, smooth bone handles, color etch, gift box, value $20.

Frost Cutlery Tennessee Vols 100th Anniversary, Manufacturer - Frost, Pattern - 4" lockback, smooth bone handles, color print, gift box, value $20.

Frost Cutlery The Old West–Butch Cassidy and The Sundance Kid, Manufacturer - Frost, Pattern - 3-1/2" fixed blade clips, engraved handles, quantity 2,400, price $70, 1987, value $50.

Frost Cutlery The Old West –Wyatt Earp and Doc Holliday, Manufacturer - Frost, Pattern - 3-1/2" folders, pen, bone handles, quantity 2,400, price $70, 1987, value $50.

Frost Cutlery Ty Cobb, Manufacturer - Frost, Pattern - 3 5/8" lockback, smooth bone handles, color print, serial numbered, gift box, value $20.

Cutlery University of Tennessee, Manufacturer - Frost, Pattern - 3-5/8" custom lockback, smooth bone handles, orange "Vols" etch, black etch of UT logo with orange flame, gift box, value $20.

Frost Cutlery Vince Dooley, Manufacturer - Frost, Pattern - 3-5/8" lockback, smooth bone handles, color engraved with Dooley and Georgia Bulldog logo, serial numbered, gift box, value $24.

Frost Cutlery Vince Dooley, Manufacturer - Frost, Pattern - 3-3/4" 10-F206WSB, quantity 5,000, price $32.95, 1989, value $24.

Frost Cutlery Vince Dooley, Manufacturer - Hen & Rooster, Pattern - 4" 312WSB, quantity 2,500, price $112, 1989, value $70.

Frost Cutlery Vince Dooley, Manufacturer - Schrade Cutlery, Pattern - 4" 524SC, picture of Bulldog and Vince Dooley etched in handle with his signature, quantity 3,500, price $40,1989, value $30.

Frost Cutlery Vince Dooley, Manufacturer - W.R. Case, Pattern - 4-1/8" 3254Y, quantity 2,500, price $80, 1989 , value $60.

Frost Cutlery Vince Lombardi, Manufacturer - Frost, Pattern - 3-5/8" lockback, smooth bone handles, color print, serial numbered, gift box, value $20.

Frost Cutlery Zodiak Set of 12, Manufacturer - Frost, Pattern - 2-1/8" custom lockbacks, smooth bone handles, matching serial numbers, value $100.

G

Genella Spike

Genella Spike, Manufacturer - Charlie Genella, Pattern - Tear drop lockback, quantity 2,400, price $15, 1978, value $35.

*Genella Your
Little Buddy*

Genella Your Little Buddy, Manufacturer - Charlie Genella, Pattern - Lockback, clip blade, quantity 2,400, price $15, 1978, value $35.

General Store, The Limited Edition, Manufacturer - Solingen, Ger., Pattern - Trapper with clip, sheepfoot, and spear blades, mother-of-pearl handles, quantity 2,000, 1977, value $100.

Gerber 40th Anniversary, Manufacturer - Gerber, Pattern - Paul knife, metal handle with etch, price $100, 1979, value $300.

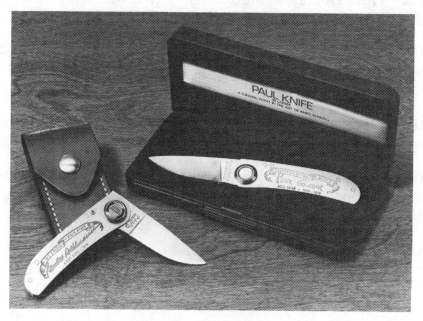

Gerber 40th Anniversary

Gerber Dupont Nylon 50th Anniversary, Manufacturer - Gerber, Pattern - One blade folder, Zytel handle, etched blade, 1984, value $90.

Gerber Dupont Nylon 50th Anniversary

Gerber Limited Edition– Mark II 20th Anniversary, Manufacturer - Gerber, Pattern - 12" Mark II with wasp-shaped waist blade, cast aluminum handles - 12 oz. weight, blade angled 5 degrees at the handle, quantity 5,000, 1987, value $150.

Gerber Limited Edition–Silver Knights, Manufacturer - Gerber, Pattern - Four lockbacks, stainless steel blades, scrimshawed handles, value $40.

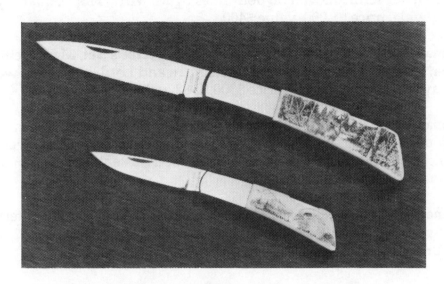

Gerber Limited Edition–Silver Knights

Gerber Texas Commemorative, Manufacturer - Gerber, Pattern - 97223 lockback, etched with Texas Seal and Lone Star State, thick stag, sheath, boxed, value $65.

Gerber Vietnam Commemorative, Manufacturer - Gerber, Pattern - Gerber Mark II, cameo handle, price $1,000, value $500.

Gordich Limited Edition Combat Set, Manufacturer - Tommy Lee, Pattern - Combat knife with Colt .45 combat commander, walnut case, pistol and knife appropriately etched with matching numbers, quantity 100, price $800, 1984, value $200.

Gutmann 4-Star Collector's Knives, Manufacturer - Puma, Pattern - 4" closed lockback, two knives with ivory/micarta handles scrimshawed with fowl scene and animal scene, price $350, value $325 set.

Gutmann Black Forest, Manufacturer - Gutmann, Pattern - Two blade stockman, pearl, Damascus blades, price $200, value $100.

Gutmann CK734 Commemorative Knife, Manufacturer - Puma, Pattern - Clip lockback, 5" closed, commemorates consecration by St. Boniface in 734, deep etching and inscriptions, quantity 734, price $950, 1978, value $550.

Gutmann Limited Edition - Explorer, Manufacturer - Gutmann, Pattern - 5" sabre, 440 stainless steel mirror polished handle sabre clip blade, genuine India stag horn handle, quantity 3,000, price $500, 1981.

Gutmann Limited Edition – Stag Collector, Manufacturer - Explorer, Pattern - 5" closed lockback folder, solid nickel silver bolster with mirror polish, quantity 3,000, price $60, 1982, value $35.

Gutmann Limited Edition, Manufacturer - Puma, Pattern - Lockback, handle hand-scrimshawed on both sides by Mr. Arno Hopp, quantity 300 world-wide, price $1,000, value $400.

Gutmann Limited Edition– Mini-Folder Collector's Set, Manufacturer - Puma, Pattern - Puma 200 series, Gentleman and Lord, handsome wood display chest, quantity 500, price $300, 1982, value $160.

Gutmann Return of the Tall Ships, Manufacturer - Puma, Pattern - Drop-point folding hunter, serial, numbered, signed by scrimshawer certificate of authenticity, American hardwood presentation box, quantity 500, price $600, 1983, value $250.

Gutmann The Tall Ships Are Coming, Manufacturer - Puma, Pattern - Drop-point folding hunter, set of three, serial numbered, quantity 2,400 sets, price $70, value $70.

H

Hen & Rooster 111th Anniversary Set, Manufacturer - Hen & Rooster, Pattern - Twelve different knives, carrying case, quantity 1,000, 1976, value $850
(1) Circa 1901, stag two blade, quantity 600, value $40,
(2) Circa 1893, pearl swell center whittler, quantity 600, value $60,
(3) Circa 1902, stag gunstock, quantity 600, value $40,
(4) Circa 1900, pearl senator whittler, quantity 600, value $60,
(5) Circa 1895, stag sheep foot whittler, quantity 600, value $52,
(6) Circa 1894, stag serpentine whittler, quantity 600, value $54,
(7) Circa 1891, stag four blade congress, quantity 600, value $56,
8) Circa 1899, stag whittler, quantity 600, value $54,
(9) Circa 1897, stag four blade congress, quantity 600, value $56,
(10) Circa 1892, pearl four blade, quantity 600, value $60,
(11) Circa 1896, pearl three blade whittler, quantity 600, value $58,
(12) Circa 1896, stag four blade congress, quantity 600, value $75.

Hen & Rooster 125th Anniversary of the Bertram Cutlery, Manufacturer - Hen & Rooster, Pattern - Large three blade stockman, genuine stag handles, frosted etch blades, value $90.

Hen & Rooster Apollo II 20th Anniversary, Manufacturer - Hen & Rooster, Pattern - Two blade trapper, white smooth bone handles, color engraved, etched, serial numbered, hardshell display case, value $42.

Hen & Rooster Archie Campbell, Manufacturer - Hen & Rooster, Pattern - Two blade trapper, white smooth bone handles, color printing, etched, serial numbered, hardshell display case, value $75.

Hen & Rooster Cale Yarborough, Manufacturer - Hen & Rooster, Pattern - Two blade trapper, white smooth bone handles, etched, serial numbered, engraved signature in handle, display box, value $90. (*See "Knives of Thunder" article in Appendix for further information*)

Hen & Rooster Coal Miners of America, Manufacturer - Hen & Rooster, Pattern - Two blade trapper, genuine stag, etched, serial numbered, hardshell display case, value $75.

Hen & Rooster Coon Hunter, Manufacturer - Hen & Rooster, Pattern - Large four blade congress, genuine stag handles, frosted blade etch, quantity 300, value $90.

Hen & Rooster Greyhound Racer, Manufacturer - Hen & Rooster, Pattern - Two blade trapper, genuine stag, etched, serial numbered, value $75.

Hen & Rooster Kentucky Thoroughbred, Manufacturer - Hen & Rooster, Pattern - Two blade trapper, genuine stag, etched, serial numbered, value $75.

Hen & Rooster Lee Petty, Manufacturer - Hen & Rooster, Pattern - Two blade trapper, white smooth bone handles, color engraved, etched, serial numbered, hardshell display case, value $110. (*See "Knives of Thunder" article in Appendix for further information*)

Hen & Rooster Moon Shiner, Manufacturer - Hen & Rooster, Pattern - Four blade congress, genuine stag handles, frosted blade etch, quantity 300, value $80.

Hen & Rooster Stock Car Legends: Dale Earnhardt, Manufacturer - Hen & Rooster for Frost Cutlery, Pattern - 4-1/8" trapper, white smoothbone handles, quantity 2,000, price $150. (*See "Knives of Thunder" article in Appendix for further information*)

Hen & Rooster Tobacco Congress, Manufacturer - Hen & Rooster, Pattern - Large four blade congress, genuine stag handles, frosted blade etch, quantity 300, value $90.

Hen & Rooster Tobacco Stockman, Manufacturer - Hen & Rooster, Pattern - Three blade sowbelly, genuine stag handles, pinched bolsters, frosted blade etch, value $90.

Hen & Rooster Tobacco Trapper, Manufacturer - Hen & Rooster, Pattern - Two blade trapper, genuine stag, etched, serial numbered, value $75.

Hen & Rooster Vince Dooley, Manufacturer - Hen & Rooster, Pattern - Two blade trapper, white smooth bone handles, engraved with picture and Georgia Bulldog logo, etched, serial numbered, hardshell display case, value $70.

Hen & Rooster World War I, Manufacturer - Hen & Rooster, Pattern - Two blade trapper, white smooth bone handles, color engraved, etched, serial numbered, hardshell display case, value $40.

Henckels 1731 Commemorative, Manufacturer - n\a, Pattern - Single blade lockback, 4-3/4" closed, black composition handle, price $100, value $65.

Henckels Bicentennial Commemorative, Manufacturer - J.A. Henckels, Pattern - Two blade folder, Capitol Building in relief on handle, 1976, value $45.

Henckels Presentation Hunter, Manufacturer - Zwilling - J.A. Henckels, Pattern - 5" Solingen hunter, three color etch of bear, trimmed with fancy gold scroll, genuine stag handles, leather spacers, brass guard, leather sheath, value $75.

Henckels Presentation Hunter, Manufacturer - Zwilling - J.A. Henckels, Pattern - 5" Solingen hunter, three color etch of boar, trimmed with fancy gold scroll, genuine stag handles, leather spacers, brass guard, leather sheath, value $75.

Henckels Bicentennial Commemorative

Henckels Presentation Hunter, Manufacturer - Zwilling - J.A. Henckels, Pattern - 5" Solingen hunter, three color etch of deer, trimmed with fancy gold scroll, genuine stag handles, leather spacers, brass guard, leather sheath, value $75.

Hickey, J.W., Manufacturer - J.W. Hickey & Sons, Pattern - Set of six metal folding hunter, 5" coke bottle with varied handles and old style blade etches, value $300.

Hickey, J.W. Limited Edition- Statesmen, Senator, Ambassador, and President, Manufacturer - J.W. Hickey & Sons, Pattern - Set of three whittlers, etched blade, German made, handles of pearl, celluloid, price $125, value $150.

Hickey, J.W. Limited Edition- Statesmen, Senator, Ambassador, and President

Holley Cutlery Connecticut Charter Oak, Manufacturer - n\a, Pattern - Holley Cutlery, congress, handles made from the wood of the Charter Oak Tree, price $1,000, 1911. One of the oldest known limited editions. Very rare.

I

Imperial/Schrade
Mark Twain Barlow

Imperial/Schrade Mark Twain Barlow, Manufacturer - Imperial/Schrade, Pattern - Folding Barlow, Staglon handle, "Mark Twain" signature engraved on bolster, value $30. (This knife was not sold through regular dealers.)

I.T.S. Trading Corp. Brama Special Edition, Manufacturer - n\a, Pattern - 8" dagger, ivory Micarta handle with inset showing a Red Stag "Bramando", quantity 5,000, price $175, 1987, value $200.

J

J. Nielsen - Mayer & Sons Cutlery Co. George Washington Valley Forge, Manufacturers - Jorgen and Nielsen-Mayer, Pattern - Three blade stag whittler, 3-13/16" closed, pinch bolsters, price $45, 1977, value $50.

K

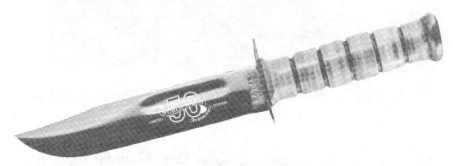

Ka-Bar 50th Anniversary of WW II, Manufacturer - Ka-Bar, Pattern - USMC fighting knife, black blade, cowhide leather grip, blade etch, price $45, 1990, value $65.

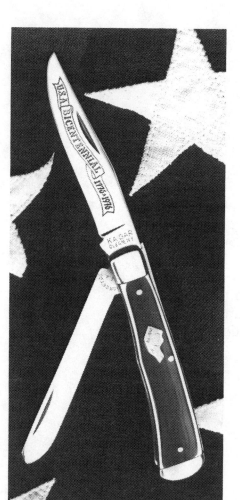

Ka-Bar Bicentennial

Ka-Bar 50th Anniversary of WW II

Ka-Bar 1986 Sunfish, Manufacturer - Ka-Bar, Pattern- Sunfish, original historical handles, 1986, value $65.

Ka-Bar Bicentennial, Manufacturer - Ka-Bar, Pattern - Dogshead trapper, two blade featuring red, white, and blue celluloid handles. One blade etched "Union Cut. Co." and the other carries the current Ka-Bar logo, price $30, 1976, value $75.

Ka-Bar Jim Bowie, Manufacturer - Ka-Bar, Pattern - 13-5/8" overall Bowie, genuine shed stag handles, bronze cross guard, leather sheath, quantity 400, price $55, 1988, value $75.

Ka-Bar Limited Edition, Manufacturer - Ka-Bar, Pattern - Two canoes, mother of pearl and stag handles, quantity 940 pearl, 915 stag, 1979, price $100 set, value $100.

Ka-Bar Limited Edition, Manufacturer - Ka-Bar, Pattern - 3-1/2" congress, mother of pearl, serialized, two blades, quantity 806, price $25, 1980, value $38.

Ka-Bar Limited Edition – Reward, Manufacturer - Ka-Bar, Pattern - Folding hunter, set of two, polished jigged bone handle, "match Striker" nail marks, nickel-silver bolsters, brass liners, quantity 885 - 1 lb., 352 - 2 lb., price $35, 1983, value $37.50.

Ka-Bar Physicians Knife, Manufacturer - Ka-Bar, Pattern - "Pillbusters" with stagged bone handles, also pearl handles with serial numbers, quantity 300, value bone $55, value pearl $80.

Ka-Bar Union Cutlery Co., Manufacturer - Ka-Bar, Pattern - Sunfish, jigged brown bone handle, value $65.

Ka- Bar Union Razor Company, Manufacturer - Ka-Bar, Pattern - Sunfish, jigged and stagged honey bone handle, value $65.

Ka-Bar WW II USMC Fighting Knife, Manufacturer - Ka-Bar, Pattern - Fighting utility knife, 7" blade, cowhide leather handle, double quillion guard, cowhide leather sheath, quantity 1,775, price $100-$300, 1975, value $120.

Keen Kutter 100th Anniversary, Manufacturer - Schrade Cutlery, Pattern - Two versions, one like an 897UH Schrade Uncle Henry, the other a three blade serpentine slightly smaller, quantity 6,000, price $10, 1969, value $65. (*See also "Schrade Keen Kutter 100th Anniversary"*)

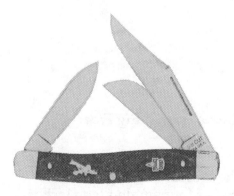

Keen Kutter Spirit of St. Louis

Keen Kutter Spirit of St. Louis, The, Manufacturer - Schrade Cutlery, Pattern - 4" stock knife, serial numbered, black saw-cut Staglon handle, brass bound, three nickel-silver shields: Keen Kutter, Airplane and Spirit of St. Louis, quantity 12,000, price $25, 1974, value $45. (*See also "Schrade Spirit of St. Louis*)

Kershaw African Game Series "Big Five", Manufacturer - Kershaw, Pattern - Ivory handled dagger, handle carved into lion, black rhino, cape buffalo, elephant or leopard, carved by Erhard Gross, quantity 100 ea., price $1500/$2500, 1989, value $1,750.

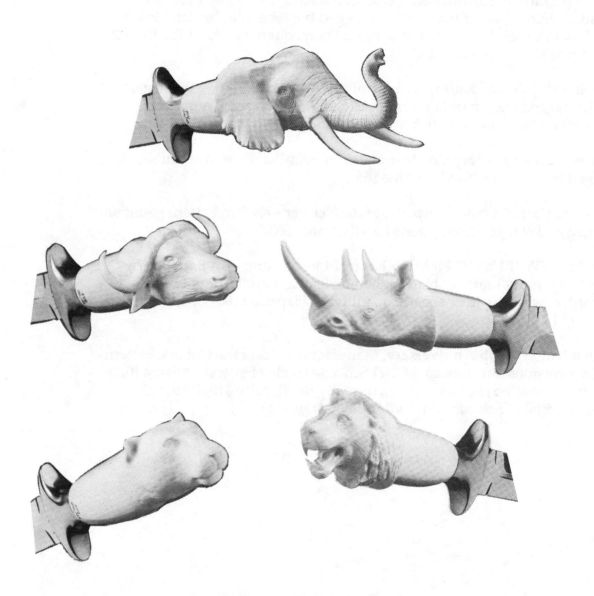

Kershaw African Game Series "Big Five"

Kershaw Endangered Species of the World: The Big Cat Series, Manufacturer - Kershaw, Pattern - Set of four single-blade lockback folders, each handle scrimshawed with a different endangered big cat.

Kershaw Limited Edition by Gary Harbour, Manufacturer - Kershaw, Pattern - 3-3/4" lockbacks, set of 3, matched serial numbers, scrimshawed handles of cougar, moose and antelope scenes, quantity 1,000, price $275, 1982, value $225.

Limited Edition Scrimshaw by Walter Alexander, Manufacturer - Kershaw, Pattern- Bald eagle color scrimshaw on handle, serial numbered, quantity 1,000, price $300, 1987, value $250.

Kershaw Limited Edition Scrimshaw by Walter Alexander, Manufacturer - Kershaw, Pattern - Humpback whale color scrimshaw on handle, serial numbered, quantity 1,000, price $300, 1987, value $250.

Kershaw Limited Edition Scrimshaw by Walter Alexander, Manufacturer - Kershaw, Pattern - Labrador retriever color scrimshaw on handle, serial numbered, quantity 1,000, price $350, 1988, value $250.

Kershaw Limited Edition Scrimshaw by Walter Alexander, Manufacturer - Kershaw, Pattern - Set of three with black and white scrimshawed handles: bald eagle, big horn sheep, grizzly bear, serial numbered, quantity 1,000, price $650, 1988, value $500.

Kershaw Limited Edition Scrimshaw, by Walter Alexander, Manufacturer - Kershaw, Pattern - Canada geese color scrimshaw on handle, serial numbered, quantity 1,000, price $350, 1988, value $200.

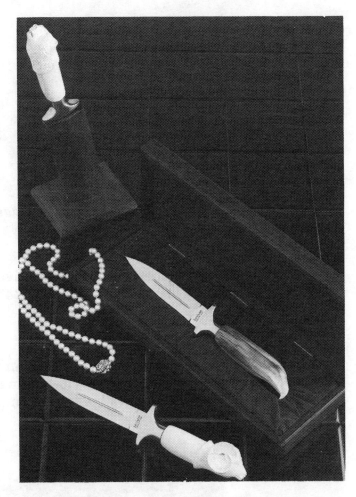

Kershaw North American Wildlife Series

Kershaw North American Wildlife Series, Manufacturer - Kershaw, Pattern - Ivory handled dagger, handles carved into bald eagle, grizzly bear, bighorn ram or polar bear, carved by Erhard Gross, quantity 100 Ea., price $900, 1986, value $550.

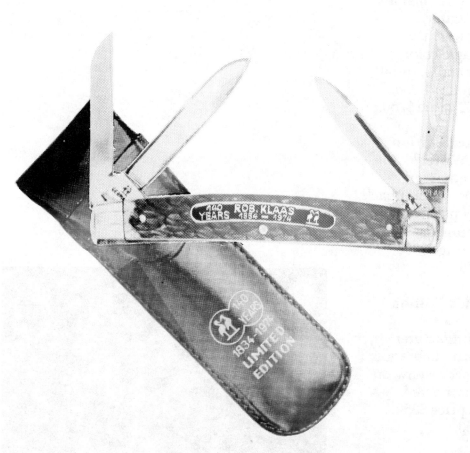

Kissing Crane/ Robert Klaas 140th Anniversary

Kissing Crane/ Robert Klaas 140th Anniversary, Manufacturer - Robert Klaas, Pattern - Four blade congress, 3-3/4" closed, red pickbone handle, etched blade, serial numbered, red enamel shield, leather slip pouch, quantity 5,000, price $30, 1974, value $65.

Kissing Crane/ Robert Klaas 145th Anniversary, Manufacturer - Robert Klaas, Pattern - Lockback, 5" closed, stag handles, three color blade etch, serial numbered, pine wall plaque, quantity 2,000, 1979, value $75.

Kissing Crane/ Robert Klaas 145th Anniversary

Kissing Crane/ Robert Klaas 150th Anniversary, Manufacturer - Robert Klaas, Pattern - Set of two, both knives feature red pick bone handles, two color blade etch, presentation case (1) Mini barlow, 2 7/8" closed, quantity 1,200, 1984, value $28. (2) 3 blade whittler, 4" closed, quantity 1,000, 1984, value $52.

Kissing Crane/ Robert Klaas 155th Anniversary, Manufacturer Robert Klaas, Pattern - One blade lockback, bowtie patterns, set of two, 3-5/8" closed, both knives feature two color blade etch (1) Genuine stag handles, quantity 1,000, 1989, value $58 (2) Red bone handles, quantity 1,000, 1989, value $48.

Kissing Crane / Robert Klaas Alabama "Roll Tide", Manufacturer - Kissing Crane, Pattern - 3-3/4" four blade congress, blue celluloid handles, etched blade, value $40.

Kissing Crane / Robert Klaas Buffalo Nickel Commemorative, Manufacturer - Robert Klaas, Pattern - Two blade copperhead, 3-3/4" closed, black composition handles with Buffalo Nickel style inlay shield, etched blades, Buffalo Nickel, quantity 500, value $50.

Kissing Crane / Robert Klaas Indian Head Penny Commemorative, Manufacturer - Robert Klaas, Pattern - Two blade copperhead, 3-3/4" closed, yellow celluloid handles with Indian Penny style inlay shield, etched blades, serial numbered on bolster, satin line presentation case with genuine Indian Head Penny, quantity 500, value $50.

Kissing Crane / Robert Klaas Kentucky Wildcats, Manufacturer - Kissing Crane, Pattern - 3-3/4" four blade congress, blue celluloid handles, etched blade, value $40.

Kissing Crane / Robert Klaas Limited Edition, Manufacturer - Robert Klaas, Pattern - 3-5/8" four blade canoe, deep-etched, 2-color filled blade, quantity 500, price $36.99, value $60.

Kissing Crane/ Robert Klaas Making Of The First Flag Bicentennial, Manufacturer - Robert Klaas, Pattern - One blade floating guard lockback, 4-3/8" closed, genuine stag handles, blade etch commemorates the first American flag, walnut display case, quantity 3,000, value $95.

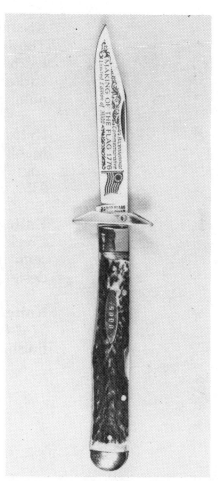

Kissing Crane/ Robert Klaas Making Of The First Flag Bicentennial

Kissing Crane / Robert Klaas Mercury Dime Commemorative, Manufacturer - Robert Klaas, Pattern - Two blade copperhead, 3-3/4" closed, red composition handles with Mercury Dime style inlay shield, etched blades, Mercury Head Dime, quantity 500, value $50.

Kissing Crane / Robert Klaas Red Baron, The, Manufacturer - Robert Klaas, Pattern - One blade folder, 5" closed, large frame, red composition handles, nickel silver airplane inlay shield, two color blade etch, satin line presentation case, quantity 600, value $60.

Kissing Crane / Robert Klaas Swamp Fox, The, Manufacturer - Robert Klaas, Pattern - Lockback, 4-1/8" closed, smooth bone handles with nickel silver running fox inlay shield, two color blade etch, walnut display box, quantity 1,200, price $65, 1976, value $45.

Kissing Crane / Robert Klaas Tennessee & Kentucky Copperhead Set, Manufacturer - Robert Klaas, Pattern - Copperheads, set of two, 3-3/4" closed, stag handles, produced by Robert Klaas Co. for Parker-Frost Cutlery, featured etched blades, matching serial numbers, satin lined presentation case, quantity 1,200 sets, value $150.

Kissing Crane/ Robert Klaas Tennessee Walking Horse & Kentucky Thoroughbred Set, Manufacturer - Robert Klaas, Pattern - Set of two lockbacks, 5" closed, stag handles, produced by Robert Klaas Co. for Parker-Frost Cutlery, featured color etched blades, matching serial numbers, satin lined presentation case, quantity 1,000 sets, value $150.

Knife Collectors Club Limited Edition – Kentucky Rifle Premier, Manufacturer - Shaw-Leibowitz, Pattern - Three blade stock, 14K gold, engraved by Lynton McKenzie, clip, sheepfoot, and spear blades, price $350, value $400.

Knife World Limited Edition - Knife World, Manufacturer - Cripple Creek, Pattern - Subscription to Knife World included with each purchase, semi-custom, hand crafted (two blade trapper with a broken blade design), quantity 2,000, price $45, 1982, value $125.

Knifemaker's Guild Limited Edition, Manufacturer - n/a, Pattern - 5-3/4" & 7-1/2" stag fighters, ATS-34 steel, stag handles, Teflon S, satin finish, quantity 100, price $575, 1987, value $575.

L

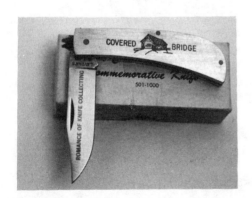

*Lavona's Cutlery Co.
Covered Bridge*

LKR Ltd. William Scagel Replica- Manufacturer - LKR Ltd., Pattern - Bowie, 1920's reproduction, custom fitted black walnut box, quantity 100, price $1,500, 1983, value $1,500.

Lavona's Cutlery Co. Covered Bridge, Manufacturer - Alcas, Pattern - One blade folder, metal handle, "Covered Bridge" etched on handle, "Romance of Knife Collecting" etched on blade, serial numbered, quantity 1,000, value $50.

Longmont Knife Works Colorado Hunter, Manufacturer - n\a, Pattern - n\a, price $35, value $40.

Longmont Knife Works Colorado Outfitter, Manufacturer - Skip Bryan, Pattern - One blade lockback, quantity 100, price $30, value $35.

M

Mac Tools 40th Anniversary of Mac Tools, Manufacturer - Schrade Cutlery, Pattern - Three blade brass, quantity 12,000, price $40, 1979, value $40.

Mac Tools Limited Edition, Manufacturer - Schrade Cutlery, Pattern - IXL bone three blade canoe, quantity 3,600, price $50, 1979, value $70.

Mareck, James Texas: From the Alamo to the Moon

Mareck, James Texas: From the Alamo to the Moon, Manufacturer - Eye Brand, Pattern - Set of two trappers, Alamo etch on one knife, Space Shuttle on the other, quantity 600, price $125, value $110 set.

Military Replica Arms 125th Anniversary of the Battle of Appamattox Cavalry Officer's Sword, Manufacturer-Imported, Pattern - Replica of Southern swordmaker Louis Froelich, North Carolina, high polished brass hilt with stylized "CSA"cutout in lower guard, black leather grip secured with brass wire, blade etched both sides, blued steel scabbard with polished brass fittings, quantity 100, $349, 1989, value $250.

Military Replica Arms 150th Anniversary – Alamo 1836 – 1986, Manufacturer - n\a, Pattern - 13-1/4" Bowie, both sides of blade are filled in gold with Alamo and "March 6, 1836", the date of the battle, polished rosewood grip, silver plated cross-guard, quantity 100, price $50, 1986, value $100.

Military Replica Arms CSA General Jo Shelby Commemorative Saber, Manufacturer - n\a, Pattern - Cavalry officer saber replica, ornate brass guard and pommel, black leather grip wrapped with twisted brass wire, polished steel blade deep etched with Confederate flag, decorated panel, blued steel scabbard with polished brass throat, center band and drag quantity 100, price $329, 1989, value $200.

Military Replica Arms Custer – Little Big Horn, Commemoratives Series, Manufacturer - n\a,

(1) 1872 7th Cavalry Officer's Saber, high carbon steel blade, deep etch both sides, gold filled, nickel silver guard, steel scabbard quantity 100, price $149.95, 1986, value $100.

(2) Deluxe 1872 Cavalry Officer's Saber, Damascus steel blade, deep etched, 24K gold plated hilt, brass scabbard, silver with 24K gold plating quantity 25, price $224.95, 1986, value $250.

(3) Tomahawk, gold filled etching panel with 7th Cavalry, Indian warrior, portrait of Custer, quantity 100, price $39.95, 1986, value $50.

(4) 13-1/2" Bowie knife, gold filled panel with 110th Year, 7th Cavalry, Custer, Indian warrior, scabbard, quantity 100, price $49.95, 1986, value $90.

(5) 1860 7th Cavalry Trooper's saber and scabbard, blade spring steel with gold filled etching inscribed 110th Year, nickel silver guard, quantity 100, price $124.95, 1986, value $100.

Military Replica Arms Custer – Little Big Horn, Commemoratives Series Tomahawk

Military Replica Arms Georgia-McElory Calvary Commemorative Cavalry Saber, Manufacturer - n\a, Pattern - Replica of very rare "W. J. McELORY/MACON, GA." cavalry officer's saber, decorative brass guard and pommel, high polished, black leather grip wrapped with single strand brass wire, carbon spring-steel blade, deep etch with maker's name with design of tobacco and cotton leaves, "C.S.", with flag, deluxe blued metal scabbard etched with military flags, etc., brass mountings, quantity 100, price $329, 1989, value $200.

Morgan & Findley 25th Anniversary Ruger Blackhawk Revolver Set, Including Bowies as part of the set, Manufacturer - Bone Knife Co., Pattern - 10" Bowie, 440C blade with design, gold plated, stag handle, 10" blades, KOA wood case, 8" Bowie for $895., quantity 250, price $1,500, 1983, value $1,500

N

National Turkey Federation 10th anniversary of the National Wild Turkey Federation, Manufacturers - Bench Mark and Knives, USA, Pattern - 4" lockback, brass medallion inset into fiddle back maple, field grade was available in cocobolo at $49.95, price $100, 1983, value $70.

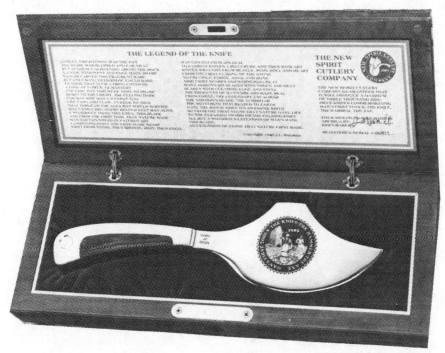

New Spirit Cutlery Company The Knife and Toolmaking Art

New Spirit Cutlery Company The Knife and Toolmaking Art,
Manufacturers - New Spirit Cutlery Company, Pattern - 12" long made
from 1/2" thick tool steel, combines elements of knife, hammer, and axe
in original design quantity 3,000, price $395, 1986, value $175.

O

Ontario Knife Co. Andrew Jackson, Manufacturer - Ontario Knife Co.,
Pattern - Old Hickory one blade lockback, price $18, value $25.

Owen's Cutlery of Hindman, KY. Coal, Kentucky's Number One
Industry, Manufacturer - Fight'n Rooster, Pattern - Stock knife, engraved
blade and black celluloid handles, serialized, quantity 600, price $32.50,
1984, value $45.

P

Pacific Cutlery Corp,. Limited Edition, Manufacturer - Pacific Cutlery Corp., Pattern - 9-1/2" dragon claw stiletto, solid bronze, quantity 600, price $125, 1986, value $100.

In reviewing Parker prices, please keep in mind that standard distributor discounts were 50% off less 25%. ($7.50 for a $20 retail). When many of these knives were issued some dealers would sell a $20.00 retail knife for $8.50. Therefore some prices shown are less than suggested retail but still show a strong appreciation in value over original market price.

Parker American Eagle Series/Set, Manufacturer - Parker Cutlery, Pattern - 4" three blade stock knives, price depended on serial number, each sets knife with different color handle, registration papers, quantity 12,000 sets, price $125, 1976, value $30. each.

Each Christmas, Jim Parker would give away a special knife as a Christmas gift. Extras were sometimes sold.

Parker Cutlery Christmas Knife 1979, Manufacturer - Parker Cutlery, Pattern - 3-3/4" pearl lockback, quantity 1,000, 1979, value $48.

Parker Cutlery Christmas Knife 1980, Manufacturer - Parker Cutlery, Pattern - 3" metal lockback, quantity 1,000, 1980, value $20.

Parker Cutlery Christmas Knife 1980, Manufacturer - Parker Cutlery, Pattern - 4" pearl lockback whittler, quantity 100, 1980, value $75.

Parker Cutlery Christmas Knife 1981, Manufacturer - Parker Cutlery, Pattern - 5" stag clasp – Lord's Supper etched illustration, quantity 1,000, 1981, value $55.

Parker Cutlery Christmas Knife 1982, Manufacturer - Parker Cutlery, Pattern - 3-1/2" two blade trapper, "Unto You A Saviour Is Born", quantity 2,000, 1982, value $40.

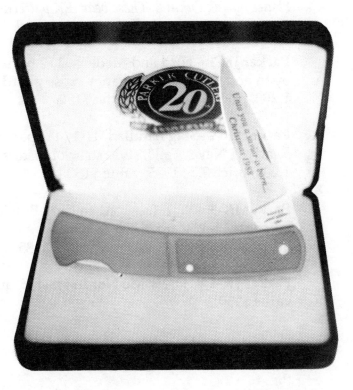

Parker Cutlery Christmas Knife 1982

Parker Cutlery Christmas Knife 1983, Manufacturer - Parker Cutlery, Pattern - 4" three blade stock knife– Matt. 4:19 etched, quantity 1,900, 1983, value $35.

Parker Cutlery Christmas Knife 1983, Manufacturer - Parker Cutlery, Pattern - 4" three blade stock – Masonic version, quantity 100, 1983, value $40.

Parker Cutlery Christmas Knife 1984, Manufacturer - Parker Cutlery, Pattern - 4" trapper, "Jesus" engraved on bolster, quantity 2,000, 1984, value $35.

Parker Cutlery Christmas Knife 1985, Manufacturer - Parker Cutlery, Pattern - 4" trapper – John 3:16, quantity 2,000, 1985, value $35.

Parker Cutlery Knife Christmas Knife 1986, Manufacturer - Parker Cutlery, Pattern - 3" lockback, scripture, quantity 1,800, 1986, value $30.

Parker Cutlery Christmas Knife 1987, Manufacturer - Parker Cutlery, Pattern - 5" lockback – Luke 2:11, quantity 2,400, 1987, value $35.

Parker Cutlery Christmas Knife 1988, Manufacturer - Parker Cutlery, Pattern - Three blade stock – Luke 2:14, quantity 2,400, 1988, value $30.

Parker Cutlery Christmas Knife 1989, Manufacturer - Parker Cutlery, Pattern - 3" lockback, "Christ Is King", quantity 4,000, 1989, value $25.

Parker Cutlery Civil War Period Or Earlier Period Dirks and Sheath Knives. *Damascus Steel, In 1985 Parker Cutlery undertook an ambitious project to reproduce old Civil War or earlier dirks and folding knives. These were made by the best Japanese makers: Same series was also issued with Damascus blades by Tak Fukuta. These bear EK pattern numbers and are valued at twice the value of the same knife in stainless steel.*

Parker JK-1 – Ford and Medley, 1/2 horse 1/2 alligator folder, 11-1/4" open and 6-3/8" closed, fancy cross guard and etched blade, quantity 1,200, price $100, 1985, value $150.

Parker JK-2 –Stag handled, 11-1/4" open, 6-1/2" closed, "Rough And Ready –I Never Fail", style struck bolsters and etched blade, quantity 1,200, price $75, 1985, value $150.

Parker JK-3 – W. F. Jackson, folding Bowie, polished wood handles, fancy bolsters, 12-3/4" open, 7-1/8" closed, etched blade, W. F. Jackson, "I Surpass", quantity 1,200, price $75, 1985, value $150.

Parker JK-4 – "Draw Me Not In Haste", quantity 875, price $75, 1985, value $130.

Parker JK-5 – Wingfield Rowbottom, second cut stag handles, fancy cross guards, 11-1/4" open, 6-1/4" closed, horsehead folder, Liberty etch, quantity 1,200, price $100, 1985, price $150.

Parker JK-6 – Made for Sears, Ft. Sumter, SC, brass framed quantity 1,200, price $99, 1985, value $175.

Parker JK-7 – C. Congreve, lockback folding Bowie, white bone handles, escutcheon plate, 10-3/4" open, 6-1/8" closed, "Ourselves We Must Defend" etching, quantity 1,200, price $85, 1985, value $125.

Parker JK-8 – "Liberty & Union", two blade folder, fancy relief bolsters, 10-3/4" open, 6-1/8" closed, quantity 1,200 $85, 1985, value $125.

Parker JK-9 –G. Woodhead, half horse, half alligator pommel, buffalo horn handles, authentic style etching "Land of Freedom, the Patriots Self Defender, protected by her brave volunteers", wall plaque included, 14-5/8" closed, 10" blade, pearl Bowie, 1985, quantity 1,200, value $150.

Parker JK-10, S. C. Scragg & Sons, "The Self Defender", Bowie, 13-1/2" long, 8-3/4" blade, authentic style Bowie fitting, Mother of pearl scales, genuine wood wall plaque included, quantity 1,200, 1985, value $125.

Parker JK-11 – Manson Bowie, "Liberty & Union" bolster, quantity 1,200, price $75, 1985, value $120.

Parker JK-12 – Reilly's Superior, "Old Dominion", complete with Virginia seal and "Real Virginia Knife" marking, two blades, smooth bone handles, 10-3/4" open, 6" closed, quantity 1,200, price $85, 1985, value $125.

Parker JK-13 - 5-1/2" closed, 2 blade folder, smooth bone scales inlaid in brass frame, copy of a knife taken off a Civil War prisoner, "C. W. Jones" scratched into handle, quantity 1,000, 1985, value $175.

Parker JK-14 – S. C. Wragg, New Orleans knife, quantity 1,000, price $75, 1986, value $125.

Parker JK-15 – Reclining lion Bowie, stag, quantity 600, price $75, 1987, value $100.

Parker JK-16 – Reclining lion folder, stag, quantity 600, price $75, 1987, value $150.

Parker JK-17 – Edward Barnes folder, quantity 600, price $100, 1987, $125.

Parker Brothers Cutlery "The Eagles", Manufacturer - n\a, Pattern - 2-1/2" two blade Barlow, quantity 200, price $12, value $20.

Parker Cutlery Abalone Eagle, Manufacturer - Parker Cutlery, Pattern - Black handle leopard with inlaid abalone eagle, quantity 300, price $60, 1984, value $85.

Parker Cutlery Civil War Whittlers, Manufacturer - Parker Cutlery, made in Japan, Pattern - Set of four whittlers, bone handles, each depicts a famous Civil War battle: Lookout Mountain, Chickamauga, Gettysburg, and Shiloh, wood box, 600, 1983, value $120.

Parker Cutlery Conquistador, Manufacturer - Parker Cutlery, Pattern - 5" folding hunter, file work blade and backspring, 200 each of black pearl, abalone, and white pearl, quantity 600, price $120, 1984, value $160.

Parker Cutlery Corvette Set, Manufacturer - Parker Cutlery, Pattern - 4" three blade stock knife, set of 12 different knives with Corvette inlaid emblem – 1953 thru 1964, etched blades, quantity 1,200, price $240, 1983, value $250.

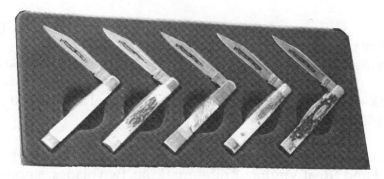

Parker Cutlery Country Doctors

Parker Cutlery Country Doctors, Manufacturer - Parker, Pattern - Doctor's knife, set of five knives with different handle materials, quantity 600, price $150, 1982, $150.

Parker Cutlery Damascus Folders "First 500 Issue", Manufacturer - Parker USA, Pattern - Set of five: (1) 3-3/4 " lockback folder, (2) 5" single blade lockback, (3) 4-1/4" lockback jumbo folder, (4) two blade 3-3/4" copperhead, (5) two blade 4" trapper with Sambar stag handles, first 500 folders made in new Parker-Edwards plant in Alabama, quantity 500, price $490, 1985, value $300.

Parker Cutlery Desperado, Manufacturer - Parker Cutlery, Pattern - Engraved by Liming, inlaid abalone, scrimshawed bird and leopard, quantity 1,985, price $220, 1984, value $200. Very Rare.

Parker Cutlery Excalibur, Manufacturer - Parker Cutlery, Pattern - 4-1/2" three blade canoe, file work, three blades etched, 200 each of abalone, black pearl, and white pearl, quantity 600, price $120, 1984, value $150. *(Very few were made because "Excalibur" was a Gerber trademark and Parker could not use it again.)*

Parker Cutlery Gone With The Wind, Manufacturer - Parker Cutlery, Pattern - 3-3/4" four blade congress, file work, 200 each of abalone, black pearl, white pearl, quantity 600 total, price $130, 1984, value $125.

Parker Cutlery Great American Generals, Manufacturer - Parker Cutlery, Pattern - Canoe, set of two, one knife has picture of Generals Eisenhower, Arnold, and MacArthur on metal handle, other knife has picture of Generals Vandergrift, Marshall, and Bradford, quantity 1,200, price $25, 1983, value $20.

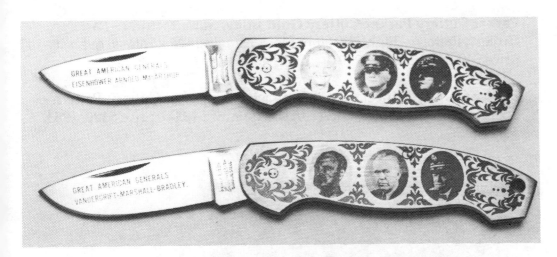

Parker Cutlery Great American Generals

Parker Cutlery Gunfighters/ Clantons, Manufacturer - Parker Cutlery, Pattern - One blade lockbacks, set of three, etched blades, serial numbered , gift box, quantity 1,000, price $80, 1979, value $65.

Parker Cutlery Gunfighters/ Daltons, Manufacturer - Parker Cutlery , Pattern - One blade lockbacks, set of three, etched blades, serial numbered, gift box, quantity 1,000, price $80, 1982, value $65.

Parker Cutlery Gunfighters / Earps, Manufacturer - Parker Cutlery, Pattern - One blade lockbacks, set of three, etched blades, serial numbered, gift box, quantity 1,000, price $80, 1980, value $65.

Parker Cutlery Hercules, Manufacturer - Parker Cutlery, Pattern - 3-1/4" coffin shape, file work, 200 each with three different pearl handle materials, quantity 600, price $60, 1984, value $90.

Parker Cutlery Limited Edition, Manufacturer - Parker USA, Pattern - Six different knives, wild life species depicted on blades, quantity 1,000, price $180, 1989, value $175. (*There were several variations of the Parker Wildlife series.*)

Cutlery Little John Set, Manufacturer - Parker Cutlery, Pattern - Mini Barlows, set of four in display box, quantity 1,200, price $50, 1982, value $55.

Parker Cutlery Little Pillbuster Sets, Manufacturer - Parker Cutlery, Pattern - Seven single blade doctor knives, quantity 1,000, price $120, 1982, value $140.

Parker Cutlery Parker & Sons, Manufacturer - Parker Cutlery, Pattern - 19-piece set, all different patterns in wall mount, second cut stag handles, "Year Of The Eagle" blade etch, 5% of proceeds donated to Wildlife Foundation, quantity 300, price $600, 1982, value $500.

Parker Cutlery Parker Cutlery Gold Inlay, Manufacturer - Parker Cutlery, Pattern - Eight different black iron with 24 k inlays, quantity 100, price $40, 1984, value $200.

Parker Cutlery Princess Set, Manufacturer - Parker Cutlery, Pattern - Six miniature toothpick knives in set, quantity 1,000, price $120, 1983, value $125.

Parker Cutlery Princess Set

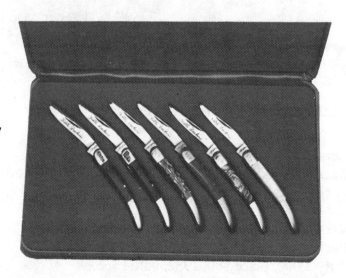

Parker Cutlery Renaissance, Manufacturer - Parker Cutlery, Pattern - 5" lockback display, each day of the week razor with mother of pearl handles, quantity 1,200, price $60 ea. $400 set, 1983, value $80 each, $350 set.

Parker Cutlery Saturday Night Special Set, Manufacturer - Parker Cutlery, Pattern - Nine piece texas toothpick set, "Saturday Night Special" etched in blades, quantity 1,200, price $240, 1983, value $250.

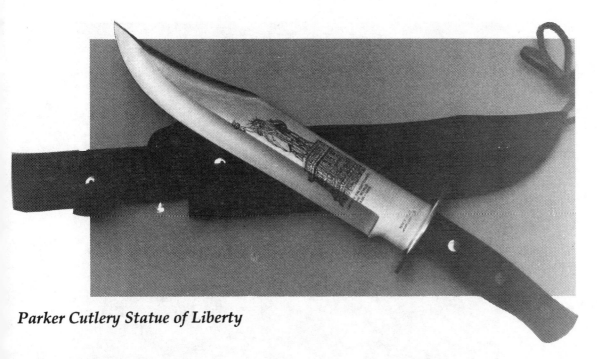

Parker Cutlery Statue of Liberty

Parker Cutlery Statue of Liberty, Manufacturer - Parker Cutlery, Pattern - 15" Bowie, Statue of Liberty etch on blade, leather sheath, quantity 1,000, 1986, value $90.

Parker Cutlery Telephone Pioneers of America, Manufacturer - Case, Pattern - 82079 pearl and eight 8220 pearl peanuts, different Bell divisions silkscreened on the handles, quantity 1,000, price $465, 1983, value $500.

Parker Cutlery Tennessee / Kentucky, Manufacturer - Winchester, Pattern - Trapper, serial numbered, both blades etched, shield bearing state name, bone stag handle, quantity 600, price $60, 1979, value $100.

Parker Cutlery Tom Seaver, Manufacturer - Parker USA, Pattern - Folding hunter, 440 surgical steel blade, genuine Indian stag bone handles, marble base, autographed baseball, quantity 1,200, price $200, 1989, value $175.

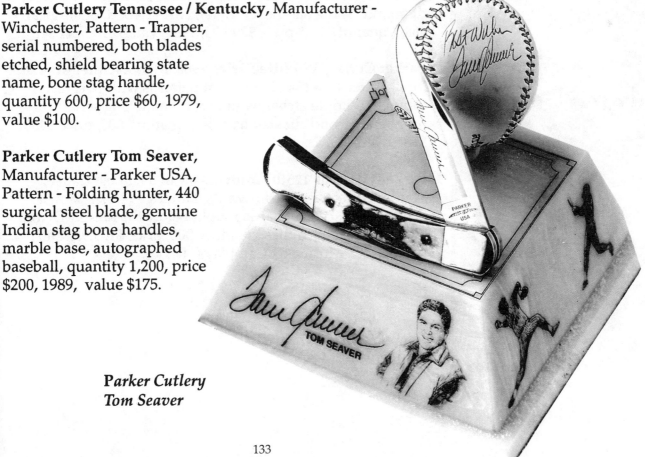

*Parker Cutlery
Tom Seaver*

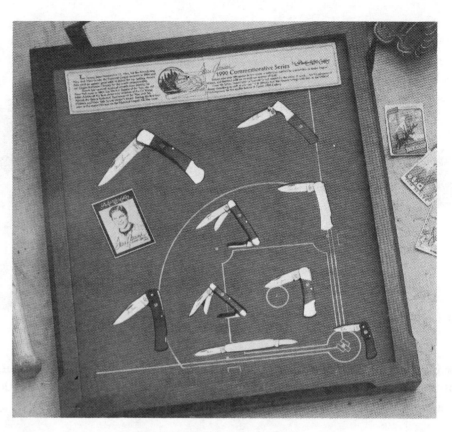

Parker Cutlery Tom Seaver Set

Parker Cutlery Tom Seaver Set, Manufacturer - Parker, Pattern - Set of 9 knives (One for each position on the baseball diamond), Blue handles of Zytel, Parkerwood, or surgical steel, quantity 500, price $299.95, 1989, value $200 per set.

Parker Cutlery Wildlife Series 1986, Manufacturer - Parker-Imai, Pattern - Set of 12 different patterns with twelve different wildlife etches, wall mount, matching serial numbers, second cut stag handles, quantity 600, price $400, 1986, value $375.

Parker-Edwards 125th Anniversary of The Lost Cause, Manufacturer - Parker-Edwards, Pattern - 14-1/4" Bowie, deep etched scene of battle fought below the Mason-Dixon line, India stag handles, quantity 300, price $179.95, 1987, value $150. Music Box Can plays "Dixie".

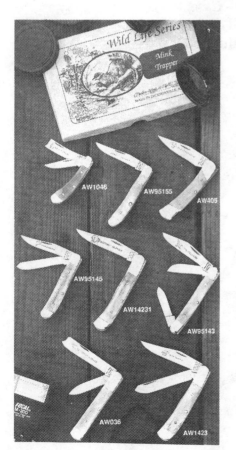

Parker Cutlery Wildlife Series 1986

Limited Edition–Bowie Knife, Manufacturer - Gilbreath, Pattern - Bench made 14-1/2" crown stag Bowie, quantity 300, price $175, 1986, value $200. (*These are listed under Parker because Parker-Frost purchased the entire run.*)

Parker-Frost American Bicentennial Series

Parker-Frost American Bicentennial Series, Manufacturer - Alcas Cutlery, Pattern - Two 5-1/2" clasp knives, one with wood handles, the other with genuine stag handles, two flags etched on blade depict the 1776 flag and the 1976 flag, knives were sold in serial numbered pairs, come with a solid walnut gold leafed box, quantity 1,500, price $200-$400 per set (depending on serial number), 1976, value $250 (set).

Parker-Frost Custer's Last Fight
See description on next page

Parker-Frost Court House Whittlers, The, Manufacturer - Fight'n Rooster, Pattern - Set of two whittlers, gold flake handles, gold etched blades, quantity 600 sets, price $80, 1977, value $125.

Parker-Frost Custer's Last Fight, Manufacturer - Schrade, Pattern - 5-1/2" single blade clasp knife, genuine stag handle, serial numbered, blade etched – art work by Frank Giorgiann, quantity 1,200, price $100, 1978, value $150.

Parker-Frost Custer, Trail of Tears Set, Manufacturer - Schrade, Pattern - 5-1/2" closed folding hunters, quantity 1,000, price $200, 1977, value $300.

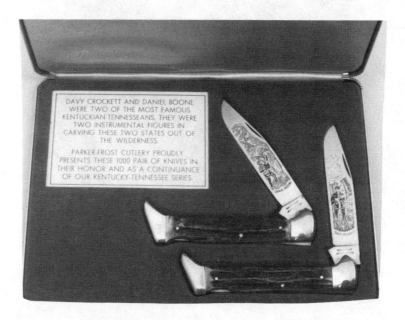

Parker-Frost Davy Crockett and Daniel Boone

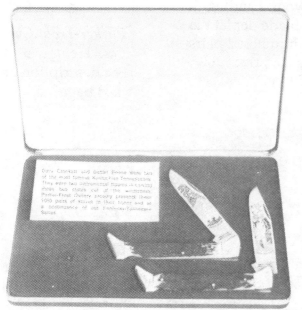

Parker-Frost Davy Crockett and Daniel Boone, Manufacturers - Robert Klaas Co. and Solingen, Ger., Pattern - Set of two 5-1/2" lockbacks, 3-color etch on stainless blades, genuine stag handles, serial numbered and packed in deluxe satin-lined display case, quantity 1,000 sets, price $135, 1977, value $150.

Parker-Frost Davy Crockett and Daniel Boone – "The Frontiersman"

Parker-Frost "Deerslayer", Manufacturer - German, Pattern - 4" closed, single blade lockback, genuine stag handles, quantity 600, price $75, 1976, value $75.

Parker-Frost Eagle Brand Bones, Manufacturer - Schrade, Pattern - 22 knives: 12 different patterns available with red, brown, or green bone handles, plus a X-mas tree canoe, two sheath knives & folding hunter with plastic handles, quantity 2,000 serial numbered sets in a salesman's case, price $450, 1977, value $500. (*These knives were also sold in a non-serial numbered edition for regular consumers.*)

Parker-Frost "Deerslayer"

Parker-Frost Fight'n Bulls, Manufacturer - Parker Cutlery, Pattern - Set of two clasp knives, handle of bone and stag, etched blade, gift boxed, quantity 1,000, price $125, 1977, value $120.

Parker-Frost Gunboat Canoes, Manufacturer - Star, Pattern - Set of two canoes, one smoothbone, one pick bone, quantity 1,800 sets, value $60.

Parker-Frost Indian Series I, Manufacturer - Parker-Frost, Pattern - Set of four trappers, two bone and two celluloid handles, etched blade, shield, quantity 1,200, price $70, 1977, value $150.

Parker-Frost Indian Series II, Manufacturer - Parker-Frost, Pattern - Four trappers, quantity 1,200, price $70, 1978, value $150.

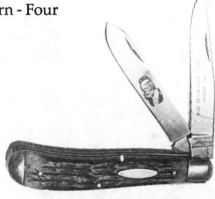

Parker-Frost Indian Series I

Parker-Frost Indian Series III

Parker-Frost Indian Series III, Manufacturer - Parker Cutlery, Pattern - Set of two lockbacks, one fixed blade, quantity 1,200, price $80, 1979, value $70.

Parker-Frost Indian Series IV, Manufacturer - Parker Cutlery, Pattern - Set of three, two lockbacks and one fixed blade, etched blade, gift box, quantity 1,200, price $80, 1980, value $70.

Parker-Frost Indian Series V, Manufacturer - Parker Cutlery, Pattern - Set of three folders, quantity 1,200, price $80, 1982, value $70.

Parker-Frost Kentucky Thoroughbred & Tennessee Walking Horse, Manufacturers - Kissing Crane /Robert Klaas, Pattern - Set of two 5-1/2" one blade lockbacks, stag handles and color etched blades, quantity 1,000 sets, price $110, 1978, value $150.

Parker-Frost Limited Edition – Deer Skinner, Manufacturer - Parker-Frost, Pattern - 4-1/2" skinner, multicolored blade etching, stag handles, quantity 600, price $45, 1980, value $55.

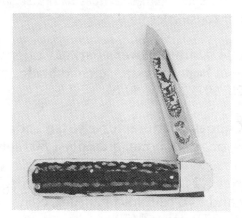

Parker-Frost Limited Edition – Deer Slayer

Parker-Frost Limited Edition – Deer Slayer, Manufacturer - Star, Pattern - 5" clasp knife, blade etch, shield engraved with Deer Slayer, quantity 1,200, price $40, 1976, value $50.

Parker-Frost Limited Edition – Longhorn, Manufacturer - Schrade, Pattern - Three blade stock, serial numbered, etched, gift boxed, quantity 1,200, price $30, 1977, value $45.

Parker-Frost North / South, Manufacturer - Kissing Crane, Pattern - Whittler, depended on serial number, red genuine stag handle, shields depicting Confederate and Union flags, satin-lined case, German made, quantity 1,500 sets, price $220, 1976, value $250.

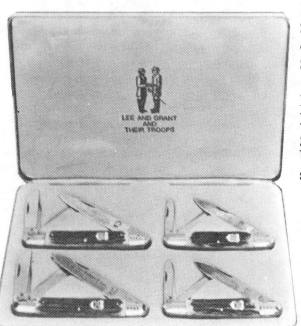

Parker-Frost North / South

Parker-Frost SEC Football Knives

Parker-Frost SEC Football Knives, Manufacturer - n\a, Pattern - 3-1/4"
single blade lockback, color etch of SEC school on blade, wooden handle
inserts, gift box, quantity 3,000, price $11, 1975, value $20 each.

Parker-Frost Service Series, 200th Birthday of the U.S. Armed Forces
See description on following page

Parker-Frost Service Series, 200th Birthday of the U.S. Armed Forces, Manufacturer - Imperial, Pattern - Set of three 4" three blade stock knives, each knife serial numbered, hammer forged blades, 8,000 sets, $12.50 per knife, 1975, value $50 per set.

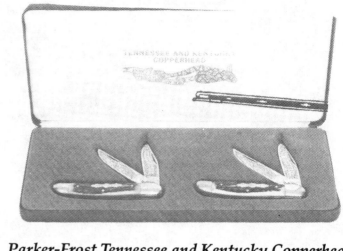

Parker-Frost Tennessee and Kentucky Copperhead

Parker-Frost Tennessee & Kentucky Stockmans

Parker-Frost Tennessee and Kentucky Copperhead, Manufacturer - Kissing Crane /Robert Klaas, Pattern - 4" two blade copperhead, genuine stag handle, both blades etched, serial numbered, deluxe satin-lined box, quantity 1,200, price $120, 1976, value $150.

Parker-Frost Tennessee and Kentucky Muskrat, Manufacturers - Fight'n Rooster and Frank Buster Cutlery, Pattern - Muskrat, 250 pair sets – red & gold celluloid, blue & gold celluloid, 100 pair Mother of Pearl, quantity 600 sets, price $80, 1977, value $150.

Parker-Frost Tennessee & Kentucky Stockmans, Manufacturer - Schrade, Pattern - Two stag stockmans, quantity 1,200 ea., price $60, 1978, value $75.

Parker-Frost Tennessee & Kentucky Whittlers, Manufacturer - Schrade, Pattern - Two whittlers, made from old parts and marked "Schrade Cut. Co.", value $95.

Parker-Frost Tiger Eye & Christmas of '41, Manufacturers - Schrade and Sheffield, Eng., Pattern - Three blade canoe, English made, quantity 1,000, price $30, 1980, value $50.

Police Marksman Association 5th Anniversary, Manufacturer - Smith & Wesson, Pattern - 8" folding hunter, gold velvet line presentation case, drop point blade, S & W seal in handles, quantity1,000, price $89, 1982, value $200.

Puma's 300th Anniversary, Manufacturer - Puma, Pattern - 5" lockback, gold embossed bolsters, gold etched blade, quantity 1,769, price $200, value $275.

Puma "The African Big Five", Manufacturer - Puma, Pattern - Clip lockbacks, animal scrimshawed, quantity 500, price $2,000, 1980, value $1500.

Puma The Defender, Manufacturer - Richard Hehn, Pattern - Fighting knife, 6-3/8" satin finished blade, stainless steel butt, quantity 500, price $650, 1990, value $500.

Puma Founding of Puma- Work in Solingen, Germany, 1769

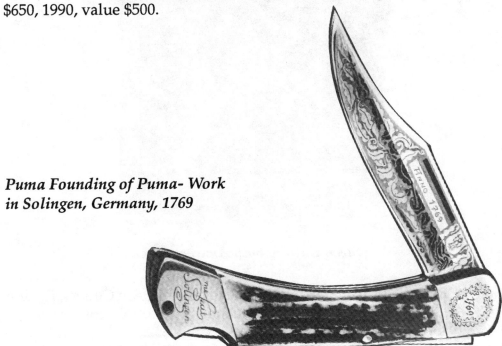

Puma Founding of Puma- Work in Solingen, Germany, 1769, Manufacturer - Puma, Pattern - Lockback, stag handle, engraved bolsters, gold-filled etched blade, serial numbered and registered, wooden presentation box, quantity 1,769, price $325, 1969, value $250.

Puma Game Warden, Manufacturer - Puma, Pattern - Lockback, Jacaranda wood handle, 4" blade, quantity 50, price $2800, value $1400.

Puma Game Warden, Manufacturer - Puma, Pattern - Saw blade instead of skinner, etched "PUMA GAME WARDEN", value $150.

Puma Limited Edition, Manufacturer - Puma, Pattern - Folding hunter, reverse etched blade with beautiful leaf design, stag handles, quantity 1,769, value $250.

Q

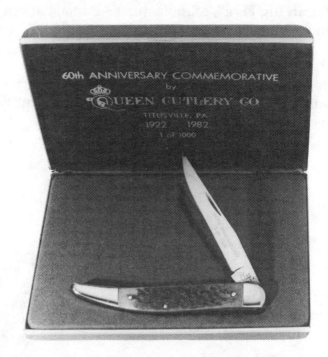

Queen Cutlery 60th Anniversary

Queen Cutlery 60th Anniversary, Manufacturer - Queen Cutlery, Pattern - 4-5/16" closed toothpick, Rogers greenbone handle, gold color deep etched blade, gift box, quantity 1,000, 1982, value $50.

Queen Cutlery 100th Running of the Kentucky Derby, Manufacturer - Queen Cutlery, Pattern - 3" two blade peanut, cardinal red handles, Kentucky shaped shield, housed in a very fragile, clear lid plastic box, price $30, value $18 for set.

Queen Cutlery 200th Birthday of Fort Harrod, Manufacturer - Queen Cutlery, Pattern - 4" two blade stock, cardinal red handles, Kentucky shaped shield, price $30, value $20.

Queen Cutlery Co. 1981 Master Cutler, Manufacturer - Queen Cutlery, Pattern - Peanut, brown bone handles, price $16, value $36.

Queen Cutlery 1982 World's Fair, Manufacturer - Schrade Cutlery, Pattern - Fixed blade hunter with inlayed stone in handle, engraved bolsters, etched blade, presented to President Ronald Reagan, quantity 1,000 1982, value $50.

*Queen Cutlery Co. 1
981 Master Cutler*

Queen Cutlery Co. Copperheads,
Manufacturer - Queen Cutlery, Pattern - Set
of two 3-3/4" copperheads, one handle
genuine stag, the other genuine pearl,
serialized bolster, photo etched blade,
matched serial numbers available, quantity
500, 1981, value, $75.

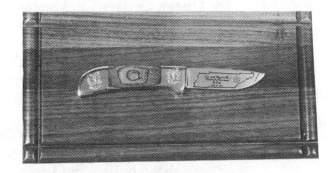

Queen Cutlery 1982 World's Fair

Queen Cutlery Drake's Oil Well,
Manufacturer - Queen Cutlery, Pattern - 3-
1/4" barlow, bone handle, blade etched
with Drake well, quantity 3,600, price $15,
1972, value $40.

Queen Cutlery Co. Limited Edition, Manufacturer - Queen Cutlery,
Pattern - 2-1/2" mini-stockman, imitation pearl, price $30, value $15.

Queen Cutlery Co. Limited Edition, Manufacturer - Queen Cutlery,
Pattern - 3-1/4" sleeveboard pen, onyx handles, price $18, value $16.

Queen Cutlery Co. Limited Edition, Manufacturer - Queen Cutlery,
Pattern - Congress, four blade, cocobolo wood handles, double crest
shield, serial numbered, oak and glass display box, value $70.

Queen Cutlery Co. Limited Stag Series, Manufacturer - Queen Cutlery,
Pattern - 4" stag handles, price $60, 1982, value $40.

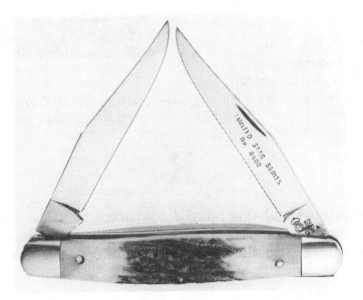

Queen Cutlery Co. Limited Stag Series

Queen Cutlery Co. Limited Edition – USA, Manufacturer - Queen
Cutlery , Pattern - 3-1/2" whittler, fine gold etch, price $57.50, 1980,
value $50.

143

Queen Cutlery Co. Master Cutler 5th Edition Knife, Manufacturer - Queen Cutlery, Pattern - Easy opener, bone handles, price $18, value $35.

Queen Cutlery Master Cutler Collection, Manufacturer - Queen Cutlery, Pattern - 3-5/16" & 4-1/8" trappers, etch bolsters, price $65, 1977, value $60. (*First of the series.*)

Queen Cutlery Co. Master Cutler Collection, Manufacturer - Queen Cutlery, Pattern - 4" closed easy opener, dyed smoothbone handle, serialized bolster, gold color deep etch on blade, gift box, quantity 3,000, 1982, value $35.

Queen Cutlery North Carolina Wildlife Enforcement Officer, Manufacturer - Queen Cutlery, Pattern - Trapper, "North Carolina Wildlife Enforcement Officer" etch on blade, quantity 300, value $65. Only available to North Carolina Game Wardens. Rare.

Queen Cutlery Co. Stag Series, Manufacturer - Queen Cutlery, Pattern - Three blade serpentine, deep etch on clip blade, genuine stag handle, 1982, value $38.

Queen Cutlery Co. Stag Series, Manufacturer - Queen Cutlery, Pattern - Muskrat, two skinning blades, deep blade etch, genuine stag handle, 1982, value $40.

Queen Cutlery Co. Texas Toothpick, Manufacturer - Queen Cutlery, Pattern - Q76 Texas toothpick, quantity 1,200, value $65.

Queen Cutlery North Carolina Wildlife Enforcement Officer

R

R & S Enterprises Hawbaker Special, Manufacturer - Case, Pattern - Muskrat, first ever made with genuine stag handle, both blades etched; with working model double spring trap, quantity 1,000, price $74, 1988, value $85.

Red Man Knives Limited Edition, Manufacturer -Parker Cutlery (Knife marked "Standing Stone") Pattern - Spear point, autographed by Chief Ross O. Swimmer, royalty went to Cherokee Nation, price $49.95, 1981, value $40.

Red Man Knives Limited Edition, Manufacturer - Standing Stone Cutlery, Pattern - 8-1/4" open pocket knife, nickel-silver bolster, brass liners, surgical steel blades, price $49.95, 1981, value $35.

Red Stag Knives

Red Stag knives are German made of high quality, low quantity, and top collectibility.

Red Stag Goodwin Enterprises 5th Anniversary, Manufacturer - Red Stag, Pattern - 63018 buffalo horn stockman, serial numbered, blade etched, quantity 250, price $30, 1988, value $40.

Red Stag Goodwin Enterprises Chattanooga 85th Anniversary Coca-Cola, Manufacturer - Red Stag, Pattern - 84034, 3-1/8" congress, smooth red cherry bone, nickel-silver inlay, deep etch, serial numbered, quantity 500, price $27.50, 1984, value $40.

Red Stag Goodwin Chattanooga Coca-Cola 91st Year, Manufacturer - Red Stag, Pattern - 52109, 1/2 whittler, imitation pearl handle, quantity 300, price $32.50, 1990, value $32.

Red Stag Goodwin Coca-Cola 100th Anniversary, Manufacturer - Red Stag, Pattern - 82025 trapper, only knife made to commemorate Coke's 100th year, red bone handle, quantity 500, price $29.50, 1986, value $50.

Red Stag Goodwin Commemorative of Chattanooga Sesquicentennial, Manufacturer - Red Stag, Pattern - 82029 trapper, green bone handles, numbered with date of each year, quantity 150, price $49.50, 1989, value $40.

Red Stag Goodwin
Enterprises
Chattanooga 85th
Anniversary Coca-Cola

Red Stag Goodwin Enterprises "First Edition", Manufacturer - Red Stag, Pattern - 82023 trapper, red bone handle, serial numbered, quantity 250, price $27.50, 1983, value $36.

Red Stag Goodwin Enterprises "First Edition", Manufacturer - Red Stag, Pattern - 84034 congress, red bone handle, serial numbered, quantity 280, price $27.50, 1984, value $40.

Red Stag Goodwin Enterprises "First Edition", Manufacturer - Red Stag, Pattern - 83065, 3-3/8" stockman, jigged red bone, carbon solingen steel, two color acid etch, serial numbered, quantity 250, price $27.50, 1985, value $36.

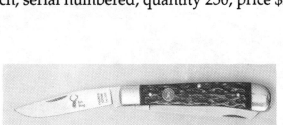

Red Stag Goodwin Enterprises "First Edition" 1983

*Red Stag Goodwin Enterprises
"First Edition" 1987*

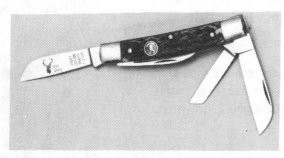

*Red Stag Goodwin Enterprises
"First Edition" 1985*

Red Stag Goodwin Enterprises "First Edition", Manufacturer - Red Stag, Pattern - 73045 whittler, green bone handle, quantity 250, price $27.50, 1985, value $38.

Red Stag Goodwin Enterprises "First Edition", Manufacturer - Red Stag, Pattern - 84065, 3-3/4" congress, jigged brown bone, two-color acid etch, serial numbered, quantity 250, $30, 1986, value $40.

Red Stag Goodwin Enterprises "First Edition", Manufacturer - Red Stag, Pattern - 72087 canoe, smooth green bone handle, carbon steel blades, serial numbered, quantity 250, price $30, 1987, value $38.

Red Stag Goodwin Enterprises "First Edition", Manufacturer - Red Stag, Pattern - 93099, 3-3/4" stockman, stag handled, serial numbered, quantity 250, price $35, 1989, value $40.

Red Stag Goodwin Enterprises Limited Edition, Manufacturer - Red Stag, Pattern - 91055, 4-1/4" stag lockback, genuine stag handle, form fit, leather sheath, quantity 50, price $75, 1985, value $65.

Red Stag Goodwin Enterprises "Premier Edition", Manufacturer - Red Stag, Pattern - 93013, 4" stag stockman, stag handles, first knife ever produced by Red Stag, quantity 300, price $30, 1983, value $45.

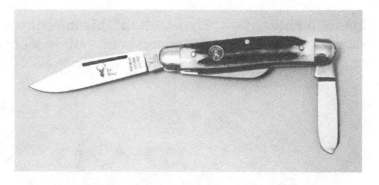

Red Stag Goodwin Enterprises "Premier Edition"

Red Stag Goodwin "Taschenkumpel", Manufacturer - Red Stag, Pattern - 93069, 3-3/8" stag stockman, quantity 100, price $35, 1989, value $40.

Red Stag Goodwin Enterprises Tennessee D. O. T., Manufacturer - Red Stag, Pattern - 73045 whittler, white bone handle, serial numbered, quantity 50, price $27.50, 1985, value $40.

Red Stag Goodwin Enterprises Tennessee D. O. T., Manufacturer - Red Stag, Pattern - 82023 trapper, red bone handle, serial numbered, quantity 50, price $27.50, 1983, value $40.

Red Stag Goodwin Enterprises Tennessee D. O. T., Manufacturer - Red Stag, Pattern - 73065, 3-3/8" stockman, green bone handles, serial numbered, quantity 50, price $27.50, 1985, 5 value $40.

Red Stag Goodwin "Tennessee Homecoming" / "Texas Sesquicentennial", Manufacturer - Red Stag, Pattern - (1) Tennessee – 82026 brown bone trapper (2) Texas – jigged white bone, blades color etched, quantity 150 sets, price $65, 1986, value $75.

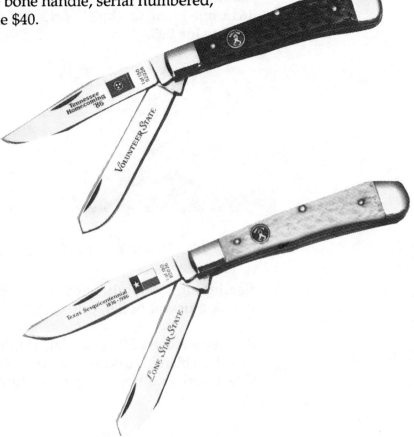

Red Stag Goodwin "Tennessee Homecoming" / "Texas Sesquicentennial"

Remington 1977 Sales Meeting, Manufacturer - Case, Pattern - Case Cheyenne hunting knife, silk screened in white, 1977, value $50.

Remington 1982 Sales Meeting, Manufacturer - Camillus, Pattern - #11 Camillus wildlife lockback, Remington logo etch, quantity 100, value $50.

Remington 1982 Year Knife, Manufacturer - Remington, Pattern - 1123, etched master blade, price $39.95, 1982, value $575.

Remington 1983 Bullet Remington Year Knife, Manufacturer - Remington, Pattern - R1173, sold with guns in a set, price $39.95, 1983, value $275.

Remington 1984 Bullet Year Knife, Manufacturer - Remington, Pattern - 1173L, 3-5/8", one blade lockback, imitation bone handles, bullet shield, price $39.95, 1984, value $200.

Remington 1985 Bullet Year Knife, Manufacturer-Remington, Pattern - R4353 woodsman, price $42, 1985, value $175.

Remington 1986 Bullet, Manufacturer - Remington, Pattern - 1263, banana shaped folding hunter, price $44.95, 1986, value $160.

Remington 1987 Bullet Year Knife, Manufacturer - Remington, Pattern - 1613, one-blade toothpick, price $44.95, 1987, value $95.

Remington 1986 Bullet

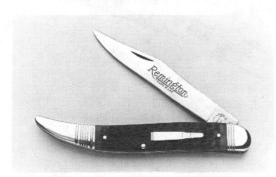

Remington 1987 Bullet Year Knife

Remington 1988 Bullet Year Knife, Manufacturer - Remington, Pattern - R4466, muskrat Bullet, price $46.95, 1988, value $100.

Remington 1988 Silver Bullet, Manufacturer - Remington, Pattern - 3-3/4" two blade muskrat, brown pick bone handles, sterling silver bullet shield, serial numbered, gift box, 1988, value $250.

Remington 1988 Bullet Year Knife

Remington 1989 Bullet Year Knife, Manufacturer - Remington, Pattern - 1128, 4-1/2" two blade trapper, cocobolo wood handles, price $62, 1989, value $55.

Remington 1989 Silver Bullet, Manufacturer - Remington, Pattern - 4-1/2" two blade trapper, brown pick bone handles, sterling silver bullet shield, serial numbered, gift box, 1989, value $160.

Remington 1990 Bullet Year Knife, Manufacturer - Remington, Pattern - Tracker, 4-1/2" one blade lockback, imitation stag, bullet shield, 1989, value $52

Remington 1990 Silver Bullet, Manufacturer - Remington, Pattern - R1306 tracker year knife, brown pick, price $54.95, 1990, value $135.

Remington 1991 Bullet Year Knife, Manufacturer - Remington, Pattern - 3-1/2" two blade baby bullet trapper, bullet shield, imitation stag handles, 1990, value $52.

Remington 1992 Bullet Year Knife, Manufacturer - Remington, Pattern - R1253 "Guide", single blade lockback, saber-ground clip blade, nickel-silver ringed bolsters, DuPont Delrin handle, "Remington" logo etched on blade, 1992, value $73.95.

Remington Baby Bullet Series, Manufacturer - Remington, Pattern - Muskrat, RE44 silver bullet, genuine bone handles, serial numbered, engraved bolsters, quantity 500, value $325.

Remington Baby Bullet Series, Manufacturer - Remington, Pattern - R303 lockback, 1984, value $250.

Remington Fisherman Toothpick, Manufacturer - Remington, Pattern - 5" toothpick, candy stripe celluloid handles, old style cartridge shield, old style box, quantity 10,000, value $60.

Remington Limited Edition, Manufacturer - Remington, Pattern - R1303, "Made Specially for Remington Pro, 1984 NRA Convention, Milwaukee, WI" etch, 1984, value $275.

Remington Limited Edition, Manufacturer - Remington, Pattern - Two blade teardrop jack, "Emdicott Johnson Shoes" shield, value $100.

Remington Replica of the R-1128 "Trapper Bullet", Manufacturer - Remington, Pattern - Two blade trapper, clip & spey blades, both 3-5/8" long, price $46.95, 1989, value $55. (*See also "Remington 1989 Bullet Year Knife"*)

Remington Sportsman Presentation Set, Manufacturer - Remington, Pattern - R5 lockback, 3-1/8" closed, multi-wildlife scene etch, quantity 10,000, price $100, 1989, value $100.

Remington Sportsman Series: Outdoorsman, The, Manufacturer - Remington, Pattern - Folding hunter, single blade lockback, 4" clip blade, 5" closed, 1990, value $55.

Remington Sportsman Series: Stockman Knife, Manufacturer - Remington, Pattern - Premium serpentine stock, three blades, 3-1/8" clip, 2-1/8" spey, and 2-3/16" scalloped sheep foot, price $34.95, 1990, value $35.

Remington Sweepstakes Winner Knife, Manufacturer - Remington, Pattern - R4466 muskrat, premium knives from Remington contest, value $300.

Remington Turkey Hunter's Gift Set, Manufacturer - Remington, Pattern - 4-1/4" closed bird knife, Delrin shinbone handles, quantity 4,000, price $100, 1989, value $100.

Rigid Knives Trophy Whitetail, Manufacturer - Rigid, Pattern - Two blade folding hunter, mother of pearl handles, deep color etch, hand made in Germany, value $145.

Risner, Clarence The Deer Skinner, Manufacturer - n\a, Pattern - Bolster shaped like a deer head, quantity 1,200, price $30, 1977, value $60.

A.G. Russell Collector's Set Entebbe Raid, Manufacturer - Hen & Rooster, Pattern - 2-3/4" closed pocket knife, one blade, screwdriver/caplifter, engraved on one side "July 1976 - Entebbe Airport", on other side in Hebrew name of American born Colonel who led and died in raid, "On Wings Of Eagles" and date in Hebrew, sterling silver quantity 100, price $43, 1976, value $140, stainless quantity 400, price $25, 1976, value $70.

A.G. Russell Collector's Set Hen & Rooster 111 Year Anniversary Set (Set of 10 Anniversary Knives), Manufacturer - Hen & Rooster, Pattern - Four ivory knives, two pearl, two horn, two stag, all with special markings, special presentation case, advance orders, quantity 250 sets, price $850, 1976, value $2,000.
(1) 562H, horn, even end, 2 blades, quantity 250, 1976, value $125.
(2) 575P, pearl congress, 4 blades, quantity 250, 1976, value $275.
(3) 1753HH, stag whittler, 3 blades, quantity 250, 1976, value $250.
(4) 573E, ivory congress, 4 blades, quantity 250, 1976, value $355.
(5) 725P, pearl, premium stock, 3 blades, quantity 250, 1976, value $295.
(6) 1750E, ivory whittler, 3 blades, quantity 250, 1976, value $265.
(7) 556HH, stag, even end, 2 blades, quantity 250, 1976, value $265.
(8) 562H, horn, even end, 2 blades, quantity 250, 1976, value $125.
(9) 556HH, stag, even end, 2 blades, quantity 250, 1976, value, $150.
(10) 574H, horn, congress, 4 blades, quantity 250, 1976, value $250.

A.G. Russell Collector's Set Russell Barlow, Manufacturer - Schrade Cutlery, Pattern - Two blade jack, bone Delrin handles, bolster marked with original hob with "R" and arrow, serial numbers under 200 with cedar box, quantity 12,000, 1976, value $50.

A.G. Russell Collector's Set The Spirit of St. Louis, Manufacturer - Schrade Cutlery, Pattern - 4" closed premium stock, special etch, bolsters and three inlays of nickel silver, serial numbered, quantity 12,000, price $20, 1976, value $45.

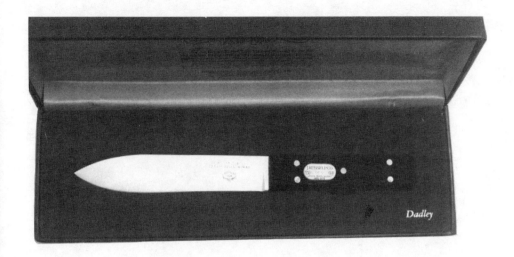

J. Russell & Co. Skinning Knife

Russell Limited Edition, Manufacturer - A.G. Russell,   Pattern - CM-4, 2-3/8" single blade folder, ivory with bullet shield, price $42, value $42.

A.G. Russell Limited Edition, Manufacturer - A.G. Russell, Pattern - CM2 daddy Barlow, price $55, value $55.
J. Russell & Co. Skinning Knife, Manufacturer - Green River Knife Works, Pattern - Skinning knife, One of three different styles made in the 1970's, value $110.

Russell-Harrington Co. Russell Barlow Commemorative, 1875-1975, Manufacturer - Schrade contract for Russell-Harrington Co., Pattern - Barlow, etched, serial numbered, cedar display box, quantity 2,000, price $35, 1975, value $90.

S

Sargent Iwo Jima, Manufacturer - n\a, Pattern - Canoe, etched in gold "Iwo Jima/March 1945", stag, flag raising etch, quantity 300, price $65, value $45.

Sargent Three Blade Stock, Manufacturer - n\a, Pattern - Stock, 4" closed, imitation ivory handles, back springs, quantity 100, price $65, 1979, value $65.

Schrade Cutlery 60th Anniversary of Ace Hardware, Manufacturer - Schrade Cutlery, Pattern - 507 lockback hunter, engraved bolsters, price $135, value $65.

Schrade Cutlery 70th Anniversary Stockman, Manufacturer - Schrade Cutlery, Pattern - Stockman, serialized, black saw cut Delrin handles, price $24, 1974, value $36.

Schrade Cutlery 75th Anniversary, Schrade, Manufacturer - Schrade Cutlery, Pattern - Clasp knife, stag handle, sterling silver bolsters and shield-engraved, display box, price $100, 1979, value $375.

Schrade Cutlery 75th Anniversary Presentation Knife, Manufacturer - Schrade Cutlery, Pattern - 5-1/2" clasp knife, Staglon handles, deep etched blade, price $135, value $125.

Schrade 80th Anniversary, Manufacturer - Schrade Cutlery, Pattern - Daddy Barlow, quantity 8,000, price $75, 1984, value $125.

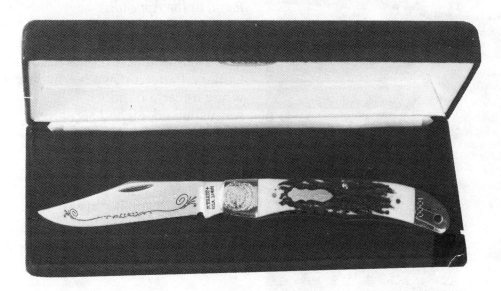

Schrade 80th Anniversary

Schrade 85th Anniversary, Manufacturer - Schrade Cutlery, Pattern - Stag whittler, 3-7/8" closed, quantity 1,000, value $200.

Schrade Cutlery 100 Years of Beef Cattle1875 - 1975, Manufacturer - Schrade Cutlery, Pattern - Three blade stockman, 4" closed, "Long Horn to Pure Bred", price $45, 1975, value $40.

Schrade Cutlery 1984 Los Angeles Games, Manufacturer - Schrade Cutlery, Pattern - Two 1/2" lockbacks, each knife individually serialized, certificate of authenticity, simulated whale tooth Delrin handle, quantity 5,000, price $7.95, 1984, value $20.

Schrade Cutlery 1984 Los Angeles Summer Games, Manufacturer - Schrade Cutlery, Pattern - Sharpfinger, etched blade, Delrin handle, quantity 500, price $40, 1984, value $60.

Schrade Cutlery 1990 Scrimshaw Set, Manufacturer - Schrade Cutlery, Pattern - Complete set of seven, matching serial numbers, wood display case, value (set) $150.

Schrade Cutlery 1991 Scrimshaw Set, Manufacturer - Schrade Cutlery, Pattern - Complete set of seven, matching serial numbers, wood display case, 1991, value (set) $150.

Schrade Cutlery 1992 Scrimshaw Set, Manufacturer - Schrade Cutlery, Pattern - Complete set of seven, matching serial numbers, wood display case, 1992, value (set) $150.

A complete listing of Schrade Scrimshaw sets and their values can be found in the Appendix.

Schrade Cutlery Abe Lincoln Barlow, Manufacturer - Schrade Cutlery, Pattern - Two blade Barlow, white micarta handles, scrimshawed, etched signature, serial numbered, fancy bolsters, 1975, value $36.

Schrade Scrimshaw Sets

Schrade Cutlery American Indian Series, Thunderbird, Manufacturer - Schrade Cutlery, Pattern - Lockback folding hunter, scrimshaw of American Indian on horse, 3-1/2" blade, Delrin handle, beaded leather sheath, serial numbered, quantity 10,000, price $70, 1981, value $200.

Schrade Cutlery American Indian Series, Morningstar, Manufacturer - Schrade Cutlery, Pattern - 511/4" folding hunter, includes beaded leather sheath, quantity 10,000, price $70, 1982, value $100.

Schrade Cutlery American Indian Series, Kachina, Manufacturer - Schrade Cutlery, Pattern - 5-1/4" folding hunter, includes beaded leather sheath, quantity 10,000, price $65, 1983, value $50.

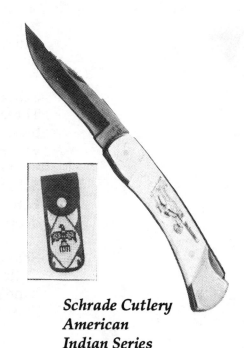

Schrade Cutlery American Indian Series

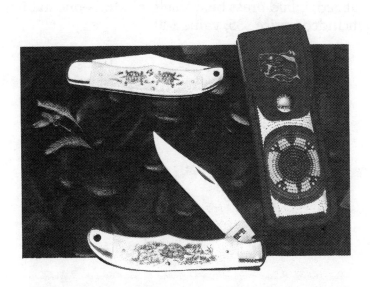

Schrade Cutlery American Indian Series, Turtle

Schrade Cutlery American Indian Series, Turtle, Manufacturer - Schrade Cutlery , Pattern - 5-1/4" folding hunter, turtle scrimshawed on both sides of handle, leather sheath with suede finish and symbol of turtle with hand sewn beads, quantity 10,000, price $65, 1984, value $50.

Schrade Cutlery American Indian Series, Bear Cult, Manufacturer - Schrade Cutlery, Pattern - 5-1/4" folding hunter, includes beaded leather sheath, quantity 10,000, price $70, 1985, value $60.

Schrade Cutlery American Indian Series, Sundance, Manufacturer - Schrade Cutlery, Pattern - 5-1/4" folding hunter, includes beaded leather sheath, quantity 8,000, price $70, 1986, value $60.

Schrade Cutlery Amvets 40th Anniversary, Manufacturer - Schrade Cutlery, Pattern - Clip folder, Uncle Henry signature on stag handle, value $40.

Schrade Cutlery Bald Eagle 200th Anniversary, Manufacturer - Schrade Cutlery, Pattern - n\a, price $35, 1982, value $50.

Schrade Cutlery Bald Eagle Commemorative, Manufacturer - Schrade Cutlery, Pattern - LB-5SC, scrimshawed, serial numbered, quantity 5,000, price $35, value $50.

Schrade Cutlery Buffalo Bill, Manufacturer - Schrade Cutlery, Pattern - Three blade stockman, 4" closed, inlaid brass bust shield of Mr. Cody, brass token included, serialized, black sawcut Delrin handles, price $35, value $40.

Schrade Cutlery "Coal Is Freedom", Manufacturer - Schrade Cutlery, Pattern - LB-7 bear paw, imitation ivory handles, color engraved, blade deep etched, serial numbered, leather sheath, gift box, value $50.

Schrade Cutlery Daniel Boone Commemorative, Manufacturer - Schrade Cutlery, Pattern - Three blade stockman, 4" closed, maroon sawcut Delrin handles, serialized, inlaid brass bust shield of Mr. Boone in buckskin, brass token included, price $35, value $40.

Schrade Cutlery Diamond Jubilee Boy Scout and Deluxe Lockback

Schrade Cutlery Diamond Jubilee Boy Scout and Deluxe Lockback, Manufacturer - Schrade Cutlery, marked "New York Knife Co.", Pattern MS505, 4" closed, quantity, 12,000, price $35, value Diamond Jubilee Boy Scout $45, Deluxe Lockback $75.

Schrade Cutlery Dixie Collection, Manufacturer - Schrade Cutlery, Pattern - Stag handled hunter and stag lockback, "Dixie collection" etch on blade, price $65, value $65.

Schrade Cutlery "The Eagle Has Landed", Manufacturer - Schrade Cutlery, Pattern - LB-7, white handles, color scrimshaw, serial numbered, leather pouch, gift box, "The Eagle Has Landed", value $60.

Schrade Cutlery Farmer, Manufacturer - Schrade Cutlery, Pattern - 4-5/8" stockman, price $20, 1985, value $20.

Schrade Cutlery Federal Duck Stamp, Manufacturer - Schrade Cutlery, Pattern - Two blade trapper, ebony handle, antique bronze shield depicting the duck in flight, antiqued coin brass replica of the Duck Stamp, quantity 6,000, 1987-1988, value $85.

Schrade Cutlery Federal Duck Stamp 1987-1988

Schrade Cutlery Federal Duck Stamp Commemorative 1988-1989, Manufacturer - Schrade Cutlery, Pattern - Two blade trapper, clip and gut hook blades, exotic hardwood handles, deluxe wood display case 1989, value $75.

Schrade Cutlery Corp. Federal Duck Stamp, Manufacturer - Schrade Cutlery, Pattern - Ebony handled trapper, bronze shield, clip blade, bird gut hook, quantity 6,000, 1988-1989, value $75.

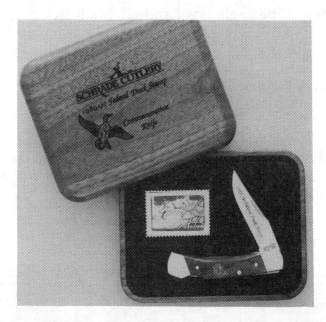

Schrade Cutlery Federal Duck Stamp 1989-1990

Schrade Cutlery Federal Duck Stamp, Manufacturer - Schrade Cutlery, Pattern - 3-3/4" lockback, DS3, Goncalo Alvez hardwood handles, quantity 6,000, 1989-1990, value $85.

Schrade Cutlery George Washington/President Set, Manufacturer - Schrade Cutlery, Pattern - Bear paw folding hunter, white micarta handles, scrimshawed, etched signature, serial numbered 1975, value $50.

Schrade Cutlery The Gold Rush, Manufacturer - Schrade Cutlery, Pattern - LB-7, white handles with full color scrimshaw, serial numbered, leather sheath, gift box, value $50.

Schrade Cutlery Grand Dad's Old Timer Barlow, Manufacturer - Schrade Cutlery, Pattern - 3-5/8" Barlow, black saw-cut Delrin handle with solid brass engraved bolster, diamond engraved back, price $25, value $25.

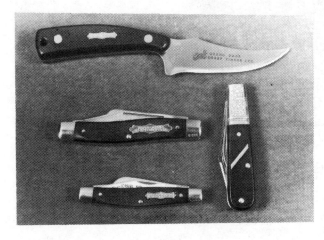

Schrade Cutlery Grand Dad's Old Timer, Manufacturer - Schrade Cutlery, Pattern - 4" stock, diamond-engraved back, serial numbered on bolster, wooden gift box, price $30, value $30.

Schrade Cutlery Grand Dad's Old Timer II, Manufacturer - Schrade Cutlery, Pattern - 3-15/16" stock, brass bolsters, Delrin handle, diamond-engraved back, serial numbered and registration card, price $25, value $35.

Schrade Cutlery "Grand Dad" Series

Schrade Cutlery Grand Dad's Sharp Finger, Manufacturer - Schrade Cutlery, Pattern - 7-1/4" sharpfinger, etched blade, black saw-cut handle fastened with brass rivets, genuine leather sheath and leatherette gift box and registration card, price $25, 1975, value $35.

Schrade Cutlery IXL Custom Limited Edition Scrimshaw Sets, Manufacturer - IXL, Pattern - 3" & 4" closed lockbacks, scrimshaw scene of sailing ship (3") and sailing ship and whale (4"), price $150.

Schrade Cutlery IXL, Manufacturer - IXL, Pattern - Two blade canoe & three blade stock, ship and lighthouse scrimshaw scene, price $72, value $100.

Schrade Cutlery IXL Prize Medal Set, Manufacturer - IXL, Pattern - Set of 5 different knives: (1) 8520 Genuine bone lockback, (2) GS30 Genuine staghorn lockback and leather sheath, (3) M40 Lockback, Ivory Micarta handles and leather sheath, (4) 8540 Three blade folder , genuine bone handles, (5) GS 50 Two blade folder, genuine staghorn handles, set commemorates Schrade IXL medal winners, etched blades, display box, value $200 (set).

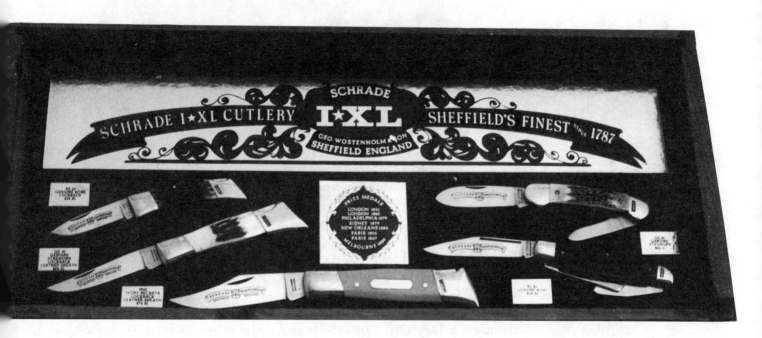

Schrade Cutlery IXL Prize Medal Set

Schrade Jim Bowie, Manufacturer - Schrade Cutlery, Pattern - Three blade stockman, striated staglon handle, brass linings, nickel-silver bolsters, antiqued handle shields—Bowie knife and oval shield "Jim Bowie Limited Edition", quantity 18,000, price $20, value $30.

Schrade Cutlery Keen Kutter 100th Anniversary, Manufacturer - Schrade Cutlery, Pattern - Two versions, one like an 897UH Schrade Uncle Henry, the other a three blade serpentine slightly smaller, quantity 6,000, price $10, 1969, value $65. (*See also "Keen Kutter 100th Anniversary "*)

Schrade Cutlery Liberty Bell, Manufacturer - Schrade Cutlery, Pattern - 3-5/8" Stockman, black composition handle, Liberty Bell shield, comes in acetate box with registration form, quantity 24,000, price $12.50, value $27.50.

Schrade Cutlery Limited Edition, Manufacturer- Schrade Cutlery, Pattern - 261SC two blade folding hunter, 5-1/4" closed, words "Eagle" and "Liberty-Justice" scrimshawed on handle, price $40, value $40.

Schrade Cutlery Limited Edition, Manufacturer - Schrade Cutlery, Pattern - 260SC two blade folding hunter, 5-1/4" closed, American Eagle on handle, price $40, value $40.

Schrade Cutlery Limited Edition Salesman's Knife, Manufacturer - Schrade Cutlery, Pattern - Set of two: One fixed blade hunter, one single blade folding canoe, Staglon handles on both, etched blade, comes with display box, these knives were sold only by salesmen, value n/a.

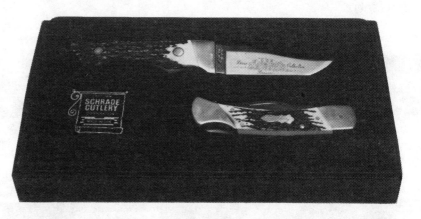

Schrade Cutlery Limited Edition Salesman's Knife

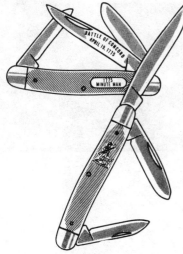

Schrade Cutlery Minuteman

Schrade Cutlery Minuteman, Manufacturer - Schrade Cutlery, Pattern - 3-5/8" Stockman, black composition handle, Minuteman shield, comes in acetate box with registration form, quantity 24,000, price $12.50, value $20.

Schrade Cutlery Old Timer Silver Anniversary, Manufacturer - Schrade Cutlery, Pattern - 340T, sterling silver shield and bolsters, price $35, value $60.

Schrade Cutlery Oliver North, Manufacturer - Schrade Cutlery, Pattern - LB-7 bear paw, imitation ivory handles color engraved, deep etched blade, serial numbered, leather sheath, gift box, value $50.

Schrade Cutlery Paul "Bear" Bryant, Manufacturer - Schrade Cutlery, Pattern - Three blade stockman, white bone handle, etched blade, Coach Bryant's picture on handle, comes in collectors box with desk plaque. (*Schrade manufactured two different Bear Bryant commemoratives. Each was contracted by a different organization. There were 3,000 of one manufactured in 1981 for Collegiate Concepts, and another was manufactured in a quantity of 2,400 for an unrecorded company. These commemoratives were sold by these two organizations, so there is no record of retail or current collector value at this time. Estimate: $35- $40.*)

Schrade Cutlery Paul Revere, Manufacturer - Schrade Cutlery, Pattern - 3-5/8" Stockman, red composition handle, Paul Revere shield, comes in acetate box with registration form, quantity 24,000, price $12.50, value $20.

Schrade Cutlery Pony Express, Manufacturer - Schrade Cutlery, Pattern - Lockback, serialized and registered, blade is etched on both sides, suede leather sheath branded with a horse head, quantity 8,000, value $70.

Schrade Cutlery Rawhide 1875-1975, Manufacturer - Parker-Frost, Pattern - 4" premium stock cattleman's knife, three blades, clip, sheep foot, and spey, quantity 3,000, price $15, 1977, value $35.

Schrade Cutlery Silver Anniversary, Manufacturer - Schrade Cutlery, Pattern - 34OT, sterling bolster and shield, price $45, value $80.

Schrade Cutlery Spirit of St. Louis, Manufacturer - Schrade-Walden, Pattern - Three blade stockman, etched blade, each knife has one of three special shields: the airplane, a Keen Kutter emblem, and on the back of the black handled knife, a shield with the date of the flight, serial numbered, quantity 12,000, price $20, 1974, value $30. (*See also "Keen Kutter Spirit of St. Louis"*)

Schrade Cutlery Teddy Roosevelt, Manufacturer - Schrade Cutlery, Pattern - 3-5/16" stockman, price $80, 1975, value $45.

Schrade Cutlery Paul "Bear" Bryant

Schrade Cutlery Pony Express

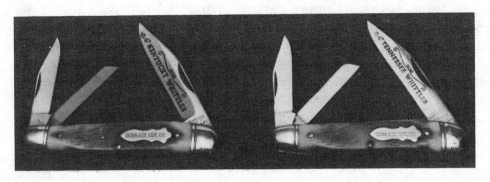

Schrade Cutlery Tennessee / Kentucky

*Schrade
Cutlery Teddy
Roosevelt*

Schrade Cutlery Tennessee / Kentucky, Manufacturer - Schrade Cutlery, Pattern - Two whittlers, etched blades, Schrade Cutlery Co. shield made from all old parts except handles, made exclusively for Parker-Frost, quantity 3,000, value $95.

Schrade Cutlery Tradesman Series, Manufacturer - Schrade Cutlery, Pattern - Set of five knives, three folding stockmans, two folding trappers, each knife has a different blade etch: The Farmer, The Lumberman, The Miner, The Rancher, and The Fisherman, quantity 6,000, price $200 (set), 1982, value $350.

Schrade Cutlery True Value Hardware "American Eagle", Manufacturer - Schrade Cutlery, Pattern - n\a, price $25, 1984, value $40.

Schrade Cutlery U.S. Shooting Team, Manufacturer - Schrade Cutlery, Pattern - Fixed blade hunter, scrimshawed blade commemorates U.S. shooting team, comes with certificate of authenticity and leather sheath, quantity 1,000, price $69.95, 1984, value $70.

Schrade Cutlery Village of Walden, Manufacturer - Schrade Cutlery, Pattern - Two blade 3" equal end, metal handle engraved "New York Knife Works", quantity 5,000, price $28, 1976, value $40.

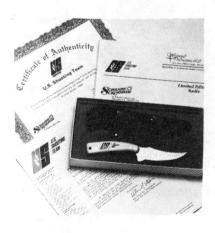

*Schrade
Cutlery U.S.
Shooting
Team*

Schrade Cutlery Village of Walden

Schrade Cutlery Vince Dooley – Head Coach University of Georgia 1964 - 1989, Manufacturer - Schrade Cutlery, customized by Frost Cutlery, Pattern - One blade, white handles, color, engraving, serial numbered 1989, value $30.

Schrade Cutlery Warren Tool, Manufacturer - Schrade Cutlery, Pattern - Pair of 2 special whittlers, price $40, value $40.

Schrade Cutlery Warren Tool

Schrade Cutlery Whaling Knife, Manufacturer - ΩSchrade Cutlery, Pattern - Loveless drop point, beautifully scrimshawed handle and two-toned etched blade, price $400.

Schrade Cutlery Will Rogers, Manufacturer - Schrade Cutlery, Pattern - 340T, plastic handles, reportedly produced exclusively for Otasco stores and not sold through normal discounters, price $20, value $35.

Schrade Cutlery Will Rogers

Schrade-Loveless

Schrade-Loveless, Manufacturer - Schrade Cutlery, Pattern - Hunter, custom ground, Delrin handle, handle custom fitted to blade, steerhide sheath, personally designed by Bob Loveless, price $100.

Sears 75th Anniversary of the Scouts Start, Manufacturer - Schrade Cutlery, Pattern - Scout knife, exact reproduction including can opener, punch and bottle opener, diamond jubilee coin is included, price $25, value $45.

Sears Alwilda - The Legendary Female Pirate

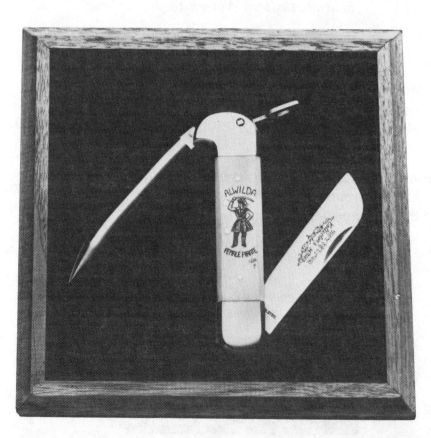

Sears Alwilda - The Legendary Female Pirate, Manufacturer - n\a, Pattern - Carbon-dated, 25,000-year-old mammoth tusk handle, scrimshaw of Alwilda—female pirate, walnut display case, price $50, value $50.

Sears Currier & Ives Collector's Knife, Manufacturer - Schrade Cutlery, Pattern - One blade folding hunter, etch of 1864 scene "The 'Lightning Express Trains' Leaving The Junction", quantity 2,000, price $90, 1984, value $90.

Sears Endangered Species Of The World, Manufacturer - Kershaw, Pattern - Set of four lockbacks, scrimshawed handles of a cheetah, Siberian tiger, snow leopard or puma, quantity 1,000, price $80 set, 1984, value $80.

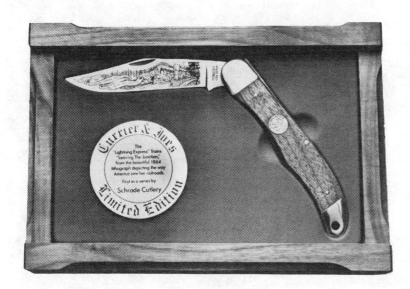

Sears "The Lighting Express Trains "

Sears "The Lighting Express Trains ", Manufacturer - Currier & Ives, Pattern - Stockman, clip blade, reproduction of 1864 scene of the trains, quantity 2,000, price $90, 1984, value $75.

Sears Morgan Knife, Manufacturer - n/a, Pattern - Walrus tusk ivory handle featuring an etch of the ship and signed by the artist, quantity 3,000, price $50, value $50. (*See picture on following page*)

Sears Wildlife Collectors Series, Manufacturer - W.R. Case, Pattern - Classic Case trapper with multi-color earthwood handles, duck etch on blades, fancy enamel color shield, serial numbered, hinged plastic display case, value $40.

Shaw-Leibowitz & Bill's For Knives The Squirrel, Manufacturer - n/a, Pattern - Two blade trapper, 2-1/2" closed, set of three, etched squirrel, bronze, silver, or gold plate on sterling silver, quantity 600, 1981, price $45 (Bronze), $65 (Silver), $90 (Gold), $170 (Set).

Shaw-Leibowitz Grizzly Bear Family, Manufacturer - Case, Pattern - Case I278, five knives, high relief sterling silver handles, walnut display box, quantity 400, $100 each.

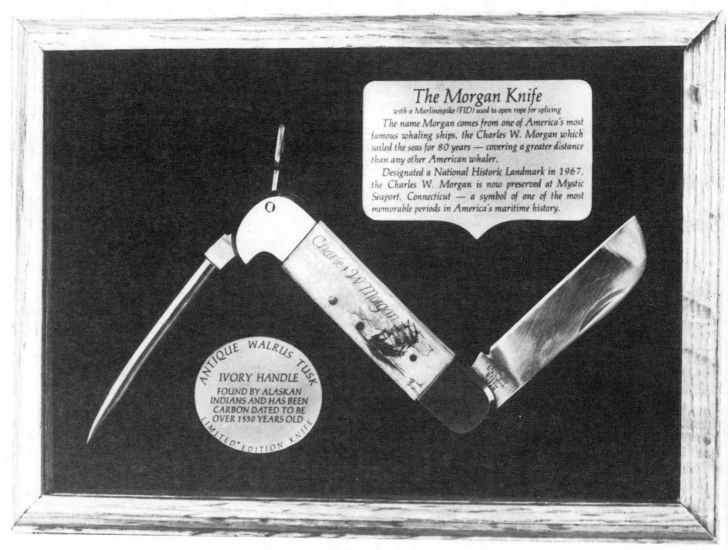

The Morgan Knife

with a Marlinespike (FID) used to open rope for splicing

The name Morgan comes from one of America's most famous whaling ships, the Charles W. Morgan which sailed the seas for 80 years — covering a greater distance than any other American whaler.

Designated a National Historic Landmark in 1967, the Charles W. Morgan is now preserved at Mystic Seaport, Connecticut — a symbol of one of the most memorable periods in America's maritime history.

ANTIQUE WALRUS TUSK

IVORY HANDLE

FOUND BY ALASKAN INDIANS AND HAS BEEN CARBON DATED TO BE OVER 1550 YEARS OLD

LIMITED·EDITION KNIFE

Sears Morgan Knife

Shaw-Leibowitz Rare Sterling Silver Collector Knives, Manufacturer - Case, Pattern - Shadow handle pen knife, classical scrolls surround an oval for complimentary, engravings up to 20 letters, quantity 1,000, price $128, 1982, $100.

Shaw-Leibowitz "The Fox", Manufacturer - Schrade Cutlery, Pattern - Two blade pen, 2-3/4" closed, bushy tailed fox relief with grapes & grape leaf clusters, set of four, quantity 55 sets, price $375, 1982, value $500 (*Very Rare*)

Smith & Wesson 125th Anniversary, Manufacturer - Smith & Wesson, Pattern - Folding hunter, etched portraits of the firm's founders, quantity 500, price $100, 1977, value $200.

Smith & Wesson Collector Series, Manufacturer - Smith & Wesson, Pattern - Fixed blade knife, serial numbered, acid-etch game scene on blade, hand engraved escutcheons inlaid in handle, mahogany presentation case, quantity 1,000, value $400.

Smith & Wesson Collector's Set, Manufacturer - Blackie Collins, Pattern - Four knives: survival, skinner, outdoorsman and Bowie, each blade is etched with a wildlife scene, engraved escutcheons are inlaid in each hardwood handle, quantity 1,000 sets, price $1,400, 1970's, value $200.

Smith & Wesson Collector Series

Smith & Wesson Texas Rangers 1823 - 1973, Manufacturer - Smith & Wesson, Pattern - 10-1/4" Bowie, laminated wood handles with Texas Ranger Shield, heavy brass guard and brass butt cap, 1973, value $200.

Smith & Wesson Whitetail Deer, Manufacturer - n/a, Pattern - Clip point blade or utility drop point blade, deer etching on scrimshaw, quantity 950, price $295, 1987, value $200.

Smoky Mountain Knife Works 1983 Mule Day Mini-Trapper, Manufacturer - Colonel Coon, Pattern - Mini-trapper, quantity 500, 1983, value $90.

Smoky Mountain Knife Works 1985 Mule Day Knife, Manufacturer - Colonel Coon, Pattern - Trapper, stag handles, 1985, value $95.

Smoky Mountain Knife Works Coin Pattern, Manufacturer - Sheffield, Eng., Pattern - Patterned like a coin with two worked back blades, rooster scrimshaw in center, quantity 20, price $450, value $450.

Smoky Mountain Knife Works Grizzly Folding Knife, Manufacturer - Shaw-Leibowitz & Case, Pattern - Case 278, two stainless steel blades, nickel silver liners, quantity 400, 1980, value $90.

Smoky Mountain Knife Works Limited Edition, Manufacturer - Case, Pattern - Three blade stockman, 4" closed, coal black silkscreened handle, quantity 5,000, price $16.99, 1990, value $16.99.

Smoky Mountain Knife Works Limited Edition, Manufacturer - n\a, Pattern - 5-1/4" clasp knife, quantity 600, price $40, value $40.

Smoky Mountain Knife Works Limited Edition, Manufacturer - Case, Pattern - Pearl peanut 8220SS, quantity 5,000, price $42.50, value $55.

Smoky Mountain Knife Works Limited Edition, Manufacturer - Case, Pattern - Three knife set: 6254, 6254SS, & 3254 trappers, quantity 600 sets, price $110, value $110.

Smoky Mountain Knife Works Little Smoky, Manufacturer - n\a, Pattern - Mini boot knife, genuine mother-of-pearl and genuine India stag, quantity 1,000, price $89.95, 1980, value $100.

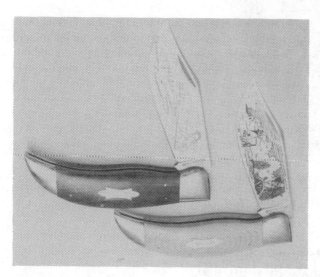

Smoky Mountain Knife Works The Mariner

Smoky Mountain Knife Works The Mariner, Manufacturer - Smoky Mountain Knife Works, Pattern -   Two 5" clasp knives, Mariner shield, fully-etched blades, quantity 600, price $50, value $45.

Smoky Mountain Knife Works "The Mountaineer, " Manufacturer - n/a, Pattern - #7 folding clasp, smoothbone handle, quantity 600, 1979, value $55.

Smoky Mountain Knife Works Old Man & The Sea, Manufacturer - Case, Pattern -Sheepfoot and manicure, quantity 600, 1981, value $100.

Smoky Mountain Knife Works Stock Car Legends: Dale Earnhardt , Manufacturer - Case, Pattern - 4-1/8" closed trapper, white smoothbone handle, 2,000, price $150, value $150. (*See "Knives of Thunder" article in Appendix for further information*)

Smoky Mountain Knife Works Stock Car Legends: Dale Earnhardt , Manufacturer - Case, Pattern - 5-1/4" closed folding hunter, red pickbone handles, quantity 2,000, price $175, value $175. (*See "Knives of Thunder" article in Appendix for further information*)

Smoky Mountain Knife Works Stock Car Legends: Glenn "Fireball" Roberts, Manufacturer - Case, Pattern - 4-1/8" closed trapper, Rogers bone handles, quantity 1,000, price $150, value $150. (*See "Knives of Thunder" article in Appendix for further information*)

Smoky Mountain Knife Works Stock Car Legends: Lee Petty, Manufacturer - Case, Pattern - 4-1/8" closed trapper, white smoothbone handles, quantity 2,000, price $150, value $150. (*See "Knives of Thunder" article in Appendix for further information*)

Smoky Mountain Knife Works Stock Car Legends: Lee Petty, Manufacturer - Case, Pattern - 5-1/4" closed folding hunter, red pickbone handles, quantity 500, price $175, value $175. (*See "Knives of Thunder" article in Appendix for further information*)

Smoky Mountain Knife Works "Unknown Explorer" and "White Trapper", Manufacturer - Shaw-Leibowitz, Pattern - Trapper, reproductions of two Frederick Remington paintings, quantity 500, 1981, value $100.

Smoky Mountain Knife Works "The Wilderness Part I, " Manufacturer - Smoky Mountain Knife Works, Pattern - Two gunstocks, one handled in stag, the other in mother of pearl stag, quantity 600 sets, price $85, value $85.

Smoky Mountain Knife Works "The Wilderness Part II," Manufacturer - Smoky Mountain Knife Works, Pattern - Two Texas toothpicks, handles: one of pearl and one of stag, quantity 600 sets, 1980, value $100.

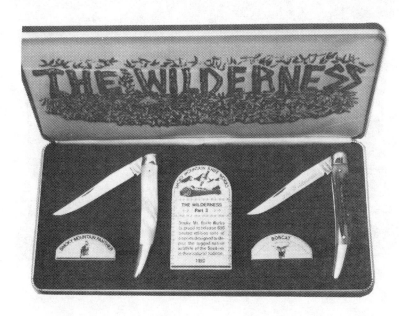

Smoky Mountain Knife Works "The Wilderness Part II "

Smoky Mountain Knife Works Yellow Gold, Manufacturer - Case, Pattern - Elephant toenail pattern, yellow handles, etched with miner panning for gold, quantity 600, 1980's, value $95.

SOG Specialties Vietnam Special Forces, Manufacturer -SOG Specialties, Pattern - 6- 1/4" SOG fighter, blue steel cross guard, pommel, and nut, quantity 1.500, prices: #1-25 ($495), #26-100 ($285), #101-1500 ($199), 1987, values: #1-25 ($495), #26-100 ($285), #101-1500 ($199).

South Carolina Wildlife Magazine Limited Edition, Manufacturer - Buck, Pattern - Folding lockback, available with Sambar stag or birchwood handle, etched blades, quantity 750, 1983, value $100.

South Carolina Wildlife Magazine Little Dude Association of Knifemakers, Manufacturer - South Carolina, Pattern - George Harrons "Little Dude", South Carolina Wildlife logo etched on blade, quantity 100, price $160, 1983, value $160.

Sports Afield, Manufacturer - several different, Pattern - Seven knife set, individually scrimshawed, quantity 100, price $175, 1988, value $160.

Standing Stone Cutlery Alabama, Manufacturer - Parker USA, Pattern - David Yellowhorse on Parker USA 5" Damascus folder, quantity 100, price $160, 1989, value $250.

Standing Stone Cutlery Cherokee Knife, Manufacturer - Standing Stone, Pattern - Bone clasp knife, quantity 1,000, price $50, 1981, value $50.

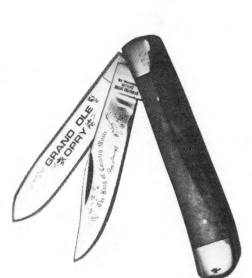

Standing Stone Cutlery Roy Acuff

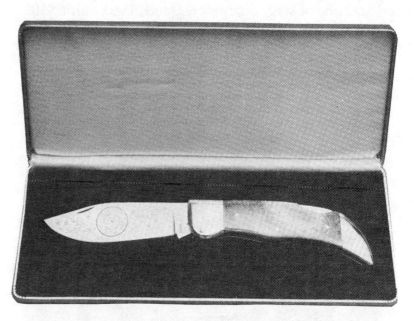

Standing Stone Cutlery Cherokee Knife

Standing Stone Cutlery Grand Ole Opry–Roy Acuff Signature Series, Manufacturer - Standing Stone, Pattern - Copperhead 4-3/4", Sambar stag handle, commemorative etching, price $29.95, 1985, value $30.

Standing Stone Cutlery Grand Ole Opry–Roy Acuff Signature Series

Standing Stone Cutlery Improved Order of Red Man, Manufacturer - Parker Cutlery, Pattern - 5" genuine stag clasp knife, full blade etch – front and rear, quantity 600, price $100, 1983, value $100.

Standing Stone Cutlery Official Cherokee Seal, Manufacturer - Parker Cutlery, Pattern - 5" smooth green bone clasp knife, quantity 600, price $60, 1984, value $90.

Standing Stone Cutlery Raccoon, Manufacturer - Parker USA, Pattern - David Yellowhorse on Parker USA 5" Damascus folder, quantity 100, price $160, 1989, value $250.

Standing Stone Cutlery Roy Acuff, Manufacturer - Standing Stone Cutlery, Pattern - Two blade folding trapper, Sambar stag handle, commemorative etching, price $29.95, 1985, value $30.

Standing Stone Cutlery The Titanic, Manufacturer - Standing Stone, Pattern - Stockman, picture of RMS Titanic, bone handles, quantity 1,000, price $40, 1981, value $40.

Star Bicentennial, Manufacturer - Star Sales, Pattern - Two blade Canoe, engraved metal handle, etched blades, serial numbered, quantity 1,776, price $35 (#100-up), $45 (#99-below), 1975, value $35.

Star Bicentennial

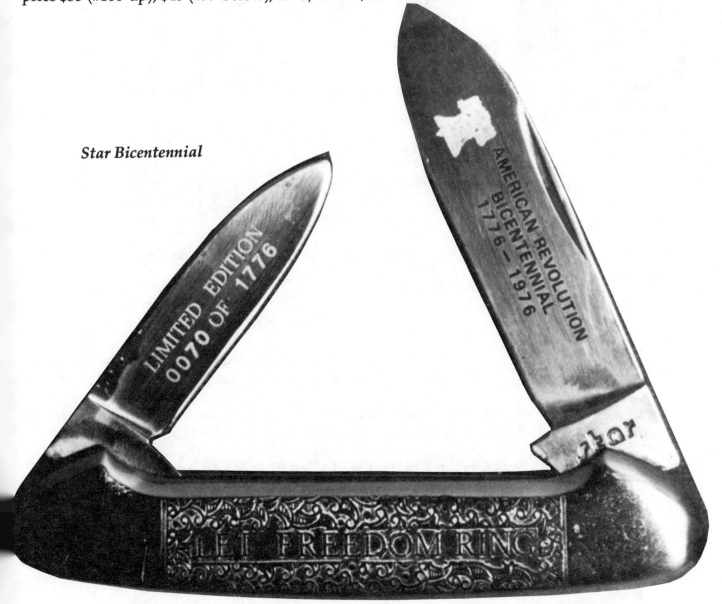

Star Coal Miner Commemorative Knife, Manufacturer - Star, Pattern - 5-3/8" swing guard lock blade, bone handles, etched, wood wall plaque, quantity 1,200, price $55, 1979, value $60.

Star Limited Edition, Manufacturer - Star, Manufacturer - Set of four: mini-jack, mother of pearl, bone, silver plate, black pearl, quantity 600, price $42, 1981, value $42.

*Stidham Knives
Bird Dog Whittler*

Stidham Knives Bird Dog Whittler, Manufacturer - Stidham Knives, Pattern - Whittler, 4-1/2" closed, stag handle, quantity 1,000, price $40, value $50.

Stidham Knives Nazi Presentation Knife, Manufacturer - Stidham Knives, Pattern - 3-3/4" whittler, deep gold leaf etched blade, German Silver handles and liners, exact replica of knife presented by Adolf Hitler to SS troops, quantity 2,400, price $40,

Stidham Knives Nazi Presentation Knife

1976, value $40.

Stud Knives

Stud Knives were marketed from England, and , shortly after they began it became hard to reach the company, thus very few ever hit these shores.

Stud Custom Knives Limited Edition, Manufacturer - Stud, Pattern - 10" Bowie, nickel-silver guard, leather sheath, price $155, 1981, value $155.

Stud Custom Knives, Ltd. Indian Scalping Knife, Manufacturer - Stud, Pattern - 237 mm Indian scalping knife, detailed scrimshaw handle commemorates the death of Jane McCrae by Burgoynes Indians in 1777, price $175, 1982, value $175.

Stud Custom Knives, Ltd. Limited Edition, Manufacturer - Stud, Pattern - 3-1/2" push dagger, duplaque ivory handle, handcrafted leather sheath, price $125, 1981, value $125.

Stud Custom Knives, Ltd. Limited Edition, Manufacturer - Stud, Pattern - 5" whaler, scrimshawed duplaque ivory, rust resistant stud steel, price $165, 1981, value $165.

Stud Custom Knives, Ltd. Wedding of Prince Charles and Lady Di, Manufacturer - Stud, Pattern - Sheepfoot & pen blades, Prince of Wales coat of arms engraving, quantity 500, price $45, 1981, value $65.

Stuyvesant Park Neighborhood Association Peter Stuyvesant, Manufacturer - Schrade Cutlery, Pattern - Granddaddy Barlow, 2 blades, clip & pen, white bone handles, quantity 200, 1987, value $80.

Swanner Cutlery Limited Edition, Manufacturer - Queen for Swanner Cutlery, Pattern - Muskrat & trapper, red bone handles, trapper also available in stag ($45) nickel-silver bolster, quantity 100 ea, 1983, value $40 each.

Swanner Cutlery Ohio Valley River Dirk, Manufacturer - Parker for Swanner Cutlery, Pattern - Dirk, brass fittings, genuine stag handles, serial numbered, quantity 200, price $50, 1980, value $50.

T

Taylor Cutlery Bonnie & Clyde, Manufacturer - Taylor Cutlery, Pattern - n\a, price $28, 1981, value $35.

Taylor Cutlery Cherry Tree Chopper, Manufacturer - Taylor Cutlery, Pattern - Knife hatchet pattern, etched picture of George Washington, quantity 1,000, price $45, 1981, value $45.

Taylor Cutlery Cherry Tree Chopper II, Manufacturer - Taylor Cutlery, Pattern - Identical to original, both smooth and picked bone handles, quantity 2,500, price $35, 1982, value $35.

Taylor Cutlery Miniature Cherry, Manufacturer - Taylor Cutlery, Pattern - 3-1/2" tree chopper, handled in smooth & picked bone, quantity 2,000, 1982, value $30.

Taylor Cutlery Deer Hunter Set, Manufacturer - Taylor Cutlery, Pattern - Set of three 2-3/8" lockbacks, white inlay in stainless handles, etched with whitetail deer, buck, and deer hunter, hardshell display case, value $75.

Taylor Cutlery Famous Men of Texas, Manufacturer - Taylor Cutlery, Pattern - Gunstock, set of two, stag handle, honor Sam Houston and Ben Milan, quantity 450 sets, price $25, 1980, value $30.

Taylor Cutlery Famous Western Judges, Manufacturer - Taylor Cutlery, Pattern - Set of two, stag handle, shows the impact of Judge Roy Bean and Judge Isaac Parker on the American West, quantity 450 sets, price $30, 1980, value $40.

Taylor Cutlery Cherry Tree Chopper

Taylor Cutlery Five Centuries of America, Manufacturer - Buck, Pattern - Clip lock blades, blade engraved with "Five Centuries of America" logo, quantity 500, 1989, value $50.

Taylor Cutlery Good Guys/Bad Guys, Manufacturer - Taylor Cutlery, Pattern - Gunstocks & canoes, price $100, 1981, value $60.

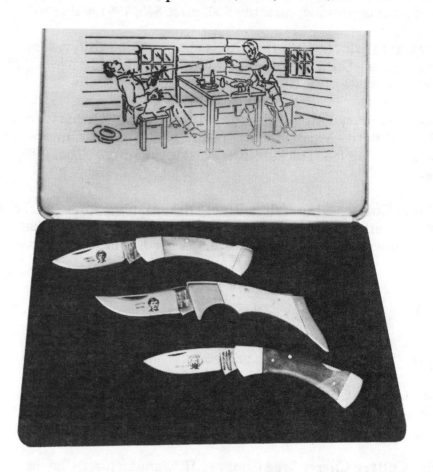

Taylor Cutlery Good Guys/Bad Guys

Taylor Cutlery Limited Edition, Manufacturer - Taylor Cutlery, Pattern - Barlows, price $75, 1981, value $60.

Taylor Cutlery Limited Edition, Manufacturer - Taylor Cutlery, Pattern - Doctors, quantity 200, price $75, 1981, value $75.

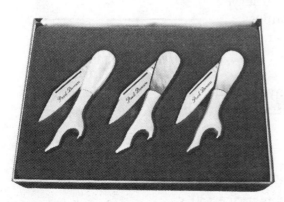

Taylor Cutlery Pearl Dancers

Taylor Cutlery Pearl Dancers, Manufacturer - Taylor Cutlery, Pattern - Set of three leg knives, white, black, or brown pearl handles, quantity 1,200, price $55, 1981, value $60.

Taylor Cutlery The People's Choice Set, Manufacturer - Taylor Cutlery, Pattern - Mini-chopper, President's Washington, Lincoln, and Reagan, price $35, 1983, value $40.

Taylor Cutlery Plainsman Series, Manufacturer - Taylor Cutlery, Pattern - Set of three gunstocks, plastic handles, Price $50, 1980, value $50.

Taylor Cutlery President Carter – Mr. Peanut, Manufacturer - Taylor Cutlery, Pattern - Peanut shaped, "Carter" embossed on one side, "Mr. Peanut" on the other, price $8, 1976, value $6.

Taylor Cutlery President's Series, Manufacturer - Taylor Cutlery, Pattern - Set of three copperheads, price $50, 1980, value $45.

Taylor Cutlery Republic of Texas, Manufacturer - Taylor Cutlery, Pattern - Set of two trappers, blade etch: Republic of Texas, 1836-1845, value $40.

Taylor Cutlery Robert E. Lee, Manufacturer - Taylor Cutlery, Pattern - Stag folding hunter (Japan), quantity 1,250, price $45, 1979, value $38.

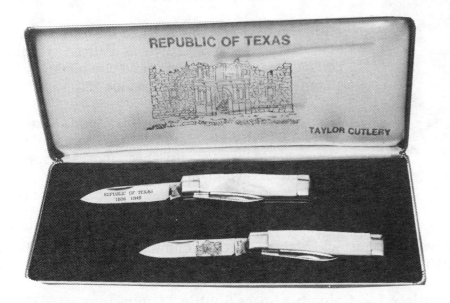

*Taylor Cutlery
Republic of Texas*

Taylor Cutlery "Scouts of the Prairies", Manufacturer - Bear Creek, Pattern - Stockman, quantity 600 sets, price $50, 1980, value $48.

Taylor Cutlery Stonewall Jackson, Manufacturer - Taylor Cutlery, Pattern - Bone Barlow, quantity 1,200, price $30, 1979, value $30.

Taylor Cutlery Tennessee Bicentennial, Manufacturer - Taylor Cutlery, Pattern - Elephant toenail pattern, 1976, value $32.

*Taylor Cutlery
Tennessee
Bicentennial*

Taylor Cutlery Tennessee Bicentennial, Manufacturer - Taylor Cutlery, Pattern - Sunfish, Tennessee inlay shield, rosewood handle, etched blade, presentation box, quantity 1,000, price depended on serial number, 1976, value $38.

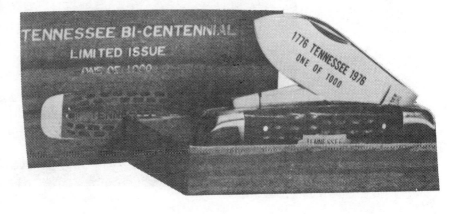

Taylor Cutlery TN/KY/VA Sunfish, Manufacturer - Taylor Cutlery, Pattern - Set of three sunfish, two wood, one stag quantity 1,000, price $40, 1976, value $50.

Taylor Cutlery Texas-Oklahoma, Manufacturer - Taylor Cutlery, Pattern - Two Barlows, razor blades, value $40.

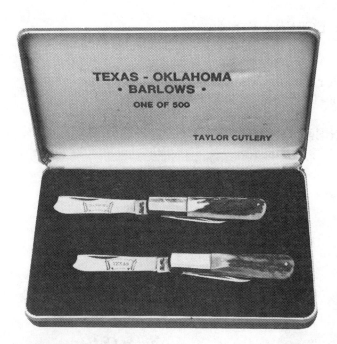

Taylor Cutlery Texas-Oklahoma

Taylor Cutlery Virginia and West Virginia, Manufacturer - Taylor Cutlery, Pattern - Two copperheads, stag handles, quantity 600, price $70, 1979, value $48.

Tennessee B-17 Flying Fortress, Manufacturer - Case, Pattern - Two blades: spear & penblade layered in 14k gold, deep commemorative etching, custom hardwood presentation case, quantity 500, price $64.95, 1986, value $70.

Thomson/Center Arms Limited Edition, Manufacturer - Parker-Edwards, Pattern - Folding knife, Damascus steel, razor and clip blades, quantity 250, price $60, 1990, value $80.

Timber Wolf Cutlery & Sporting Goods Coach Paul "Bear" Bryant, Manufacturer - Schrade, Pattern - Three blade trapper, clip, sheep foot, and spear, certificate of ownership, lifetime guarantee, signature on blade, head stamp on handle, price $39.95, value $50.

Ken Tolle The Gunstock, Manufacturer - Columbia, Pattern - Two blade stockman, quantity 2,400, price $15, 1977, value $15.

TSCO Cutlery, Inc. Columbia Space Shuttle, Manufacturer - TSCO Cutlery, pattern - n\a, price $19.95, 1981, value $16.

TSCO Cutlery, Inc. The "Corvette", Manufacturer - TSCO Cutlery, Pattern - 4" stockman, 23 knives: one for each year from 1953-1976, DuPont Delrin handle, quantity 2,000 of each, value $16 each.

TSCO Cutlery, Inc. The "Corvette"

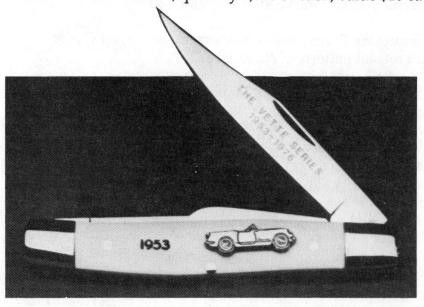

U

United-Boker 1803 U. S. Flintlock, Manufacturer - United- Boker, Pattern - 4-1/8" two blade trapper, wood handles, inlay rifle shield, etched and serial numbered, hardshell display box, value $40.

United-Boker American Eagle, Manufacturer - United-Boker, Pattern - 4-1/8" two blade trapper, smooth red bone handles, enamel flag shield, etched, serial numbered, display box with silver eagle U. S. silver dollar, value $70.

United-Boker Blue Tick Hound, Manufacturer - United-Boker, Pattern - 4-1/8" two blade trapper, smooth blue bone handles, color etched blade and serial numbered, gift box, value $25.

United-Boker Classic Car Series 1957 Chevy, Manufacturer - United-Boker, Pattern - 3-3/4" two blade copperhead, red pick bone handles, etched, serial numbered, value $55.

United-Boker Classic Car Series 1957 Corvette, Manufacturer - United-Boker, Pattern - 3-3/4" two blade copperhead, red pick bone handles, etched, serial numbered, value $55.

United-Boker Classic Car Series 1957 T-Bird, Manufacturer - United-Boker, Pattern - 3-3/4" two blade copperhead, red pick bone handles, etched, serial numbered, value $55.

United-Boker Great Season's Greetings, Manufacturers - Boker and United, Pattern - Copperhead, Christmas tree handles and deluxe blade etching, price $39.99, value $30.

United-Boker Red Bone Hound, Manufacturer - United-Boker, Pattern - 4-1/8" two blade trapper, smooth red bone handles, color etched blade and serial numbered, gift box, value $40.

United-Boker Santa Claus, Manufacturers - Boker and United, Pattern - Trapper, pearl handles, price $99.95, value $70.

United-Boker U.S. Armed Services Series National Guard, Manufacturer - United-Boker, Pattern - 4-1/8" two blade trapper, green pick bone handles, value $55.

United Cutlery Indiana Jones Khyber Bowie Knife, Manufacturer - United Cutlery, Pattern - 24" overall khyber Bowie, Indiana Jones signature etched on blade, hardwood handle, solid brass finger guard and eagle-head pommel, high relief cobras cast into finger guard, 1989, value $135.

United States Historical Society American Fighting Forces of World War II, Manufacturer - n/a, Pattern - V-J Day fighting knife, banded ivory grip, 24-k gold etched scenes, brass pommel, velvet lined case, price $195, 1985, value $200.

United States Historical Society Jim Bowie Vidalia Sandbar Knife, Spanish, Pattern - Bowie, picture and name etch of James Bowie and Rezin Bowie on Searles style Bowie, value $150.

United States Historical Society Jim Bowie Vidalia Sandbar Knife

Utica 75th Anniversary, Manufacturer - Utica, Pattern - Three office knives, metal handles, presentation case, quantity 1,500 sets, price $75 set, 1985, value $65.

Utica 75th Anniversary

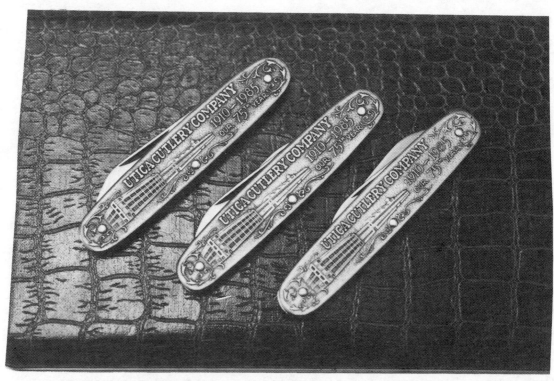

Utica Gary Hawk Signature Series, Manufacturer - Kutmaster, Pattern - Model #131B21, 2-1/4" blades, "Mallards On Manns Cove" etch, quantity 2,500, price $32, $160 per set, 1990, value $30.

Utica Gary Hawk Signature Series, Manufacturer - Kutmaster, Pattern - Model #131B23, 2-1/4" blades, "On Point" etch, quantity 2,500, price $32 $160 set, 1990, value $30 each or $90 per set.

Utica Gary Hawk Signature Series, Manufacturer - Kutmaster, Pattern - Model #131B24, 2-1/4" blades, "Just Fishin" etch, Pattern - 2,500, price $32, $160 set, 1990, value $30 each or $90 per set.

Utica Gary Hawk Signature Series, Manufacturer - Kutmaster, Pattern - Model #131B22, 2-1/4" blades, "Whitetail Country" etch, quantity 2,500, price $32, $160 per set, 1990, value $30, $120 per set.

Utica Kutmaster Full Color Scrimshaw, Manufacturer - Kutmaster, Pattern - Model #131S51, 3" long, whitetail-deer scene, bone handles, quantity 1,000 annually, price $29.95, value $29.95.

Utica Kutmaster Full Color Scrimshaw, Manufacturer - Kutmaster, Pattern - Model #131S53, 3" long, mallard scene, bone handles, quantity 1,000 annually, price $29.95, value $29.95.

Utica Kutmaster Full Color Scrimshaw, Manufacturer - Kutmaster, Pattern - Model #131S54, 3" long, bass scene, bone handles, quantity 1,000 annually, price $29.95, value $29.95.

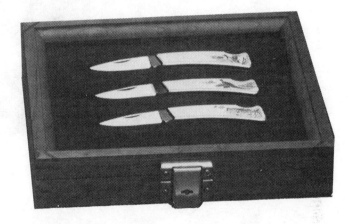

Utica Kutmaster Full Color Scrimshaw

Utica Kutmaster Scrimshaw Series, Manufacturer - Kutmaster, Pattern - Model #181322, 3" long, whitetail deer scene, bone handles, quantity 1,500 annually, price $29.95, value $29.95.

Utica Kutmaster Scrimshaw Series, Manufacturer - Kutmaster, Pattern - Model #181323, 3" long, trout scene, bone handles, quantity 1,500 annually, price $29.95 value $29.95.

Utica Kutmaster Scrimshaw Series, Manufacturer - Kutmaster, Pattern - Model #181324, 3" long, mallard in flight scene, bone handles, quantity 1,500 annually, price $29.95, value $29.95.

Utica Kutmaster Scrimshaw Series, Manufacturer - Kutmaster, Pattern - Model #181325, 3" long, bass scene, bone handles, quantity 1,500 annually, price $29.95, value $29.95.

Utica Kutmaster Scrimshaw Series, Manufacturer - Kutmaster, Pattern - Model #181326, 3" long, eagle scene, bone handles, quantity 1,500 annually, price $29.95, value $29.95.

Utica Wildlife Series, Manufacturer - Kutmaster, Pattern - Model #131A01, 3" long, lithograph of deer on bone handles, serial numbered and signed, quantity 2,000 sets annually, price $30, $120 set, 1990

Utica Wildlife Series, Manufacturer - Kutmaster, Pattern - Model #131A02, 3" long, lithograph of pheasant on bone handles, serial numbered and signed, quantity 2,000 annually sets, price $120 set, $30, 1990.

Utica Wildlife Series, Manufacturer - Kutmaster, Pattern - Model #131A03, 3" long, lithograph of mallard on bone handles, serial numbered and signed, quantity 2,000 sets annually, price $120 set $30, 1990.

Utica Wildlife Series, Manufacturer - Kutmaster, Pattern - Model #131A04, 3" long, lithograph of bass on bone handles, serial numbered and signed, quantity 2,000 sets annually, price $120 set, $30, 1990.

Utica Wildlife Series

V

Virginia City Knife Shop Limited Edition, Manufacturer - Bill Duff and Hoyt Axton, Pattern - 11-3/4" Bowie, handmade by Bill Duff, engraved by George Sherwood and scrimshawed by Mr. Myer, quantity 100, price $1,500, 1984.

Voyles Cutlery Cottonmouth

Voyles Cutlery Black Bear, Manufacturer - Queen Cutlery, Pattern - Sodbuster, blade etched with Black Bear Skinner, quantity 600, price $12, 1978, value $20.

Voyles Cutlery Cottonmouth, Manufacturer - Queen Cutlery, Pattern - Two blade copperhead, imitation pearl handle, quantity 1,200, price $12, 1978, value $25.

Voyles Cutlery Limited Edition, Manufacturer - Queen Cutlery, Pattern - Peanut, pearl handle, quantity 600, price $22, 1977, value $65.

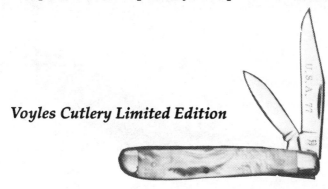

Voyles Cutlery Limited Edition

W

Voyles Cutlery Black Bear

W. G. Willey Knives Lem & Steve Ward, Manufacturer - Buck, Pattern - Buck 110 (blue bill), etched by Aurum and scrimshawed by Bonnie Schulte, gold plated, genuine stag handles, quantity 250, price $180, 1989, value $150.

W. G. Willey Knives Lem & Steve Ward, Manufacturer - Buck, Pattern - 526 dress lockback (barber pole), with gold engraved handle, quantity 250, price $42.50, 1989, value $70.

W . G. Willey Knives Lem & Steve Ward, Manufacturer - Buck, Pattern - Buck 110 (workshop knife), etched by Aurum & scrimshawed by Bonnie Schulte, prehistoric mastodon ivory, glass topped walnut box, quantity 100, price $595, 1989, value $500.

Warren Whittlers Set, Manufacturer - Schrade Cutlery, Pattern - Set of Warren whittlers, serial numbered, East Indian rosewood handles, wharncliffe and modified pen blades, quantity 1,500 sets, price $39.95, 1984, value $40.

Wenoka America's First Underwater Park, Manufacturer - Wenoka Seastyle, Pattern - Diving knife, etch of the world famous Christ of the Deep Statue, quantity 2,000, price $300, 1986, value $200. *(See photo on next page)*.

Wenoka Birth of Sport Diving, Manufacturer - Wenoka Seastyle, Pattern - Diving knife, etching of first breathing apparatus in 1942, quantity 2,000, price $300, 1981, value $200.

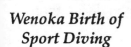

Wenoka Birth of Sport Diving

Wenoka Hard Hat Diving, Manufacturer - Wenoka Seastyle, Pattern - Diving knife, "The first diving knife" etch, quantity 2,000, price $300, 1983, value $300.

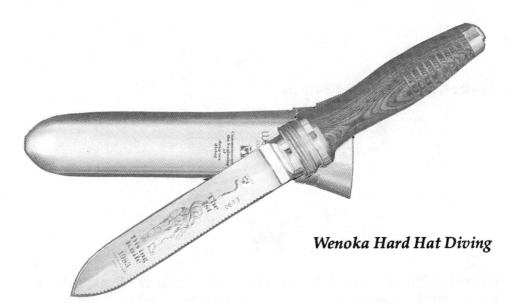

Wenoka Hard Hat Diving

Wenoka Sea Lab, Manufacturer - Wenoka Seastyle, Pattern - Diving knife, honors the first three sea lab projects, quantity 2,000, price $300, 1985, value $300.

*Wenoka
America's
First
Underwater
Park*

Wenoka Sea Lab

Wenoka UDT, Manufacturer - Wenoka Seastyle, Pattern - Fighting knife, replica of the famous UDT used on the beaches of Normandy, quantity 2,000, price $300, 1985, value $300.

Wenoka UDT

Western - Limited Edition – Series 54 matched sets, Manufacturer - Western, Pattern - #54 lockbacks, stag wood, quantity 2,000, price $100, 1981, value $100.

Western Limited Edition Western Series Collectors Edition, Manufacturer - Western, Pattern - Set of two, 5" single blade folding lockbacks, one with wood handle and one with imitation stag handles, quantity 2,000, value $100 (Set).

Western First Collector's Edition – Series 54 matched sets, Manufacturer - Western, Pattern - Clip, hardwood or buckhorn handle, 5" closed, stag, collector's edition etching on blades, quantity 2,000, price $100, 1981, value $110.

Westwinds Productions, Ltd. Aircraft of Vietnam, Manufacturer - Camillus for Westwinds Productions, Pattern - Sheath knife, sheath, etched blade, signed letter from Camillus verifying issue, quantity 1,000, price $39.95, 1984, value $40.

Winchester Kentucky & Tennessee, Manufacturer -German, Pattern - 5-1/2" muskrat trapper, bone handles, price $40, value $70.

Winchester
The Kentuckian
and The Tennessean

Winchester Red Letter Set, Manufacturer - Bluegrass Cutlery, Pattern - 2-5/8" two blade pen knives, set of five, bone handles, blades etched 12-gauge through .410 gauge with model 37 shotguns, serial numbered, display case, price $150, value $150.

Winchester The Kentuckian and The Tennessean, Manufacturer - German, Pattern - Set of two folding trappers, fancy scroll etched blades, "Winchester, Tennessee Trapper" and "Kentucky Trapper" etched in gold, serial numbered, value $150.

A complete listing of Winchester commemoratives and their values can be found in the Appendix.

Club Knives

The information that follows was provided by knife clubs from across the country. All prices listed are local.

Allegheny Mountain Knife Collectors Association, Hunker, PA, Pattern - Stag "Lil' Trapper", Manufacturer - Cripple Creek, quantity 55, 1983, price $54, value $175.

Allegheny Mountain Knife Collectors Association, Hunker, PA, Pattern - Bone stockman, Manufacturer - Fight'n Rooster, quantity 94, 1984, price $22.50, value $45.

Allegheny Mountain Knife Collectors Association, Hunker, PA, Pattern - Stag medium trapper Cripple Creek, quantity 61, 1985, price $53, value $125.

Allegheny Mountain Knife Collectors Association, Hunker, PA, Pattern - 2nd cut stag three blade canoe, Manufacturer - Cripple Creek, quantity 55, 1986, price $57, value $150.

Allegheny Mountain Knife Collectors Association, Hunker, PA, Pattern - 2nd cut stag five blade stockman, Manufacturer - Cripple Creek, quantity 50, 1987, price $60, value $150.

Allegheny Mountain Knife Collectors Association, Hunker, PA, Pattern - Stag single blade "Saddlehorn", Manufacturer - Cripple Creek, quantity 55, 1988, price $63, value $125.

Allegheny Mountain Knife Collectors Association, Hunker, PA, Pattern - Bone "Coke bottle", Manufacturer - Cripple Creek, 1989, price $63.

American Blade Collectors Association , Chattanooga, TN, Pattern - 5288SS, two blade congress, stag handles, Manufacturer - Case, quantity 5,000, 1982, price $30, value $124.

American Blade Collectors Association , Chattanooga, TN, Pattern - Lockback whittler, 2nd cut handles, Manufacturer - American Blade, quantity 5,000, 1983, price $19, value $60.

American Blade Collectors Association , Chattanooga, TN, Pattern - Three blade trapper, black lip mother-of-pearl handles, Manufacturer - American Blade, quantity 5,000, 1984, price $24, value $70.

American Blade Collectors Association , Chattanooga, TN, Pattern - Damascus lockback, 2nd cut handles, Manufacturer - Parker-Edwards, quantity 4,000, 1985, price $59, value $140.

American Blade Collectors Association , Chattanooga, TN, Pattern - Six blade congress, black lip mother-of-pearl handles, Manufacturer - Wostenholm, quantity 4,000, 1985, price $32.99, value $90.

American Blade Collectors Association , Chattanooga, TN, Pattern - Four blade sowbelly, mother-of-pearl and abalone, Manufacturer - Parker Cutlery, quantity 3,900, 1986, price $37.50, value$80.

American Blade Collectors Association , Chattanooga, TN, Pattern - Damascus trapper, mother-of-pearl, Manufacturer - Parker-Edwards, quantity 3,990, 1986, price $57.99, value $120.

American Blade Collectors Association , Chattanooga, TN, Pattern - C51050L Folding guard hunter, stag handles, Manufacturer - Case, quantity 3,500, 1987, price $79.95, value $150.

American Blade Collectors Association , Chattanooga, TN, Pattern - Damascus trapper smooth green bone, Manufacturer - Parker-Edwards, quantity 3,500, 1987, price $56.95, value $95.

American Blade Collectors Association , Chattanooga, TN, Pattern - 61013 single blade hunter green bone, Manufacturer - Case, quantity 2,100, 1988, price $74.95, value $90.

American Blade Collectors Association , Chattanooga, TN, Pattern - Damascus and steel trapper, smooth red bone handles, Manufacturer - Parker-Edwards, quantity 2,100, 1988, price $39.95, value $85.

American Blade Collectors Association , Chattanooga, TN, Pattern - 51050 coke bottle folding hunter, Manufacturer - Case, quantity 2,500, 1989, price $78.95.

American Blade Collectors Association , Chattanooga, TN, Pattern - Damascus liner lock, genuine stag handles, Michael Walker design, Manufacturer - Parker USA, quantity 2,500, 1989, price $59.95.

American Blade Collectors Association Life Member , Chattanooga, TN, Pattern - No. 1 Pearl Trapper, two blade, mother-of-pearl handles, Manufacturer - Fight'n Rooster, quantity 1,000, 1981, value $150.

American Blade Collectors Association Life Member , Chattanooga, TN, Pattern - No. 2 Sowbelly, five blade pearl and abalone, Manufacturer - American Blade, quantity 1,000, 1983, value $120.

American Blade Collectors Association Life Member , Chattanooga, TN, Pattern - No. 3 Four blade bone handled congress knife with gold etching, Manufacturer - Fight'n Rooster, quantity 600, 1984, value $120.

American Blade Collectors Association Life Member , Chattanooga, TN, Pattern - No. 4 Single blade Damascus trapper with salesman sample style handles (smooth bone on one side, jigged bone on the other), Manufacturer - Parker, quantity 300, 1988, value $60.

Badger Knife Club, Elm Grove, WI, Pattern - Honey bone dogleg jack, Manufacturer - Bob Cargill, quantity 45, 1986, price $45, value $95, information provided by club.

Badger Knife Club, Elm Grove, WI, Pattern - Winterbottom bone whittler, Manufacturer - Queen, quantity 75, 1987, price $30, value $35, information provided by club.

Badger Knife Club, Elm Grove, WI, Pattern - Sidelock I, Manufacturer - Mountain Forge, quantity 50, 1989, price $50, value $60, information provided by club.

Badger Knife Club, Elm Grove, WI, Pattern - Bird & Trout, Manufacturer - Dave Ricke, quantity 30, 1990, price $85, value $85, information provided by club.

Bay Area Knife Collectors Association , Freemont, CA, Pattern - Rosewood trout/bird, sheath, Manufacturer - Sornberger, quantity 52, 1980, price $70, value $125-$197, information provided by club.

Bay Area Knife Collectors Association , Freemont, CA, Pattern - FL2 folder, Micarta, Manufacturer - Centofante, quantity 50, 1981, price $155, $250-$372, information provided by club.

Bay Area Knife Collectors Association , Freemont, CA., Pattern - Rosewood semi-skinner, sheath, Manufacturer - Terrill, quantity 32, 1982, price $85, value $110- $160, information provided by club.

Bay Area Knife Collectors Association , Freemont, CA, Pattern - Folder, coin silver, Manufacturer - Corrado, quantity 50, 1983, price $83, value $150- $230, information provided by club.

Bay Area Knife Collectors Association , Freemont , CA, Pattern - Rosewood trailing point, sheath, Manufacturer - Gamble, quantity 25, 1984, price $75, value $95- $142, information provided by club.

Bay Area Knife Collectors Association , Freemont, CA, Pattern - Cocobolo drop point, sheath, Manufacturer - Norton, quantity 25, 1985, price $85, value $95- $109, information provided by club.

Bay Area Knife Collectors Association , Freemont, CA, Pattern - Folder, jigged stag, Manufacturer - Osborne, quantity 27, 1986, price $120, value $220, information provided by club.

Bay Area Knife Collectors Association, Freemont, CA, Pattern - Rosewood semi-skinner, sheath, Manufacturer - Ankrom, quantity 30, 1987, price $125, value $165, information provided by club.

Bay Area Knife Collectors Association, Freemont, CA, Pattern - Stag drop point, engraving and filework, sheath, Manufacturer - Mendenhall, quantity 49, 1988, price $125, value $250, information provided by club.

Bay Area Knife Collectors Association, Freemont, CA, Pattern - Small lock back folder, cocobolo handles, nickel bolsters, Manufacturer - Buguszewski, quantity 39, 1989, price $135, value $225, information provided by club.

Bay Area Knife Collectors Association , Freemont, CA, Pattern - Fixed blade (4-1/4") ATS 34, desert ironwood handle, tapered tang, sheath, Manufacturer - Crowder, quantity 38, 1990, price $145, value $160, information provided by club.

Bechtler Mint Knife Club, Rutherfordton, NC, Pattern - Copperhead, Manufacturer - Case, quantity 150, 1983, price $38, value $125, information provided by club.

Bechtler Mint Knife Club, Rutherfordton, NC, Pattern - Barlow razor, Manufacturer - Case, quantity 95, 1983, price $30, value $175, information provided by club.

Bechtler Mint Knife Club, Rutherfordton, NC, Pattern - Lockback, Manufacturer - Colonel Coon, quantity 50, 1984, price $42.50, value $75, information provided by club.

Bechtler Mint Knife Club, Rutherfordton, NC, Pattern - Trapper, Manufacturer - Case, quantity 145, 1984, price $45, value $150, information provided by club.

Bechtler Mint Knife Club, Rutherfordton, NC, Pattern - Small stockman, Manufacturer - Case, quantity 129, 1985, price $50, value $130, information provided by club.

Bechtler Mint Knife Club, Rutherfordton, NC, Pattern - Congress, Manufacturer - Case, quantity 128, 1986, price $55, value $150, information provided by club.

Bechtler Mint Knife Club, Rutherfordton, NC, Pattern - Canoe, Manufacturer - Case, quantity 125, 1987, price $50, value $75, information provided by club.

Bechtler Mint Knife Club, Rutherfordton, NC, Pattern - Canoe, Manufacturer - Case, quantity 100, 1988, price $55, value $100, information provided by club.

Bechtler Mint Knife Club, Rutherfordton, NC, Pattern - Canoe, Manufacturer - Case, quantity 103, 1989, price $55, value $100, information provided by club.

Bechtler Mint Knife Club, Rutherfordton, NC, Pattern - Canoe, Manufacturer - Case, 1990, price $50, value $75, information provided by club.

Bold City Knife Collectors , Jacksonville, FL, Pattern - G6154 green bone single blade trapper, Manufacturer - Case, 1982, information provided by club.

Case Collector's Club, Bradford, PA, Pattern - Two blade trapper, smooth handles, etched blade, Case shield, Manufacturer - Case, 1987.

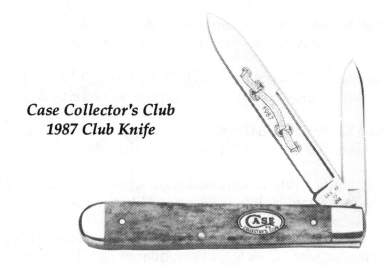

*Case Collector's Club
1987 Club Knife*

Case Collector's Club, Bradford, PA, Pattern - Two blade Daddy Barlow, one spey blade, one clip blade, stag handles, etched blade, Case shield, Manufacturer - Case, 1988.

Central Kentucky Knife Club, Lexington, KY, Pattern - Stag canoe, three blade, Manufacturer - Case, quantity 125, 1983, price $40, value $125.

Central Kentucky Knife Club, Lexington, KY, Pattern - Stag lockback folding hunter, Manufacturer - Case, quantity 172, 1984, price $50, value $75.

Central Kentucky Knife Club, Lexington, KY, Pattern - Stag trapper, two blade, Manufacturer - Case, quantity 201, 1985, price $40, value $50.

Central Kentucky Knife Club, Lexington, KY, Pattern - Stag stockman, three blade, Manufacturer - Bulldog, quantity 108, 1986, price $45, value $90.

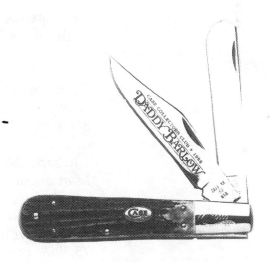

*Case Collector's
Club 1988 Club
Knife*

Central Kentucky Knife Club, Lexington, KY, Pattern - Stag lockback whittler, Manufacturer - Fight'n Rooster, quantity 101, 1987, price $50, value $75.

Central Kentucky Knife Club, Lexington, KY, Pattern - Saddle-horn, single blade, Manufacturer - Cripple Creek, quantity 100, 1988, price $60, value $90.

Chesapeake Bay Knife Club, Baltimore, MD, Pattern - Custom folder, Manufacturer - Ray Beers, quantity 50, 1980, price $100, value $200.

Chesapeake Bay Knife Club, Baltimore, MD, Pattern - Standard folder, Manufacturer - Al Mar, quantity 4, 1980, price $50, value $100.

Chesapeake Bay Knife Club, Baltimore, MD, Pattern - Engraved folder, Manufacturer - Al Mar, quantity 18, 1980, price $77, value $150.

Chesapeake Bay Knife Club, Baltimore, MD, Pattern - Skinner, Manufacturer - William Antonio, quantity 30, 1981, price $120, value $200.

Chesapeake Bay Knife Club, Baltimore, MD, Pattern - Full-tang hunter, Manufacturer - Ray Beers, quantity 40, 1982, price $150, value $250.

Chesapeake Bay Knife Club, Baltimore, MD, Pattern - Silver dollar, Manufacturer - Gary Barnes, quantity 80, 1982, price $88, value $125.

Chesapeake Bay Knife Club, Baltimore, MD, Pattern - Green bone Mako, Manufacturer - Case, quantity 100, 1983, price $40, value $40.

Chesapeake Bay Knife Club, Baltimore, MD, Pattern - German drop-point folder, Manufacturer - G. & S. Cutlery, quantity 80, 1984, price $35, value $45.

Chesapeake Bay Knife Club, Baltimore, MD, Pattern - Folder, Manufacturer - Kas Knives, quantity 40, 1985, price $125, value $175.

Chesapeake Bay Knife Club, Baltimore, MD, Pattern - Black plastic multi-blade, Manufacturer - Victorinox, quantity 40, 1986, price $35, value $35.

Chesapeake Bay Knife Club, Baltimore, MD, Pattern - Hunter, Manufacturer - Ray Beers, quantity 35, 1987, price $95-$140, value $120-$160.

Chesapeake Bay Knife Club, Baltimore, MD, Pattern - Three blade folder, Manufacturer - Beretta, quantity 20, 1988, price $85, value $110.

Chesapeake Bay Knife Club, Baltimore, MD, Pattern - Folder, Trapper, red stag with stag head, Manufacturer - Goodwin Enterprises, quantity 75, 1989, price $40, value $50.

Chesapeake Bay Knife Club, Baltimore, MD, Pattern - Dagger, 10th Anniversary, Manufacturer - Ray Beers, 1990, price $135-$300, value $135-$300.

Chesapeake Bay Knife Club, Baltimore, MD, Pattern - Folder, blade engraved "CBKC", Manufacturer - G. Smith, 1990, price $30, value $30.

Choo Choo Knife Club, Chattanooga, TN, Pattern - Two blade trapper, Manufacturer - Case, Quantity 150, 1982.

Choo Choo Knife Club, Chattanooga, TN, Pattern - Smoke pearl trapper, Manufacturer - Case, quantity 150, 1983.

Choo Choo Knife Club
1982 Club Knife

Choo Choo Knife Club, Chattanooga, TN, Pattern - Green bone trapper, Manufacturer - Case, quantity 150, 1984.

Flint River Knife Club, Jonesboro, GA, Pattern - Two blade folding trapper, Manufacturer - Case, quantity 150, 1982, value $50.

Flint River Knife Club, Jonesboro, GA, Pattern - Two blade folding trapper, smooth bone handle, Manufacturer - Case, quantity 150, 1983, value $50.

Flint River Knife Club 1982 Club Knife

Fort City Knife Collectors Club, Cincinnati, OH, Pattern - Pearl whittler, Manufacturer - Fight'n Rooster, quantity 150, 1981, price $39.50, value $115-125.

Fort City Knife Collectors Club, Cincinnati, OH, Pattern - "Founders" gold plated blades, Manufacturer - Fight'n Rooster, quantity 20, 1981, price $44.50, value $150-160.

Fort City Knife Collectors Club, Cincinnati, OH, Pattern - Stag trapper, Manufacturer - Case, quantity 220, 1982, price $37.50.

Fort City Knife Collectors Club, Cincinnati, OH, Pattern - Etched "Club Officer", Manufacturer - Case, quantity 15, 1982, price $37.50, value $65.

Fort City Knife Collectors Club, Cincinnati, OH, Pattern - Golden bone Barlow, Manufacturer - Cripple Creek, quantity 135, 1983, price $43, value $80-90, $95-115.

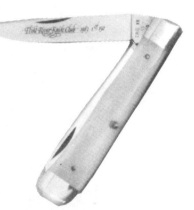

Flint River Knife Club 1983 Club Knife

Fort City Knife Collectors Club, Cincinnati, OH, Pattern - Etched "Club Officer", Manufacturer - Cripple Creek, quantity 15, 1983, price $43, value $100-110.

Fort City Knife Collectors Club, Cincinnati, OH, Pattern - Honey bone gunstock jacks, Manufacturer - Swanner, quantity 100, 1984, price $32, value $35.

Fort City Knife Collectors Club, Cincinnati, OH, Pattern - Etched "Club Officer", Manufacturer - Swanner, quantity 15, 1984, price $32, value $40.

Fort City Knife Collectors Club, Cincinnati, OH, Pattern - Stag congress, four blade, Manufacturer - Hen & Rooster, quantity 65, 1985, price $41, quantity $60.

Fort City Knife Collectors Club, Cincinnati, OH, Pattern - Etched "Club Officer",Manufacturer - Hen & Rooster, quantity 10, 1985, price $41, value $75.

Fort City Knife Collectors Club, Cincinnati, OH, Pattern - Pearl lockback whittler, Manufacturer - Fight'n Rooster, quantity 100, 1986, price $52.55, value $65.

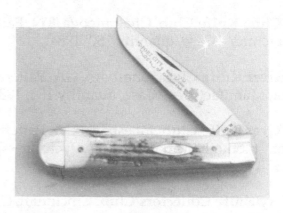

Fort City Knife Collectors Club 1982 Club Knife

Fort City Knife Collectors Club, Cincinnati, OH, pattern - Etched "Club Officer", Manufacturer - Fight'n Rooster, quantity 11, 1986, price $61, value $80.

Fort City Knife Collectors Club, Cincinnati, OH, Pattern - Pearl stockman, five blade "5th Anniversary", Manufacturer - Fight'n Rooster, quantity 35, 1986, price $72, $100.

Fort City Knife Collectors Club, Cincinnati, OH, Pattern - Stag canoe, four blade, Manufacturer - Fight'n Rooster, quantity 75, 1987, price $42.50, value $45.

Fort City Knife Collectors Club, Cincinnati, OH, Pattern - Pearl "Club Officer", Manufacturer - Fight'n Rooster, quantity 10, 1987, price $68, value $100.

Fort City Knife Collectors Club, Cincinnati, OH, Pattern - Red bone "Copperhead", Manufacturer - Kissing Crane, quantity 50, 1988, price $28, value $35.

Fort City Knife Collectors Club, Cincinnati, OH, Pattern - Pearl "Club Officer", Manufacturer - Kissing Crane, quantity 10, 1988, price $50, value $75.

Fort Myers Knife Club, Fort Myers, FL, Pattern - Two blade folding trapper, bone handle, Manufacturer - Case, quantity 100, 1984, value$50.

Fort Myers Knife Club, Fort Myers, FL, Pattern - Two blade folding trapper, Manufacturer - Case, quantity 150, 1985, value $55.

Fort Myers Knife Club, Fort Myers, FL, Pattern - Two blade folding trapper, Manufacturer - Case, quantity 100, 1986, value $55.

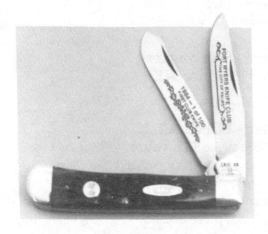

Fort Myers Knife Club 1984 Club Knife

Gator Cutlery Club, Tampa, FL, Pattern - Stag toothpick, Manufacturer - Fight'n Rooster, quantity 300, 1979, price $27, value $100.

Gator Cutlery Club, Tampa, FL, Pattern - Pearl toothpick, Manufacturer - Parker, quantity 350, 1980, price $30, value $40.

Gator Cutlery Club, Tampa, FL, Pattern - Smooth bone toothpick, Manufacturer - Colonel Coon, quantity 350, 1981, price $30, value $40.

Gator Cutlery Club, Tampa, FL, Pattern - Smooth green bone toothpick, Manufacturer - Case, quantity 350, 1982, price $27.50, value $45.

Gator Cutlery Club, Tampa, FL, Pattern - Stag toothpick, Manufacturer - Ka-Bar, quantity 200, 1983, price $32, value $65.

Gator Cutlery Club, Tampa, FL, Pattern - #3235 stag whittler, Manufacturer - Robert Klaas, quantity 250, 1984, price $35, value $45.

Gator Cutlery Club, Tampa, FL, Pattern - Pearl whittler, Manufacturer - Robert Klaas, quantity 150, 1985, price $35, value $45.

Gator Cutlery Club, Tampa, FL, Pattern - Red jigged bone whittler, Manufacturer - Fight'n Rooster, quantity 150, 1986, price $35, value $40.

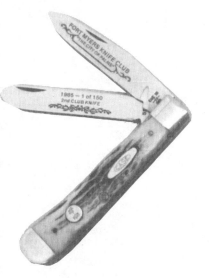

Fort Myers Knife Club 1985 Club Knife

Gator Cutlery Club, Tampa, FL, Pattern - Red jigged bone whittler, Manufacturer - Case, quantity 50, 1987, price $30, value $40.

Gator Cutlery Club, Tampa, FL, Pattern - X-mas tree celluloid whittler, Manufacturer - Fight'n Rooster, quantity 75, 1988, price $45, value $50.

Gator Cutlery Club, Tampa, FL, Pattern -Ivory custom physician's pattern (10th Anniversary), Manufacturer - Bill Simmons, quantity 50, 1989, price $75, value $125.

Gator Cutlery Club, Tampa, FL, Pattern - Coke bottle, Manufacturer - Cripple Creek, 1989.

GEM Capital Knife Club, Franklin, NC, Pattern - Pearl powderhorn with two blades, Manufacturer - Fight'n Rooster, quantity 150, 1980, price $41, value $200, $225, $300+.

GEM Capital Knife Club, Franklin, NC, Pattern - Pearl five blade stockman with two sapphires, Manufacturer - Fight'n Rooster, quantity 250, 1981, price $52, value $125, $150.

GEM Capital Knife Club, Franklin, NC., Pattern - Pearl four blade canoe with two emeralds, Manufacturer - Fight'n Rooster, quantity 300, 1982, price $52, value $80, $125.

GEM Capital Knife Club, Franklin, NC, Pattern - Pearl muskrat with two garnets, Manufacturer - Fight'n Rooster, quantity 300, 1983, price $52, value $85, $125.

Fort Myers Knife Club 1986 Club Knife

GEM Capital Knife Club, Franklin, NC, Pattern - Black pearl equal end jack with one diamond, Manufacturer - Fight'n Rooster, quantity 200, 1984, price $65, value $125, $225.

GEM Capital Knife Club, Franklin, NC, Pattern - Pearl three blade cattleman with one ruby, Manufacturer - Fight'n Rooster, quantity 200, 1985, price $65, price $80, $125.

GEM Capital Knife Club, Franklin, NC, Pattern - Pearl three blade stockman with one sapphire, Manufacturer - Fight'n Rooster, quantity 150, 1986, price $65, value $125.

Golden Circle Knife Club, Jackson, TN, Pattern - Stag serpentine whittler, Manufacturer - Klaas, quantity 300, 1978, price $18.50, value $75,$100, $60.

Golden Circle Knife Club, Jackson, TN, Pattern - Stag four blade sleeveboard, Manufacturer - Klaas, quantity 300, 1979, price $30, value $50,$90,$60.

Golden Circle Knife Club, Jackson, TN, Pattern - White equal end whittler, Manufacturer - Klaas, quantity 500, 1980, price $30, value $50, $60.

Golden Circle Knife Club, Jackson, TN, Pattern - Stag muskrat, Manufacturer Col. Coon, quantity 500, 1981, price $30, $50, $65.

Golden Circle Knife Club, Jackson, TN, Pattern - 6265 SAB red bone folding hunter, Manufacturer - Case, quantity 500, 1982, price $35, value $50, $75.

Golden Circle Knife Club, Jackson, TN, Pattern - 4254 white composition trapper, Manufacturer - Case, quantity 300, 1983, price $30, value $40, $60.

Golden Circle Knife Club, Jackson, TN, Pattern - Stag trapper, Manufacturer - Col. Coon, quantity 50, 1984, price $40, value $100.

Golden Circle Knife Club, Jackson, TN, Pattern - Stockman, three blade, Manufacturer - Col. Coon, quantity 65, 1985, price $45, value $100.

Golden Circle Knife Club, Jackson, TN, Pattern - Stockman, four blade, Manufacturer - Col. Coon, quantity 60, 1986, price $45, value $100.

Golden Circle Knife Club, Jackson, TN, Pattern - Stag canoe, Manufacturer - Bulldog, quantity 70, 1987, price $45, value $70.

Golden Circle Knife Club, Jackson, TN, Pattern - 6199 green bone jack, Manufacturer - Case, quantity 44, 1988, price $42.50, value $50.

Hardeman County Knife Collectors Association , Toone, TN, Pattern 3254 trapper, Manufacturer - Case, 1982.

Hardeman County Knife Collectors, Toone, TN, Pattern - 6254SSP, Manufacturer - Case, quantity 100, 1984.

Hawkeye Knife Collectors, Earlham, IA, Pattern - Stag whittler, Manufacturer - Cripple Creek, quantity 100, 1986, price $60, value $75.

Hawkeye Knife Collectors, Earlham, IA, Pattern - Stag three spring Eureka, Manufacturer - Cripple Creek, quantity 100, 1987, price $65, value $75.

Hawkeye Knife Collectors, Earlham, IA, Pattern - #280 Pearl whittler, Manufacturer - Boker, quantity 100, 1988, price $48, value $55.

Indiana Knife Collectors, Anderson, IN, Pattern - 3254 trappers, Manufacturer - Case, 1981.

Jefferson County Custom Knife Club, Mt. Vernon, IL, Pattern - Mexican cocobolo boot knife, Manufacturer - Frank Hargis, quantity 10, 1986, price $118.00, information provided by club.

Jefferson County Custom Knife Club, Mt. Vernon, IL, Pattern - Coffin handle folder, Manufacturer - Paul Myers, quantity 10, 1987, price $112.00., information provided by club

Jefferson County Custom Knife Club, Mt. Vernon, IL, Pattern - Bocote leaf dagger, Manufacturer - Rick Hill, quantity 10, 1988, price $135.00, information provided by club.

Jefferson County Custom Knife Club, Mt. Vernon, IL, Pattern - White pearl folder, Manufacturer - Raymond A. Cover, quantity 10, 1989, price $150.00, information provided by club.

Jefferson County Custom Knife Club, Mt. Vernon, IL, Pattern - Double edge boot knife, Manufacturer - Doug Casteel, quantity 10, 1990, price $178.00, information provided by club.

Johnny Appleseed Knife Collectors, Mansfield, OH, Pattern - 3254, Manufacturer - Case, quantity 40, 1984, price $27.50, information provided by club.

Johnny Appleseed Knife Collectors, Mansfield, OH, Pattern - Two blade, jigged bone Congress, Manufacturer - Ka-Bar, quantity 40, 1985, price $35, information provided by club.

Johnny Appleseed Knife Collectors, Mansfield, OH, Pattern - Three blade Stockman, Manufacturer - Fight'n Rooster, quantity 50, 1986, price $29, information provided by club.

Johnny Appleseed Knife Collectors, Mansfield, OH, Pattern 6275, Manufacturer - Case, quantity 50, 1987, price $30., information provided by club.

Johnny Appleseed Knife Collectors, Mansfield, OH, Pattern - 6249, 5th Anniversary Knife, Manufacturer - Case, quantity 54, 1988, price $36, information provided by club.

Johnny Appleseed Knife Collectors, Mansfield, OH, Pattern - 6265, Manufacturer - Case, quantity 55, 1988, price $50, information provided by club.

Johnny Appleseed Knife Collectors, Mansfield, OH, Pattern - Two blade, pearl handled canoe, Manufacturer - Fight'n Rooster, quantity 60, 1989, price $60, information provided by club.

Johnny Appleseed Knife Collectors, Mansfield, OH, Pattern - Two blade, stag handled trapper, Manufacturer - Queen, quantity 60, 1990, information provided by club.

Ka-Bar Collectors Club 1975 Club Knife

Ka-Bar Collectors Club, Olean, NY, Pattern - USMC WWII Fighting Knife, Manufacturer - Ka-Bar, 1975, price $100-$300, value $200, information provided by club.

Ka-Bar Collectors Club, Olean, NY, Pattern - Trapper, Manufacturer - Ka-Bar, 1976, price $30-$100, value $120, information provided by club.

Ka-Bar Collectors Club, Olean, NY, Pattern - Folding Hunter, Manufacturer - Ka-Bar, 1977, price $200, value $200 set, information provided by club.

Ka-Bar Collectors Club, Olean, NY, Pattern - 5" Folding hunter, Manufacturer - Ka-Bar, 1978, price $35, value $80, information provided by club.

Ka-Bar Collectors Club, Olean, NY, Pattern - 5" Folding hunter, Manufacturer - Ka-Bar, 1978, price $40, value $100., information provided by club.

Ka-Bar Collectors Club, Olean, NY, Pattern - Lockback, Manufacturer - Ka-Bar, 1979, price $27.50, value $70, information provided by club.

Ka-Bar Collectors Club, Olean, NY, Pattern - Giant jack, Manufacturer - Ka-Bar, 1979, price $31.50, value $75, information provided by club.

Ka-Bar Collectors Club, Olean, NY, Pattern - Canoe, Manufacturer - Ka-Bar, 1979, price $33, value $55, information provided by club.

Ka-Bar Collectors Club, Olean, NY, Pattern - Folding hunter, Manufacturer - Ka-Bar, 1979, price $80, value $170, information provided by club.

Ka-Bar Collectors Club, Olean, NY, Pattern - Folding hunter, Manufacturer - Ka-Bar, 1979, price $80, value $150, information provided by club.

Ka-Bar Collectors Club, Olean, NY, Pattern - Swingguard, Manufacturer - Ka-Bar, 1979, price $35, value $70, information provided by club.

Ka-Bar Collectors Club, Olean, NY, Pattern - Gunstock, Manufacturer - Ka-Bar, 1980, price $27.50, value $60, information provided by club.

Ka-Bar Collectors Club, Olean, NY, Pattern - Lockback hunter, Manufacturer - Ka-Bar, 1980, price $65, value $80, information provided by club.

Ka-Bar Collectors Club, Olean, NY, Pattern - Engraved bolster, Manufacturer - Ka-Bar, 1980, price $67.50, value $100, information provided by club.

Ka-Bar Collectors Club, Olean, NY, Pattern - Lockback hunter, Manufacturer - Ka-Bar, 1980, price $45., value $90, information provided by club.

Ka-Bar Collectors Club, Olean, NY, Pattern - Congress, Manufacturer - Ka-Bar, 1980, price $25, value $50, information provided by club.

Ka-Bar Collectors Club, Olean, NY, Pattern - Coke bottle #1, Manufacturer - Ka-Bar, 1981, price $35, value $85, information provided by club.

Ka-Bar Collectors Club, Olean, NY, Pattern - gunstock, Manufacturer - Ka-Bar, 1981, price $125 set, value $160 set , information provided by club.

Ka-Bar Collectors Club, Olean, NY, Pattern - Coke bottle #2, Manufacturer - Ka-Bar, 1982, price $37.50, value $90, information provided by club.

Ka-Bar Collectors Club, Olean, NY, Pattern - Trapper, Manufacturer - Ka-Bar, 1982, price $125, value $140 set , information provided by club.

Ka-Bar Collectors Club, Olean, NY, Pattern - Giant trapper, Manufacturer - Ka-Bar, 1982, price $35.65, value $50, information provided by club.

Ka-Bar Collectors Club, Olean, NY, Pattern - Coke bottle #3, Manufacturer - Ka-Bar, 1983, price $37.50, value $90, information provided by club.

Ka-Bar Collectors Club, Olean, NY, Pattern - Folding hunter, Manufacturer - Ka-Bar, 1983, price $35, value $65, information provided by club.

Ka-Bar Collectors Club, Olean, NY, Pattern - Folding hunter, Manufacturer - Ka-Bar, 1983, price $37.50, value $70, information provided by club.

Ka-Bar Collectors Club, Olean, NY, Pattern - Barlow, Manufacturer - Ka-Bar, 1983, price $18.75, value $55, information provided by club.

Ka-Bar Collectors Club, Olean, NY, Pattern - Coke bottler #4, Manufacturer - Ka-Bar, 1984, price $37.50, value $90, information provided by club.

Ka-Bar Collectors Club, Olean, NY, Pattern - Whittler, Manufacturer - Ka-Bar, 1984, price $23.50, value $65, information provided by club.

Ka-Bar Collectors Club, Olean, NY, Pattern - Whittler, Manufacturer - Ka-Bar, 1984 , price $50, value $125, information provided by club.

Ka-Bar Collectors Club, Olean, NY, Pattern - Texas toothpick, Manufacturer - Ka-Bar, 1984, price $22.50, value $75, information provided by club.

Ka-Bar Collectors Club, Olean, NY, Pattern - Texas toothpick, Manufacturer - Ka-Bar, 1984, price $50, value $150, information provided by club.

Ka-Bar Collectors Club, Olean, NY, Pattern - Congress, Manufacturer - Ka-Bar, 1984, price $27.50, value $75, information provided by club.

Ka-Bar Collectors Club, Olean, NY, Pattern - Congress, Manufacturer - Ka-Bar, 1984, price $57.50, value $120, information provided by club.

Ka-Bar Collectors Club, Olean , NY, Pattern - Stockman, Manufacturer - Ka-Bar, 1984, price $25.50, value $65, information provided by club

Ka-Bar Collectors Club, Olean, NY, Pattern - Stockman, Manufacturer - Ka-Bar, 1984, price $55.50, value $110, information provided by club.

Ka-Bar Collectors Club, Olean, NY, Pattern - Coke bottle #5, Manufacturer - Ka-Bar, 1985, price $45, value $130, information provided by club.

Ka-Bar Collectors Club, Olean, NY, Pattern - Plowman, Manufacturer - Ka-Bar, 1985, price $29, value $60, information provided by club.

Ka-Bar Collectors Club, Olean, NY, Pattern - Plowman, Manufacturer - Ka-Bar, 1985, price $52.50, value $100, information provided by club.

Ka-Bar Collectors Club, Olean, NY, Pattern - Swingguard, Manufacturer - Ka-Bar, 1985, price $28.50, value $70, information provided by club.

Ka-Bar Collectors Club, Olean, NY, Pattern - Swingguard, Manufacturer - Ka-Bar, 1985, price $52.50, value $100, information provided by club.

Ka-Bar Collectors Club, Olean, NY, Pattern - Sleeveboard, Manufacturer - Ka-Bar, 1985, price $20, value $40, information provided by club.

Ka-Bar Collectors Club, Olean, NY, Pattern - Sleeveboard, Manufacturer - Ka-Bar, 1985, price $39.50, value $75, information provided by club.

Ka-Bar Collectors Club, Olean, NY, Pattern - Barlow, Manufacturer - Ka-Bar, 1985, price $24, value $60, information provided by club.

Ka-Bar Collectors Club, Olean, NY, Pattern - Barlow, Manufacturer - Ka-Bar, 1985, price $47, value $75, information provided by club.

Ka-Bar Collectors Club, Olean, NY, Pattern - Coke bottle, Manufacturer - Ka-Bar, 1985, price $72.50, value $140, information provided by club.

Ka-Bar Collectors Club, Olean, NY, Pattern - Grizzly #1, Manufacturer - Ka-Bar, 1986, price $42, value $100, information provided by club.

Ka-Bar Collectors Club, Olean, NY, Pattern - Ladies leg, Manufacturer - Ka-Bar, 1986, price $32.50, value $70, information provided by club.

Ka-Bar Collectors Club, Olean, NY, Pattern - Ladies leg/Diamond Lil, Manufacturer - Ka-Bar, 1986, price $75, value $135, information provided by club.

Ka-Bar Collectors Club, Olean, NY, Pattern - Sunfish, Manufacturer - Ka-Bar, 1986, price $32.50, value $65, information provided by club.

Ka-Bar Collectors Club, Olean, NY, Pattern - Sunfish, Manufacturer - Ka-Bar, 1986, price $110 set, value $65 each, $220 set, information provided by club.

Ka-Bar Collectors Club, Olean, NY, Pattern - Sunfish, Manufacturer - Ka-Bar, 1986, value $65, information provided by club.

Ka-Bar Collectors Club, Olean, NY, Pattern - Sunfish, Ka-Bar, 1986, price $65, information provided by club.

Ka-Bar Collectors Club, Olean, NY, Pattern - Swingguard, Manufacturer - Ka-Bar, 1986, quantity 251, price $45, value $120, information provided by club.

Ka-Bar Collectors Club, Olean, NY, Pattern - Swingguard, Manufacturer - Ka-Bar, quantity 890, 1986, price $35, value $70, information provided by club.

Ka-Bar Collectors Club 1986 Club Knife Swingguard

Ka-Bar Collectors Club, Olean, NY, Pattern - Grizzly #2, Manufacturer - Ka-Bar, quantity 1.643, 1987, price $42, value $90, information provided by club.

Ka-Bar Collectors Club 1987 Club Knife Grizzly #2

Ka-Bar Collectors Club, Olean, NY, Pattern - Pillbuster, Manufacturer - Ka-Bar, quantity 684, 1987, price $25, value $50, information provided by club

Ka-Bar Collectors Club, Olean, NY, Pattern - Pillbuster, Manufacturer - Ka-Bar, quantity 293, 1987, price $39, value $85, information provided by club.

Ka-Bar Collectors Club, Olean, NY, Pattern - Bomb, Manufacturer - Ka-Bar, quantity 605, 1987, price $28, value $60, information provided by club

Ka-Bar Collectors Club, Olean, NY, Pattern - Bomb, Manufacturer - Ka-Bar, quantity 475, 1987, price $33, value $75, information provided by club.

Ka-Bar Collectors Club 1987 Club Knife Pillbusters

Ka-Bar Collectors Club, Olean, NY, Pattern - Whittler aerial, Manufacturer - Ka-Bar, quantity 698,, 1987, price $32, value $65, information provided by club.

Ka-Bar Collectors Club, Olean, NY, Pattern - Whittler aerial, Manufacturer - Ka-Bar, quantity398, 1987, price $35, value $70, information provided by club.

Ka-Bar Collectors Club, Olean, NY, Pattern - Axe/knife combo, Manufacturer - Ka-Bar, quantity 637, 1987, price $32.50, value $125, information provided by club.

Ka-Bar Collectors Club, Olean, NY, Pattern - Axe/knife combo, Manufacturer - Ka-Bar, quantity 441, 1987, price $37.50, value $125, information provided by club.

Ka-Bar Collectors Club 1988 Club Knife Grizzly #3

Ka-Bar Collectors Club, Olean, NY, Pattern - Grizzly #3, Manufacturer - Ka-Bar, quantity 1,165, 1988, price $42, value $90, information provided by club.

Ka-Bar Collectors Club, Olean, NY, Pattern - Grizzly/scrimshaw, Manufacturer - Ka-Bar, quantity 400, 1988, price $55, value $120, information provided by club.

Ka-Bar Collectors Club, Olean, NY, Pattern - Bowie, Manufacturer - Ka-Bar, quantity 389, 1988, price $67.50, value $150, information provided by club.

Ka-Bar Collectors Club, Olean, NY, Pattern - Bowie, Manufacturer - Ka-Bar, quantity 723, 1988, price $55, value $140, information provided by club

Ka-Bar Collectors Club, Olean, NY, Pattern - Center lock, Manufacturer - Ka-Bar, quantity 673, 1988, price $31, value $60, information provided by club.

Ka-Bar Collectors Club, Olean, NY, Pattern - Center lock, Manufacturer - Ka-Bar,quantity 399, 1988, price $37.50, value $65, information provided by club.

Ka-Bar Collectors Club, Olean, NY, Pattern - Coffin jack/gunfighter, Manufacturer - Ka-Bar, quantity 711, 1988, price $29, value $55, information provided by club.

Ka-Bar Collectors Club, Olean, NY, Pattern - Coffin jack/banker, Manufacturer - Ka-Bar, quantity 406, 1988, price $34, value $60, information provided by club.

Ka-Bar Collectors Club 1987 Club Knife Axe/Knife Combo

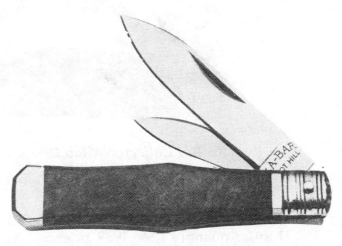

Ka-Bar Collectors Club 1988 Club Knife Coffin/jack Banker

Ka-Bar Collectors Club, Olean, NY, Pattern - Congress/congressman, Manufacturer - Ka-Bar, quantity 636, 1988, price $32.50, value $60, information provided by club.

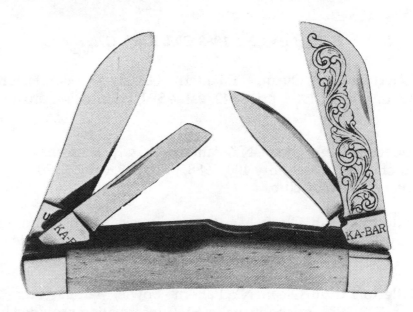

Ka-Bar Collectors Club 1988 Club Knife Congress/ congressman

Ka-Bar Collectors Club, Olean, NY, Pattern - Congress/senator, Manufacturer - Ka-Bar, quantity 401, 1988, price $37.50, value $65, information provided by club.

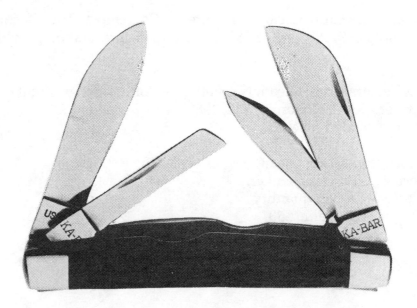

Ka-Bar Collectors Club 1988 Club Knife Congress/senator

Ka-Bar Collectors Club, Olean, NY, Pattern - Grizzly #4, Manufacturer - Ka-Bar, quantity 1,566,1989, price $42, value $90, information provided by club.

Ka-Bar Collectors Club, Olean, NY, Pattern - Dolphin, Manufacturer - Ka-Bar, quantity 784, 1989, price $34, value $60, information provided by club.

Ka-Bar Collectors Club, Olean, NY, Pattern - Dolphin, Manufacturer - Ka-Bar, quantity 488, 1989, price $37.50, value $65, information provided by club.

Ka-Bar Collectors Club, Olean, NY, Pattern - Humpback, Manufacturer - Ka-Bar, quantity 776, 1989, price $33, value $60, information provided by club.

Ka-Bar Collectors Club, Olean, NY, Pattern - Humpback, Manufacturer - Ka-Bar, quantity 475, 1989, price $38, value $65, information provided by club.

Ka-Bar Collectors Club, Olean, NY, Pattern - One hand opener, Manufacturer - Ka-Bar, quantity 766, 1989, price $29.50, value $55, information provided by club.

Ka-Bar Collectors Club, Olean, NY, Pattern - One hand opener, Manufacturer - Ka-Bar, quantity 431, 1989, price $32.50, value $60, information provided by club.

Ka-Bar Collectors Club, Olean, NY, Pattern - Whaler, Manufacturer - Ka-Bar, quantity 774, 1989, price $31, value $55, information provided by club.

Ka-Bar Collectors Club, Olean, NY, Pattern - Whaler, Manufacturer - Ka-Bar, quantity 496, 1989, price $38.50, value $65, information provided by club

Ka-Bar Collectors Club, Olean, NY, Pattern - Long john, Manufacturer - Ka-Bar, quantity 762, 1990, price $38, value $65, information provided by club.

Ka-Bar Collectors Club, Olean, NY, Pattern - Long john, Manufacturer - Ka-Bar, quantity 500, 1990, price $43, value $70, information provided by club.

Ka-Bar Collectors Club, Olean, NY, Pattern - Rancher, Manufacturer - Ka-Bar, quantity 800 , 1990, price $39, value $75, information provided by club.

Ka-Bar Collectors Club, Olean, NY, Pattern - Rancher, Manufacturer - Ka-Bar, quantity 500, 1990, price $42, value $80, information provided by club.

Ka-Bar Collectors Club 1990 Club Knife Grizzly #5

Ka-Bar Collectors Club, Olean, NY, Pattern - Grizzly #5, Manufacturer - Ka-Bar, quantity 1,700, 1990, price $45, value $90, information provided by club.

Ka-Bar Collectors Club, Olean, NY, Pattern - Boxcar whittler, Manufacturer - Ka-Bar, quantity 800, 1990, price $37, value $75, information provided by club.

Ka-Bar Collectors Club, Olean, NY, Pattern - Boxcar whittler, Manufacturer - Ka-Bar, quantity 500, 1990, price $42, value $80, information provided by club.

Ka-Bar Collectors Club, Olean, NY, Pattern - Bent Barlow, Manufacturer - Ka-Bar, quantity 800, 1990, value $55, information provided by club.

Ka-Bar Collectors Club, Olean, NY, Pattern - Bent Barlow, Manufacturer - Ka-Bar, quantity 500, 1990, value $60, information provided by club.

King Coal Knife Club, Madisonville, KY, Pattern - Two blade folding trapper, Manufacturer - Case, quantity 150, 1983, value $75.

*King Coal Knife Club
1983 Club Knife*

Lone Star Knife Club, Waco, TX, Pattern - 6275SP moose, Manufacturer - Case, quantity 50, 1983, price $40, value $100.

Lone Star Knife Club, Waco, TX, Pattern - Pearl toothpick, Manufacturer - Fight'n Rooster, quantity 100, 1984, price $45, value $45.

Lone Star Knife Club, Waco, TX, Pattern - Founders' Knife, bone folding hunter, Manufacturer - Ka-Bar, 1984, price $45, value $75.

Lone Star Knife Club, Waco, TX, Pattern - 5254 stag trapper, Manufacturer - Case, quantity 58, 1985, price $45, value $75.

Lone Star Knife Club, Waco, TX, Pattern - Bone plowman, shield, Manufacturer - Ka-Bar, quantity 50, 1986, price $35, value $50.

Lone Star Knife Club, Waco, TX, Pattern - Bone toenail, shield, Manufacturer - Ka-Bar, quantity 55, 1987, price $45, value $100.

Lone Star Knife Club, Waco, TX, Pattern - R62131SS canoe, Manufacturer - Case, quantity 55, 1988, price $45, value $60.

Lone Star Knife Club, Waco, TX, Pattern - Smooth bone congress, four blade, Manufacturer - Ka-Bar, 1989, price $45.

Mahoning Valley Knife Collectors Association, Newton Falls, OH, Pattern - 6254SS bone trapper, Manufacturer - Case, quantity 125, 1986, price $25, value $60.

Mahoning Valley Knife Collectors Association, Newton Falls, OH, Pattern - B6254SS black bone trapper, Manufacturer - Case, quantity 125, 1987, price $37, value $60.

Mahoning Valley Knife Collectors Association, Newton Falls, OH, Pattern - R6294 S red bone equal end, Pattern - Case, quantity 125, 1988, price $40, value $60.

Mahoning Valley Knife Collectors Association, Newton Falls, OH, Pattern - 52131SS stag canoe, Manufacturer - Case, 1989, price $45, value $50.

Mason-Dixon Knife Club, Quincy, PA, Pattern - White jigged bone 6165 folding hunter, Manufacturer - Case, quantity 75, 1984, price $42, value $125-$150.

Mason-Dixon Knife Club, Quincy, PA, Pattern - Chestnut jigged bone plowman, Manufacturer - Ka-Bar, quantity 75, 1985, price $39, value $50.

Mason-Dixon Knife Club, Quincy, PA, Pattern - Winterbottom bone canoe, Manufacturer - Queen, quantity 75, 1986, price $35, value $50.

Mason-Dixon Knife Club, Quincy, PA, Pattern - Chestnut jigged bone sunfish, Manufacturer - Ka-Bar, quantity 75, 1987, price $39, value $50.

Mason-Dixon Knife Club, Quincy, PA, Pattern - Stag large trapper, Manufacturer - Alcas, quantity 100, 1988, price $48, value $100.

Memphis Knife Collectors, Pattern - 6254SSP trapper, Manufacturer - Case, 1983.

Music City Knife Collectors, Goodlettsville, TN, Pattern - 3254 trapper, Manufacturer - Case, 1977.

Music City Knife Collectors, Goodlettsville, TN, Pattern - 6254 trapper, Manufacturer - Case, quantity 75, 1983.

National Knife Collectors Association, Chattanooga, TN, Pattern - Stag oval whittler, Manufacturer - Klaas, quantity 1,200, 1975, price $12, $600, $475, value $750.

National Knife Collectors Association , Chattanooga, TN, Pattern - White composition whittler, Manufacturer - Case, quantity 3,000, 1976, price $15, $150, $145, value $250.

National Knife Collectors Association , Chattanooga, TN, Pattern - Stag canoe cattle knife, Manufacturer - Klaas, quantity 5,000, 1977, $17.50, $100, $75, value $125.

National Knife Collectors Association , Chattanooga, TN, Pattern - Bone canoe cattle knife, Manufacturer - Rodgers-Wostenholm, quantity 6,000, 1978, price $18.25, $55, $65, value $100.

National Knife Collectors Association , Chattanooga, TN, Pattern - Stag single blade "trapper", Manufacturer - Case, quantity 12,000, 1979, price $22, $55, $60, value $85.

National Knife Collectors Association , Chattanooga, TN, Pattern - Stag gunstock cattle, Manufacturer - Klaas, quantity 12,000, 1980, price $21.75, $45, value $65.

National Knife Collectors Association , Chattanooga, TN, Pattern - Stag equal end cattle, Manufacturer - Queen, quantity 12,000, 1981, price $24.50, $40, value $65.

National Knife Collectors Association , Chattanooga, TN, Pattern - Stag trapper, Manufacturer - Schrade, quantity 10,000, 1982, price $25.50, value $60, $65.

National Knife Collectors Association , Chattanooga, TN, Pattern - Case 6592 stockman, Manufacturer - Case, quantity 1,600, 1982.

National Knife Collectors Association , Chattanooga, TN, Pattern - Bone lockback hunter,. Manufacturer - Case, quantity 7,000, 1983, price $45, value $100, $150.

National Knife Collectors Association Limited Edition, Pattern - 5-3/8" lockback, Manufacturer - Case, quantity 7,000, price $150, 1983, value $150.

Knife Collectors Association , Chattanooga, TN, Pattern - Single blade lockback, Manufacturer - Bertram, quantity 7,000, 1984, price $38, value $50, $80.

National Knife Collectors Association , Chattanooga, TN, Pattern - 6240 bone light trapper, Manufacturer - Case, quantity 7,000, 1985, price $40, value $75.

National Knife Collectors Association , Chattanooga, TN, Pattern - Lockback folding hunter, Manufacturer - Gerber, quantity 6,200, 1986, price $39, value $125.

National Knife Collectors Association , Chattanooga, TN, Pattern - 6345 1/2 green bone cattle, Manufacturer - Case, quantity 7,000, 1987, price $42.95, value $85.

National Knife Collectors Association , Chattanooga, TN, Pattern - 1123 bone large trapper, Manufacturer - Camillus, quantity 6,500, 1988, price $41.95, value $150.

National Knife Collectors Association , Chattanooga, TN, Pattern - Full set 975, 1988.

National Knife Collectors Association , Chattanooga, TN, Pattern - Modified sunfish, Manufacturer - Case, 1989, price $50.

National Knife Collectors Association , Chattanooga, TN, Pattern - 103 Skinner (fixed), Manufacturer - Buck, 1989, price $80.

National Knife Collectors Association , Chattanooga, TN, quantity 1,500, 1990.

National Knife Collectors Association , Chattanooga, TN, Pattern - fixed hunter, quantity 1,500, 1990.

National Knife Collectors Association 15th Anniversary of National Knife Collectors Association, Pattern - 5" coke bottle, Manufacturer - Case, quantity 1,500, 1989, value $90.

National Knife Collectors Association Decade Of Growth, Pattern - (1) 3-3/4" Case; price $125, 1982, value $120. (2) 4-1/4" Queen, Manufacturer - Assorted, price $100, 1982, value $80.

National Knife Collectors Association Dedication Set, Pattern - Set of two 4" Case knives, Manufacturer - Case, price $175, 1981, value $150.

National Knife Collectors Association Dedication Set, Pattern - R6380 ssp whittler, SR6488 congress; alligator case, Manufacturer - Case, value $150.

National Knife Collectors Association First In A Series Museum Knives, Pattern - 5" coke bottle, Manufacturer - Case, quantity 1,500, price $6, 1990, value $100.

National Knife Collectors Association Founder's Set, Manufacturer - Set of four Assorted Brands (1) 4-1/2" Case; (2) 5-1/2" Schrade; (3) 4" Kissing Crane; (4) 3-3/4" Fight'n' Rooster, price $300, 1980, value $300.

National Knife Collectors Association Limited Edition, Pattern - 4-1/2" stag whittler, Manufacturer - Kissing Crane, quantity 1,200, price $750, 1975, value $750.

National Knife Collectors Association Limited Edition, Pattern - 3-7/8" serpentine, Manufacturer - Case, price $195, 1976, value $225.

National Knife Collectors Association Limited Edition, Pattern - 3-7/8" serpentine, Manufacturer - Case, quantity 3,000, price $250, 1976, value $225.

National Knife Collectors Association Limited Edition, Pattern - 4-1/2" three blade canoe, Manufacturer - Kissing Crane, quantity 5,000, price $125, 1977, value $150.

National Knife Collectors Association Limited Edition, Pattern - 3-5/8" blade canoe, Manufacturer - Rodgers-Wostenholm, quantity 6,000, price $100, 1978, value $75.

National Knife Collectors Association Limited Edition, Pattern - 4-1/8" one blade trapper, Manufacturer - Case, quantity 12,000, price $85, 1979, value $80.

National Knife Collectors Association Limited Edition, Pattern - 4" gunstock, Manufacturer - Kissing Crane, quantity 12,000, price $65, 1980, value $60.

National Knife Collectors Association Limited Edition, Pattern - 4-1/2" big cigar Manufacturer - Queen, quantity 12,000, price $65, 1981, value $60.

National Knife Collectors Association Limited Edition, Pattern - 3-7/8" two blade trapper, Manufacturer - Schrade, quantity 10,000, price $65, 1982, value $70.

National Knife Collectors Association Limited Edition, Pattern - 4-1/4" slant bolster, Manufacturer - Hen & Rooster, quantity 7,000, price $80, 1984, value $80.

National Knife Collectors Association Limited Edition, Pattern - G6240SS 4-7/16" giant two blade Peanut, Manufacturer - Case, quantity 7,000, price $75, 1985, value $100.

National Knife Collectors Association Limited Edition, Pattern - 3-5/8" single blade lockback, Manufacturer - Gerber, quantity 6,200, price $125, 1986, value $100.

National Knife Collectors Association Limited Edition, Pattern - G6345 1/2, Manufacturer - Case, quantity 7,000, price $85, 1987, value $100.

National Knife Collectors Association Limited Edition, Pattern - 4-7/16"
giant trapper, Manufacturer - Camillus, quantity 6,500, price $150, 1988,
value $160.

National Knife Collectors Association Museum Knives– First In A Series,
Pattern - 5" coke bottle, Manufacturer - Case, quantity 1,500, price $65,
1990, value $85.

National Knife Collectors Association USMC Beirut Commemorative
Fighter, Pattern - Fighting knife; money goes to families who lost loved
ones in that tragic event, Manufacturer - Jim Pugh, quantity 1,000, price
$500, value $800.

North Carolina Cutlery Club, Fuquay Varina, NC, Pattern - Pearl mini-
trapper, Manufacturer - Parker, quantity 150, 1981, price $27.50, value $65,
information provided by club.

North Carolina Cutlery Club, Fuquay Varina, NC, Pattern - Pearl sway-
back whittler, Manufacturer - Parker, quantity 150, 1982, price $20, value
$55, information provided by club.

North Carolina Cutlery Club, Fuquay Varina, NC, Pattern - Gray smooth
bone trapper, Manufacturer - Boker/Germany, quantity 200, 1983, price
$24, value $75, information provided by club.

North Carolina Cutlery Club, Fuquay Varina, NC, Pattern - Gray smooth
bone canoe, Manufacturer - Boker/Germany, quantity 200, 1984, price $24,
value $70, information provided by club.

North Carolina Cutlery Club, Fuquay Varina, NC, Pattern - Red jigged
bone mini-trapper, Manufacturer - Hen & Rooster, quantity 200, 1984,
price $27, value $60, information provided by club.

North Carolina Cutlery Club, Fuquay Varina, NC, Pattern - Gray smooth
bone copperhead, Manufacturer - Boker/Germany, quantity 200, 1985,
price $24.50, value $60, information provided by club.

North Carolina Cutlery Club, Fuquay Varina, NC, Pattern - Antique
Green Bone Trapper - 5th Anniversary Knife, Manufacturer - Case,
quantity 100, 1985, price $38, value $45, information provided by club.

North Carolina Cutlery Club, Fuquay Varina, NC, Pattern - Burnt bone
6380 whittler, Manufacturer -Case, quantity 166, 1986, price $39, value
$45, information provided by club.

North Carolina Cutlery Club, Fuquay Varina, NC, Pattern - Gray smooth
bone folding hunter, Manufacturer - United Boker, quantity 175, 1987,
price $29.50, value $40, information provided by club.

North Carolina Cutlery Club, Fuquay Varina, NC, Pattern - Gray smooth
bone stockman, Manufacturer - United/Boker, quantity 175, 1988, price
$28.75, value $35, information provided by club.

North Carolina Cutlery Club, Fuquay Varina, NC, Pattern - Gray smooth bone lockback hunter, Manufacturer - United/Boker, quantity 150, 1989, price $32, value $37, information provided by club.

North Carolina Cutlery Club, Fuquay Varina, NC, Pattern - Yellow Composition 31400LSS — Fuquay–Varina Show Knife, Manufacturer - Case, quantity 25, 1989, price $17, value $20, information provided by club.

North Carolina Cutlery Club, Fuquay Varina, NC, Pattern - Smooth Grey Bone Congress, Manufacturer - Boker/Germany, quantity 175, 1990, price $30, value $40, information provided by club.

North Carolina Cutlery Club, Fuquay Varina, NC, Pattern - Smooth Grey Bone Whittler, Manufacturer - Boker/Germany, quantity 150, 1991, price $29.50, value $35, information provided by club.

Northeast Cutlery Collectors Association, Wollaston, MA, Pattern - White bone 62131 canoe, scrimshaw, Manufacturer -Case, quantity 150, 1982, price $50, value $130, information provided by club.

Northeast Cutlery Collectors Association, Wollaston, MA, Pattern - Red jigged bone stockman, Manufacturer - Cripple Creek, quantity 75, 1986, price $55, value $95, information provided by club.

Northeast Cutlery Collectors Association, Wollaston, MA, Pattern - Stag dog-leg whittler, Manufacturer - Cripple Creek, quantity 62, 1987, price $60, value $95, information provided by club.

Northeast Cutlery Collectors Association, Wollaston, MA, Pattern - Jigged bone "Coke bottle", Manufacturer - Cripple Creek, quantity51, 1989, price $68, value $90, information provided by club.

Northeast Cutlery Collectors Association, Wollaston, MA, Pattern - Red jigged bone drop-point, Manufacturer - Jim Turecek, quantity 28, 1989, price $135, value $145, information provided by club.

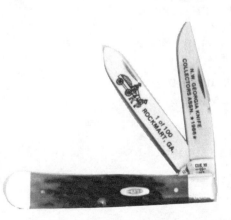

Northwest Georgia Knife Collectors Association 1986 Club Knife

Northwest Georgia Knife Collectors Association, Rockmart, GA, Pattern - Two blade folding trapper, bone handles, Manufacturer -Case, quantity 100, 1986, value $50.

Old Dominion Collectors Association , Bedford, VA, Pattern - Canoe, two blade, Manufacturer -Case, quantity 75, 1978, price $16.50, value $350.

Old Dominion Collectors Association , Bedford, VA, Pattern - Stag whittler, Manufacturer - Kissing Crane, quantity 300, 1979, price $27.50, value $65.

Old Dominion Collectors Association , Bedford, VA, Pattern - Stag, four blade, Manufacturer - Kissing Crane, quantity 250, 1980, price $29, value $55.

Old Dominion Collectors Association , Bedford , VA, Pattern - Stag trapper, Manufacturer - Bulldog, quantity 300, 1981, price $27, value $65.

Old Dominion Collectors Association , Bedford , VA, Pattern - Stag gunstock stockman, Manufacturer - Bulldog, quantity 300, 1982, price $30, value $60.

Old Dominion Collectors Association , Bedford, VA, Pattern - Stag folding hunter, two blade, Manufacturer - Bulldog, quantity 300, 1983, price $35, value $75.

Old Dominion Collectors Association , Bedford, VA, Pattern - Stag congress, four blade, Manufacturer - Bulldog, quantity 300, 1984, price $34, value $65.

Old Dominion Collectors Association , Bedford, VA, Pattern - Stag trapper, three blade, Manufacturer - Bulldog, quantity 300, 1985, price $37, value $75.

Old Dominion Collectors Association , Bedford, VA, Pattern - Stag canoe, three blade, Manufacturer - Bulldog, quantity 255, 1986, price $32, value $65.

Old Dominion Collectors Association , Bedford, VA, Pattern - Stag stockman, Manufacturer - Boker, quantity 250, 1987, price $32, value $35.

Old Dominion Collectors Association , Bedford, VA, Pattern - Stag folding hunter, Manufacturer- Fight'n Rooster, quantity 200, 1988, price $47, value $60.

Old Dominion Collectors Association , Bedford, VA, Pattern - Pearl canoe (10th Anniversary), Manufacturer - Boker, quantity 150, 1988, price $39, value $100.

Oregon Knife Collectors Association , Eugene-Springfield, OR, Pattern - 21051 LSSP lockback, Manufacturer -Case, quantity 200, 1979, price $20, value $50.

Oregon Knife Collectors Association , Eugene-Springfield, OR, Pattern - 250 SP silver knight, stag, Manufacturer - Gerber, quantity 200, 1980, price $27.50, value $50.

Oregon Knife Collectors Association , Eugene-Springfield, OR, Pattern - LST, white Micarta, Manufacturer - Gerber, quantity 100, 1981, price $30, value $40.

Oregon Knife Collectors Association , Eugene-Springfield, OR, Pattern - Single blade, Sherwood engraved, Manufacturer - Corrado, quantity 50, 1982, price $60, value $300.

Oregon Knife Collectors Association , Eugene-Springfield, OR, Pattern - Beaver scrimshaw, Manufacturer - Gerber/Paul, quantity 50, 1983, price $55, value $350.

Oregon Knife Collectors Association , Eugene-Springfield, OR, Pattern - Beaver scrimshaw, Manufacturer - Gerber Touche, quantity 50, 1984, price $30, value $75.

Oregon Knife Collectors Association , Eugene-Springfield, OR, Pattern - Beaver scrimshaw, Manufacturer - Gerber/FSII, quantity 50, 1985, price $40, value $75.

Oregon Knife Collectors Association , Eugene-Springfield, OR, Pattern - Beaver scrimshaw, Manufacturer - Gerber/Loveless, quantity 71, 1986, price $40, value $100.

Oregon Knife Collectors Association, Eugene-Springfield, OR, Pattern - Tanto, Manufacturer - Al Mar, quantity 60, 1987, price $60, value $100.

Oregon Knife Collectors Association , Eugene-Springfield, OR, Pattern - Benchmark/ Blackie Collins, Manufacturer - Gerber, quantity 60, 1988, price $67.50, value $67.50.

Oregon Knife Collectors Association , Eugene-Springfield, OR, Pattern - Stag "Coke Bottle", Manufacturer - Cripple Creek, quantity 50, 1989, price $80, value $150.

Oregon Knife Collectors Association , Eugene-Springfield, OR, Pattern - Bone English jack, Manufacturer - Terry Davis, quantity 50, 1990, price $100, value $200.

Oregon Knife Collectors Association , Eugene-Springfield, OR, Pattern - Gone gunstock jack, Manufacturer - Mark Wahlster, quantity 50, 1991, price $115, value $115.

Palmetto Cutlery Club, Greer, SC, Pattern - Pearl sleeveboard, Manufacturer - Queen, quantity 50, 1976, price $13, value $175.

Palmetto Cutlery Club, Greer, SC, Pattern - Pearl three blade canoe, Manufacturer - Fight'n Rooster, quantity 200, 1977, price $27, value $100.

Palmetto Cutlery Club, Greer, SC, Pattern - Pearl muskrat, Manufacturer -Fight'n Rooster, quantity 200, 1978, price $19.50, value $75.

Palmetto Cutlery Club, Greer, SC, Pattern - Pearl gunstock, Manufacturer - Fight'n Rooster, quantity 200, 1979, price $30, value $90.

Palmetto Cutlery Club, Greer, SC, Pattern - Pearl physician's single blade, Manufacturer - Fight'n Rooster, quantity 200, 1980, price $29.50, value $90.

Palmetto Cutlery Club, Greer, SC, Pattern - Pearl teardrop Barlow, Manufacturer - Fight'n Rooster, quantity 200, 1981, price $36.50, value $90.

Palmetto Cutlery Club, Greer, SC, Pattern - Pearl baby bullet, Manufacturer - Parker, quantity 200, 1982, price $20, quantity $40.

Palmetto Cutlery Club, Greer, SC, Pattern - Pearl sow-belly stockman, three blade, Manufacturer - Parker, quantity 200, 1983, price $27, value $30.

Palmetto Cutlery Club, Greer, SC, Pattern - Pearl congress, three blade, Manufacturer - Parker, quantity 135, 1983, price $16, value $25.

Palmetto Cutlery Club, Greer, SC, Pattern - Pearl mini-trapper, Manufacturer -Case, quantity 135, 1984, price $47.50, value $90.

Palmetto Cutlery Club, Greer, SC, Pattern - Pearl whittler, Manufacturer - Queen, quantity 140, 1985, price $40, value $75.

Palmetto Cutlery Club, Greer, SC, Pattern - Pearl copperhead, Manufacturer - Queen, quantity 105, 1986, price $45, value $60.

Palmetto Cutlery Club, Greer, SC, Pattern - Pearl half-whittler, two blade, Manufacturer - Queen, quantity 100, 1987, price $38, value $40.

Palmetto Cutlery Club, Greer, SC, Pattern - Pearl 501 squire, Manufacturer - Buck, quantity 75, 1988, price $42, value $50.

Palmetto Cutlery Club, Greer, SC, Pattern - Pearl Trapper, Manufacturer - Hen & Rooster, quantity 75, 1989, price $55, value $70.

Palmetto Cutlery Club, Greer, SC, Pattern - Pearl Copperhead, Manufacturer - United Boker, quantity 90, 1990, price $45, value $45.

Palmetto Cutlery Club, Greer, SC, Pattern - Pearl Congress four blade, Manufacturer - Sargent, 1991.

Peach State Cutlery Club, Acworth, GA, Pattern - Stag gunstock, two blade, Manufacturer - Ka-Bar, quantity 60, 1984, price $34.20.

Peach State Cutlery Club, Acworth, GA, Pattern - Second cut stag trapper, Manufacturer -Case, quantity 60, 1985, price $35.

Peach State Cutlery Club, Acworth, GA, Pattern - Ivory mini-trapper, Manufacturer -Case, quantity 55, 1986, price $35.

Peach State Cutlery Club, Acworth, GA, Pattern - Red bone congress, three blade, Manufacturer -Case, quantity 75, 1987, price $36.

Peach State Cutlery Club, Acworth, GA, Pattern - Stag canoe, Manufacturer - Case, quantity 55, 1988, price $40.

Permian Basin Knife Club, Midland, TX, Pattern - 6254 white smooth bone trapper, Manufacturer -Case, quantity 151, 1981, price $25.

Permian Basin Knife Club, Midland, TX, Pattern - 6254 blond pakkawood trapper, Manufacturer - Case, quantity 200, 1982, price $26.

Permian Basin Knife Club, Midland, TX, Pattern - 9254 dark imitation pearl trapper, Manufacturer - Case, quantity 200, 1983, price $28.

Permian Basin Knife Club, Midland, TX, Pattern - 8254 pearl trapper, Manufacturer -Case, quantity 200, 1984, price $70, value $175.

Permian Basin Knife Club, Midland, TX, Pattern - 6254 green jigged bone trapper, Manufacturer -Case, quantity 200, 1985, price $36, value $85.

Permian Basin Knife Club, Midland, TX, Pattern - 6254 Rogers style bone trapper, Manufacturer -Case, quantity 200, 1986, price $36, value $75.

Permian Basin Knife Club, Midland, TX, Pattern - IV254 ivory trapper, Manufacturer -Case, quantity 200, 1987, price $50, value $200.

Permian Basin Knife Club, Midland, TX, Pattern - B200 black bone trapper, Manufacturer -Case, quantity 200, 1988, price $30, value $75.

Permian Basin Knife Club, Midland, TX, Pattern - 6254 mesquite wood trapper, Manufacturer -Case, quantity 200, 1989, price $41, value $75.

Rebel Knife Club 1980 Club Knife

Rebel Knife Club, Tupelo, MS, Pattern - 6254SSP, Manufacturer -Case, 1980.

Rebel Knife Club, Tupelo, MS, Pattern - Two blade folding trapper, Manufacturer -Case, 1981, value $50.

Rebel Knife Club, Tupelo, MS, Pattern - 3254 trapper, Manufacturer - Case, 1982.

Rocky Mountain Blade Collectors, Louisville, CO, Pattern - Custom pearl sleeveboard whittler, Manufacturer - Case, quantity 72, 1979, price $42.50, value $125.

Rocky Mountain Blade Collectors, Louisville, CO, Pattern - Stag folding hunter, Manufacturer - Ka-Bar, quantity 100, 1980, price $30, value $100.

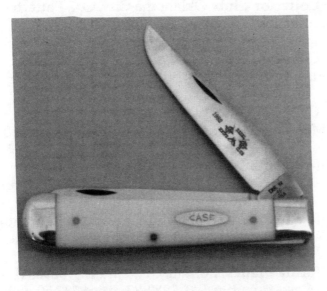

Rebel Knife Club 1982 Club Knife

Rocky Mountain Blade Collectors, Louisville, CO, Pattern - Stag jack, Manufacturer - Ka-Bar, quantity 100, 1981, price $20, value $60.

Rocky Mountain Blade Collectors, Louisville, CO, Pattern - Stag lockback, Manufacturer - Ka-Bar, quantity 100, 1982, price $37.50, value $75.

Rocky Mountain Blade Collectors, Louisville, CO, Pattern - Bone folding hunter, Manufacturer - Ka-Bar, quantity 55, 1983, price $37.50, value $125.

Rocky Mountain Blade Collectors, Louisville, CO, Pattern - Stag Barlow, Manufacturer - Ka-Bar, quantity 100, 1984, price $35, value $45.

Rocky Mountain Blade Collectors, Louisville, CO, Pattern - Custom hunter, stag Barminski, quantity 55, 1986, price $55, value $125.

Rocky Mountain Blade Collectors, Louisville, CO, Pattern - "Rocky Mt. USA" Lockback, Manufacturer - Damascus, quantity 100, 1987, price $37.50, value $60.

Rocky Mountain Blade Collectors, Louisville, CO, Pattern - Custom hunter, pakkawood, Manufacturer - Barminski, quantity 55, 1988, Price $50, value $75.

Smoky Mountain Woodcarvers Club, Pattern - 6254 bone handle trapper, Manufacturer -Case, quantity 56, 1983, price $50, value $50.

Sooner Knife Collector Club, Oklahoma City, OK, Pattern - Stag 5254 trapper, Manufacturer -Case, quantity 38, 1984, price $45, value $80.

Sooner Knife Collector Club, Oklahoma City, OK, Pattern - Lockback whittler, Manufacturer - Fight'n Rooster, quantity 50, 1985, price $50, value $60.

Sooner Knife Collector Club, Oklahoma City, OK, Pattern - Bone stockman, Manufacturer - Fight'n Rooster, 1986, value $60.

Sooner Knife Collector Club, Oklahoma City, OK, Pattern - Bone muskrat, Manufacturer - Fight'n Rooster, 1987, value $60.

Sooner Knife Collector Club, Oklahoma City, OK, Pattern - Red sawn bone Barlow, Manufacturer - Fight'n Rooster, 1988, value $50.

Southern California Blades, Lomita, CA, Pattern - Stag gunstock, Manufacturer - Queen, quantity 150, 1980, price $27.50, value $50.

Southern California Blades, Lomita, CA, Pattern - Stag trapper, Manufacturer - Queen, quantity 150, 1981, price $27.50, value $55.

Southern California Blades, Lomita, CA, Pattern - 051051LSSP lockback, Manufacturer - Case, quantity 100, 1982-83, price $32.50, value $50.

Southern California Blades, Lomita, CA, Pattern - 0591 bone folding hunter, Manufacturer - Ka-Bar, quantity 75, 1984, price $37.50, value $50.

Southern California Blades, Lomita, CA, Pattern - DH89 bone Plowman, Manufacturer - Ka-Bar, quantity 75, 1985, price $37.50, value $50.

Southern California Blades, Lomita, CA, Pattern - Buffalo skinner, Manufacturer - Cripple Creek, quantity 70, 1986, price $65, value $75.

Southern California Blades, Lomita, CA, Pattern - 4011 folding hunter, Manufacturer - Boker, quantity 75, 1987, price $55, value $55.

Southern California Blades, Lomita, CA, Pattern - Trapper, Manufacturer - Happy Jack, quantity 75, 1988, price $45, value $45.

Soy Knife Collector's Club, Decatur, IL, Pattern - "Bob Wong's Phantom" set, Manufacturer - Taylor Cutlery, quantity 30, 1982, price $38, value $45.

Soy Knife Collector's Club, Decatur, IL, Pattern - Stag mini-trapper, Manufacturer - Colonel Coon, quantity 30, 1983, price $29, value $75.

Soy Knife Collector's Club, Decatur, IL, Pattern - 6154 red bone trapper, single blade, Manufacturer -Case, quantity 30, 1984, price $24, value $34.

Soy Knife Collector's Club, Decatur, IL, Pattern - Stag mini-trapper, Manufacturer - Cargill, quantity 23, 1985, price $46.50, value $60.

Soy Knife Collector's Club, Decatur, IL, Pattern - Honey bone "butterbean" three blade, Manufacturer - Cargill, quantity 30, 1986, price $55, value $70.

Soy Knife Collector's Club, Decatur, IL, Pattern - SF86 brown bone sunfish, Manufacturer - Ka-Bar, quantity 20, 1987, price $34, value $45.

Soy Knife Collector's Club, Decatur, IL, Pattern - 163DS stag, three blade, Manufacturer - Hen & Rooster, quantity 30, 1988, price $43, value $55.

Tarheel Cutlery Club, Cleveland, TN, Pattern - Gunstock whittler, pearl, Manufacturer - Fight'n Rooster, quantity 350, 1975, value $65.

Tarheel Cutlery Club, Cleveland, TN, Pattern - Whittler, 3 blade lockback, pearl, Manufacturer - Fight'n Rooster, 1982, value $48.

Tennessee Valley Blades Knife Club, Cleveland, TN, Pattern - Wood & bone trappers set, Manufacturer - Parker-Frost, quantity 25, 1988, price $40, value $60.

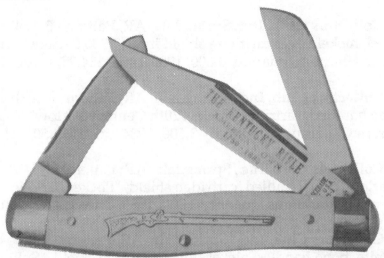

The Knife Collectors Club, Inc. 1971 Club Knife "Kentucky Rifle"

The Knife Collectors Club, Inc., Springdale, AR, Pattern -Three blade stockman, ivory Micarta handle, rifle shield inlay, "Kentucky Rifle", Manufacturer - Schrade-Walden, quantity 12,000, 1971, price $12, value $95.

The Knife Collectors Club, Inc., Springdale, AR, Pattern - Single blade 5-1/2" Barlow, Delrin handle, special Barlow knife shield inlay, "Grandaddy Barlow", Manufacturer - Camillus, quantity 12,000, 1973, price $20, value $60.

The Knife Collectors Club, Inc., Springdale, AR, Pattern - Single blade knife, genuine stag handle, pistol on shield, etched blade, honors 75th anniversary of the Luger pistol, "Luger Pistol", Manufacturer - Puma, quantity 3,700, 1974, price $34.95, value $100.

The Knife Collectors Club, Inc., Springdale, AR, Pattern - 2-1/2" Barlow, genuine ivory handle, nickel silver bolsters, cartridge shield inlay, "Baby Barlow", Manufacturer - Bertram, quantity 1,800, 1975, price $18, value $235.

The Knife Collectors Club, Inc., Springdale, AR, Pattern - 3-1/2" whittler, ebony handled, cartridge shield, nickel silver liners and bolsters, ".44 Magnum Whittler", Manufacturer - Bertram, quantity 1,200, 1977, price $39, value $175.

The Knife Collectors Club, Inc. 1974 Club Knife "Luger Pistol"

The Knife Collectors Club, Inc., Springdale, AR, Pattern - 2-7/8" coffin, one saber-ground blade, India stag handle, "Straight Arrow", Manufacturer - Bertram, quantity 2,500, 1978, price $34.95, value $165.

The Knife Collectors Club, Inc., Springdale, AR, Pattern - 3-7/16" vest pocket skinner, one blade, cocobolo handles with cartridge shield, "Long Colt", Manufacturer - Bertram, quantity 2,800, 1979, price $34.95, value $135.

The Knife Collectors Club, Inc., Springdale, AR, Pattern - 2-7/8" Barlow, ebony handled, .219 cartridge shield, ".219 Zipper", Manufacturer - Bertram, quantity 2,200, 1979, price $34.95, value $135.

The Knife Collectors Club, Inc., Springdale, AR, Pattern - 3-1/4" canoe, stainless steel, nickel silver cartridge shield inlay, ".300 Savage Canoe, Manufacturer - Bertram, quantity 3,000, 1980, price $34.95, value $75.

The Knife Collectors Club, Inc., Springdale, AR, Pattern - Lockback Barlow, bone handled, cartridge shield, "20th Century Barlow", Manufacturer - Cattaraugus, quantity 3,600, 1984, price $24.50, value $45.

The Knife Collectors Club, Inc., Springdale, AR, Pattern - 2-5/8" lockback Barlow, bone handled, cartridge shield, "Pocket Barlow" Manufacturer - Cattaraugus, quantity 3,000, 1986, price $24.50, value $35.

The Knife Collectors Club, Inc., Springdale, AR, Pattern - Single blade liner-lock knife, bone handles, nickel silver cartridge shield, "Split Bolster Jack", Manufacturer - Cattaraugus, quantity 3,000, 1988, price $24.50, value $40.

The Knife Collectors Club, Inc., Springdale, AR, Pattern - Sleeveboard whittler, Manufacturer - Cattaraugus, quantity 1,500, 1990, price $50, value $70.

The Knife Collectors Club, Inc., Springdale, AR, Pattern - 2-7/8" Muskrat bone scales, Manufacturer - Cattaraugus, quantity 1,000, 1991, price $40, value $50.

The Knife Collectors Club, Inc., Springdale, AR, Pattern - 3-3/8" Muskrat bone scales, Manufacturer - Cattaraugus, quantity 1,000, 1991, price $45, value $55.

Three Rivers Knife Club, Rome, GA, Pattern - 6254 Brown bone, Manufacturer -Case, quantity 100, 1980, price $125, information provided by club.

Three Rivers Knife Club, Rome, GA, Pattern - G6207 Green bone, Manufacturer -Case, quantity 150, 1981, price $100, value $70, information provided by club.

Three Rivers Knife Club, Rome, GA, Pattern - 5207 Stag, Manufacturer - Case, quantity 150, 1982, price $100, value $75, information provided by club.

Three Rivers Knife Club, Rome, GA, Pattern - 8207 Pearl, Manufacturer - Case, quantity 150, 1983, price $145, value $170, information provided by club.

Three Rivers Knife Club, Rome, GA, Pattern - 5207 second cut stag, Manufacturer - Case, quantity 100, 1984, price $95, value $75, information provided by club.

Three Rivers Knife Club, Rome, GA, Pattern - 6207 Rogers bone, Manufacturer - Case, quantity 125, 1985, price $85, value $70, information provided by club.

Three Rivers Knife Club, Rome, GA, Pattern - IV207 Ivory, Manufacturer - Case, quantity 100, 1986, price $175, value $200, information provided by club.

Three Rivers Knife Club, Rome, GA, Pattern - 3207 Yellow, Manufacturer - Case, quantity 100, 1987, price $75, value $50, information provided by club

Three Rivers Knife Club, Rome, GA, Pattern - WR6207 Red/White bone, Manufacturer -Case, quantity 100, 1988, price $95, value $65, information provided by club

Three Rivers Knife Club, Rome, GA, Pattern - 5207D Stag, Manufacturer -Case, quantity 75, 1989, price $160, value $125, information provided by club.

Three Rivers Knife Club, Rome, GA, Pattern - P8207 Pink pearl, Manufacturer -Case, quantity 75, 1990, price $165, value $200, information provided by club

Tulsa Knife Club, Tulsa, OK, Pattern - 3254 Case trapper, Manufacturer - Case, quantity 100, 1982.

Western Reserve of Ohio Cutlery Association, Doylestown, OH, Pattern - 6254 Case Trapper, Manufacturer -Case, quantity 100, 1977, price $24, value $60.

Western Reserve of Ohio Cutlery Association, Doylestown, OH, Pattern - 6249 Case Copperhead, Manufacturer -Case, quantity 118, 1978, price $20, value $70.

Western Reserve of Ohio Cutlery Association, Doylestown, OH, Pattern - Hunter, stag handles, Manufacturer - Ka-Bar, quantity 35, 1978, price $50, value $150.

Western Reserve of Ohio Cutlery Association, Doylestown, OH, Pattern - 6383 whittler jigged bone, Manufacturer -Case, quantity 100, 1979, price $20, value $50.

Western Reserve of Ohio Cutlery Association, Doylestown, OH, Pattern - Canoe, 2 blade, jigged stag, Manufacturer - Cargill, quantity 40, 1980, price $40, value $75.

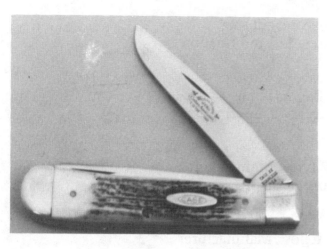

Western Reserve of Ohio Cutlery Association
1982 Club Knife

Western Reserve of Ohio Cutlery Association, Doylestown, OH, Pattern - Marked 6254 Case Trapper (some marked correctly 5254), Manufacturer - Case, quantity 150, 1982, price $33, value $55.

Western Reserve of Ohio Cutlery Association, Doylestown, OH, Pattern - 5149 Case copperhead, stag, Manufacturer -Case, quantity 60, 1983, price $35, value $60.

Western Reserve of Ohio Cutlery Association, Doylestown, OH, Pattern - Custom Bowie, 1/2 scale (20 with African blackwood handles, 40 leather), Manufacturer - Dale Warther, quantity 60, 1984, price $75, value $250.

Western Reserve of Ohio Cutlery Association, Doylestown, OH, Pattern - Side lever, stag handles, Manufacturer - Hubertus, quantity 65, 1985, price $65, value $150.

Western Reserve of Ohio Cutlery Association, Doylestown, OH, Pattern - Side lever, stag handles, Manufacturer - Hubertus, quantity 65 plain, 1986, price $65, value $150.

Western Reserve of Ohio Cutlery Association, Doylestown, OH, Pattern - 335 with gold wash banner, Manufacturer - Hubertus, quantity 35 gold, 1986, price $75, value $190.

Western Reserve of Ohio Cutlery Association, Doylestown, OH, Pattern - SG86 lockback India stag, Manufacturer - Ka-Bar, quantity 125, 1987, price $42, value $75.

Western Reserve of Ohio Cutlery Association, Doylestown, OH, Pattern - "10th Anniversary Special", large Warther pocket knife, elephant ivory, silver dollar bolsters, Manufacturer - Warther, quantity 54, 1987, price $240, value $750.

Western Reserve of Ohio Cutlery Association, Doylestown, OH, Pattern - Barlow, jigged bone, dog's head shield, Manufacturer - Ka-Bar, quantity 100, 1988, price 37, value $60.

Western Reserve of Ohio Cutlery Association, Doylestown, OH, Pattern - Three blade stockman, Damascus, powdered ivory handles, Manufacturer - Parker USA, quantity 100, 1989, price $60, value $130.

Western Reserve of Ohio Cutlery Association, Doylestown, OH, Pattern - Two blade copperhead stag, Manufacturer - Cripple Creek, quantity 71, 1990, price $70, value $90.

Western Reserve of Ohio Cutlery Association, Doylestown, OH, Pattern - One blade toothpick show knife, black polished bone, Manufacturer - Queen, quantity 85, 1990, price $25, value $40.

Wolverine Knife Collectors Club, Taylor, MI, Pattern - Stag gunstock, Manufacturer - Queen, quantity 100, 1980, price $25, value $200, information provided by club.

Wolverine Knife Collectors Club, Taylor, MI, Pattern - White bone gunstock, Manufacturer - Queen, quantity 120, 1981, price $20, value $65, information provided by club.

Wolverine Knife Collectors Club, Taylor, MI, Pattern - Pearl gunstock, Manufacturer - Queen, quantity 150, 1982, price $45, value $75, information provided by club.

Wolverine Knife Collectors Club, Taylor, MI, Pattern - Second cut stag gunstock, Manufacturer - Queen, quantity 121, 1983, price $32, value $45, information provided by club.

Wolverine Knife Collectors Club, Taylor, MI, Pattern - Second cut stag trapper, Manufacturer -Case, quantity 106, 1984, price $45, value $85, information provided by club.

Wolverine Knife Collectors Club, Taylor, MI, Pattern - Second cut stag mini- trapper, Manufacturer - Case, quantity 100, 1985, price $45, value $65, information provided by club.

Wolverine Knife Collectors Club, Taylor, MI, Pattern - Second cut stag trapper, Manufacturer - Queen, quantity 115, 1986, price $32, value $40, information provided by club.

Wolverine Knife Collectors Club, Taylor, MI, Pattern - Pearl trapper, Manufacturer - Queen, quantity 100, 1987, price $48, value $85, information provided by club.

Wolverine Knife Collectors Club, Taylor, MI, Pattern - Green bone doctors, Manufacturer - Queen, quantity 89, 1988, price $36, value $45, information provided by club.

Wolverine Knife Collectors Club, Taylor, MI, Pattern - Jigged green bone doctors, Manufacturer - Bob Enders, quantity 30, 1988, price $105, value $175, information provided by club.

Wolverine Knife Collectors Club, Taylor, MI, Pattern - Pearl doctors, Manufacturer - Fight'n Rooster, quantity 100, 1989, price $50, value $65, information provided by club.

Wolverine Knife Collectors Club, Taylor, MI, Pattern - Christmas tree doctors, Manufacturer - Fight'n Rooster, quantity 100, 1990, price $35, value $50, information provided by club.

Knife Club Addresses

The club addresses in this section are the most current ones available.
Addresses and club contacts are subject to change without notice.

Alabama

American Coin and Knife Collectors, Rt. 7, Russellville, AL, contact Lacy Berryman, Dept. E, Russellville, AL 35653.

Circle City Cutlery Club of Dothan, contact Buzz Breer, The Knife Place, Dept. E, 2975 Ross Clark Circle SW, Dothan, AL 36301.

Noccalula Knife Collectors Association, contact Bob Hodo, Dept. E, Rt. 1, Box 520, Gadsden, AL 35901.

Sand Mountain Cutlery Club, contact Joe Pell, Dept. E, Rt. 5, Albertville, AL 35905.

Wheeler Basin Knife Club, contact W.B.K.C., POB 346, Dept. E, Hartselle, AL 35640.

Arizona

Arizona Knife Collectors Club, contact Bob Wheeler, Dept. E, POB 26178, Phoenix, AZ 85068.

Arkansas

The Knife Collectors Club, Inc., contact A. G. Russell, 1705 Highway 71 North, Springdale, AR, 72764.

California

Bay Area Knife Collectors Association, contact, 39594 Koma Ct., Fremont, CA 94537.

Orange County Knife Club, contact Gus Marsh, Dept. E, 8761 Anthony Dr., Huntington Beach, CA 92647.

Southern California Blades Knife Collectors Club, contact Lowell Shelhart, Dept. E, POB 1140, Lomita, CA 90717.

Colorado

Rocky Mountain Blade Collectors, contact Gordon Smith (303) 465-4744 or Barry Carithers (303) 422-0443 or write: RMBC, Dept. E, POB 115, Louisville, CO 80027.

Florida

Bold City Knife Club, contact Delores D. Bomar, secretary, POB 37241, Jacksonville, FL 32236-7241.

Florida Knife Collectors, contact Dennis Conley, Dept. E, Delaware Ave., Titusville, FL, 32780.

Fort Meyers Knife Club, contact Stan Thomas, president, Dept. E, POB 1274, Ft. Meyers, FL 33902.

Gator Cutlery Club, Contact Gator Cutlery Club, 71 Noon Dr., Spring Hill FL 34610.

Gold Coast Chapter of the Florida Knife Collectors Association, contact Doug Ford (305) 947-3955 or Leo Dodier (305) 771-3168.

Leesburg Chapter FKCA, contact Dennis Conley, Dept. E, 3301 Delaware Ave., Titusville, FL 32780.

Randall Knife Society of America, PO Box 539, Dept. E, Roseland, FL 32957.

Riverland Knife Collectors Club, contact Charley Piper at (904) 489-8138.

Georgia

Chattahoochee Cutlery Club of Atlanta, Chattahoochee Cutlery Club, Dept. E, POB 568, Tucker, GA 30084.

Flint River Knife Club, contact Paul Grimes, Dept. E, 8013 Fisher, Jonesboro, GA.

Northwest Georgia Knife Collectors Association, contact Dr. Harold H. Moore, Dept. E, POB 166, Rockmart, GA 30153.

Ocmulgee Knife Collectors, contact Joseph P. Wilson, Dept. E, Rt. 27, Box 185, Macon, GA 31211.

Three Rivers Knife Club, contact Jimmy Green, Dept. E, 783 Jones Mill Rd. NE, Rome, GA 30161.

Idaho

Idaho Knife Collectors Association, contact IKCA, 824 Vista, Boise, ID 83705.

Illinois

American Edge Collectors Association, contact AECA, Dept. E, POB 2565, Country Club Hills, IL 60478-8565.

Bunker Hill Pocketknife Collectors and Trade Club, contact Cecil M. Turner, Dept. E, RR 2, Bunker Hill, IL 62014.

Jefferson County Custom Knife Club, contact Larry Hancock, Dept. E, Rt. 8, Mt. Vernon, IL 62864.

River to River Knife Club, contact Dale Baker, Dept. E, Rt. 5, Box 104, Marion, IL 62959.

Soy Knife Collectors, contact Jerome Greive, Dept. E, Box 1752, Decatur, IL 62525.

Indiana

Evansville Knife Collectors Club of Indiana, contact Dr. Ken Helm, Dept. E, 670 Darmstadt Rd., Evansville, IN 47710 (812) 867-2114.

Indiana Knife Collectors, contact Gordon Kinnaman, RR3 Box 348, Alexandria, IN 46001.

Northern Indiana Knife Club, contact Rudy Stanley, NIKC, Dept. E, 8911 Park Valley Ct., Hobart, IN 46342.

Iowa

Hawkeye Knife Collectors Club. Contact Dean Swenson, Dept. E, Box 184, Callender, IA 50523.

Kentucky

Central Kentucky Knife Club, contact the CKKC, 4499 Muddy Ford Rd, Georgetown, KY 40324.

Chief Paduke Knife Collectors Club, contact CPKC, Dept. E, POB 1955, Paducah, KY 42001.

Eagle Creek Knife Club, contact Eagle Creek Knife Club, c/o K.F. Ballard Jr., 214 Seminary St., Owenton, KY 40359.

Kentucky Cutlery Association, contact the KCA, Dept. E, POB 58012, Louisville, KY 40258.

Yellow Banks Cutlery Club, contact Rick Graham, Dept. E, 4737 Leitchfield, Rd., Owensboro, KY 43201.

Maryland

Chesapeake Bay Area Knife Club, contact Glenn Paul Smith, 3206 E. Fairmount Ave., Baltimore, MD 21221.

Massachusetts

Northeast Cutlery Collectors Association, contact Cindy Taylor, PO Box 624, Mansfield, MA 02048.

Michigan

Flint Knife Club, contact C. Judson, Dept. E, 1572 Ward Dr., Flint, MI 48504.

Wolverine Knife Collectors Club, contact Ed Duprey, 5698 Lafayette, Dearborne Heights, MI 48127.

Minnesota

Nordic Cutlery Collectors Club, contact NCCC, Dept. E, POB 41, Wolf Lake, MN 56593.

North Star Blade Collectors, POB 20523, Dept. E, Bloomington, MN 55420.

Mississippi

Rebel Knife Club of Tupelo , contact Dan Westmoreland, Dept. E, 1121 Chapman Dr., Tupelo, MS 38801.

Missouri

Gateway Area Knife Club, contact John Brown, #5 Cedar Park, Florissant, MO.

North Carolina

Albemarle Cutlery Club, contact Ronnie Ray, c/o Albemarle Cutlery Club, Dept. E, Box 424, Albemarle, NC 28001.

Associated Southern Knifemakers, contact ASK, Dept. E, POB 10035, Winston-Salem, NC 27108.

Bechtler Mint Knife Club, contact Bill Steene, 2110 Jefferson Ave., Gastonia, NC 28056.

Catawba Valley Knife Club, contact Catawba Valley Knife Club, Rt. #11 Box 113, Morgantown, NC 28655.

Gem Capital Knife Club, contact Nolan Smathers or Ken Mashburn, Dept. E, POB 233, Franklin, NC 28734.

Kotton Country Knife Collectors, contact Milton Flowe, 8215 Chandos Place, Hunterville, NC 28078.

Mountain Whittler Knife Club, contact MWKC, Dept. E, POB 6734, Asheville, NC 28816.

North Carolina Cutlery Club, contact Gene Abernethy, Dept. E, 113 Powell Dr., Fuquay Varina, NC 27625.

Tarheel Cutlery Club, contact Tarheel Cutlery Club, Dept. E, 2730 Tudor Rd., Winston-Salem, NC 27106.

Ohio

Fort City Knife Collectors Club, contact Bill Powell, 681 Riesling Knoll, Cincinnati, OH 45226.

Johnny Appleseed Knife Collectors Club, contact Rick Allen, Dept. E, 323 Buckeye Ave., Mansfield, OH 44906.

Mahoning Valley Knife Collectors Association , write to: MVKCA, POB 781, Dept. E, Canfield,, OH 44406 (216) 457-7520.

Western Reserve Cutlery Association, contact Glen Graham, Box 352, Canal Fulton, OH 44614.

Oklahoma

Tulsa Knife Collectors Club, contact Tulsa Knife Club, c/o Dale Gerschutz, Dept. E, POB 54275, Tulsa, OK 74155.

Sooner Knife Collectors Club, contact Les Chaffin, Dept. E, 3125 Oakbrook, Del City, OK 73115.

Oregon

Oregon Knife Collectors Association, contact the OKCA, POB 2091, Dept. E, Eugene, OR 97440..

Pennsylvania

Allegheny Mountain Knife Collectors, contact Allegheny Mountain Knife Collectors Association, Dept. E, POB 23, Hunker, PA 15639.

Delaware Valley Knife Collectors Club, contact Charles Estadt, Dept. E, 52 Mood Dr., Fallsington, PA 18347.

Keystone Blade Association, contact KBA, POB 486, Dept. E, Lewisburg, PA 17837.

Mason-Dixon Knife Club, contact club at Box 196, Dept. E, Quincy, PA 17247.

Susquehanna Knife Collectors Association Contact John Glass, 839 Beaver Ln., Dept. E, Mt. Penn, PA 19606 or call (215) 779-5523.

South Carolina

Palmetto Cutlery Club of the Spartanburg/Greenville area, contact Gene Ravan, Dept., E, POB 1356, Greer, SC 29561.

Tennessee

American Blade Collectors Association, PO Box 22007, Chattanooga, TN 37422.

East Tennessee Knife Collectors, contact J.C. Presnell, Dept. E, 2515 Volunteer Parkway, Bristol, TN 37620 (615) 968-7543.

Hardeman County Knife Collectors, contact Roy Hanna, Rt. #1 Box 19A, Hornsby, TN 38044.

Memphis Knife Collectors Club, contact Wayne Koons, Dept. E, 1439 Elmgrove, Burlison, TN 38015.

Middle Tennessee Knife Collectors Club, contact MTCC, Dept. E, 1510 Maymont, Murfreesboro, TN 37130.

Music City Knife Collectors, contact Music City Knife Collectors, Dept. E, 210 Goodlettsville Plaza, Goodlettsville, TN 37072.

Northwest Tennessee Knife Collectors Association, contact NWTKCA, Dept. E, Harrell Ave., Dyersburg, TN 38024.

Smoky Mountain Knife Collectors, contact the club at POB 1176, Dept. E, Maryville, TN 37801.

Tennessee Valley Blades, contact Bob Cargill, Rt. #1 Box 501B, Old Fort, TN 37362.

Texas

Gulf Coast Knife Club, contact Gulf Coast Knife Club, 10510 Sagepine, Houston, TX 77275-0542.

Lone Star Knife Club, contact Lone Star Knife Club, Rt. #12 Box 443, Waco, TX 76714.

Texas Knife Collectors Association of Austin, contact TKCA, POB 4754, Dept. E, Austin, TX 78765-4754.

West Texas Knife Club, contact Billie Williams, Dept. E, Rt. 1, Box 98, Hamlin, TX 79520.

Virginia

Northern Virginia Knife Collectors, contact the club at POB 501, Dept. E, Falls Church, VA 22046.

Old Dominion Knife Collectors Association, contact John Riddle, 4236 Lakeridge Cr., Troutville, VA 24175.

Shenandoah Valley Knife Collectors, contact Larry Gray, POB 22, Singers Glen, VA 22850.

Wisconsin

Badger Knife Club, contact Bob Schrap, Dept. E, POB 511, Elm Grove, WI 53122.

Alliance of Local Knife Clubs

Contact G. T. Williams, Dept. E, 4499 Muddy Ford Rd., Georgetown, KY 40324.

Australia

Australian Knife Collectors Club, contact the AKC, Dept. E, POB 268, Morely, 6062, Western Australia.

Canada

Canadian Knife Collectors Club of Ontario, contact W. C. White, Dept. E, 148 Islington Ave., Apt.. 208, Toronto, Ontario M8V 3B6 CANADA.

Israel

IEWC Israeli Edged Weapon Collectors, Kiryat Ono Golomb St. 39 55000

Factory Knife Clubs

Buck Collectors Club, PO Box 1267, El Cajon, CA 92022.

Bulldog Knife Club, Dept. E, POB 453, Maysville, KY 41056 (513) 549-2709.

Case Collectors Club, Dept. E, Owens Way, Bradford, PA 16701.

Ek Commando Knife Collectors Club, 601 N. Lombardy St., attn: Pat Sylvia, Dept. E, Richmond, VA 23220.

International Fight'n Rooster Cutlery Club, Dept. E, Box 936, Lebanon, TN 37087.

Ka-Bar Knife Collectors Club, P.O. Box 406, Olean, NY 14760.

Swiss Army Knife Society, PO Box 91157, San Diego, CA 92109.

Bulldog Knife Value Chart

by Clarence Risner   As of Feb. 1, 1995

From *Edges,* Spring 1995

Style	Size	Handles	Main Bld	Blds	Bolster	Shield	No.	Year	Etching	Then	Now
Gunstock	3 1/2	pearl	clip	2		none	300	1980	Bulldog brand	$90.00	$150.00
Gunstock	3 1/2	pearl	spear	2		none	300	1980	Bulldog brand	$90.00	$150.00
Gunstock	3 1/2	butter & molasses	clip	3		rifle	310	1980	Henry Repeater	$75.00	$175.00
Gunstock	3 1/2	butter & molasses	spear	3		rifle	310	1980	Henry Repeater	$75.00	$175.00
Gunstock	3 1/2	pearl	clip	2		none	300	1980	Bulldog brand	$80.00	$150.00
Gunstock	3 1/2	pearl	spear	2		none	300	1980	Bulldog brand	$80.00	$150.00
Gunstock	3 1/2	brown bone	clip	3		banner	261	1981	Pit Bull Trademark	$70.00	$110.00
Gunstock	3 1/2	brown bone	spear	3		banner	261	1981	Pit Bull Trademark	$70.00	$110.00
Gunstock	3 1/2	pearl	razor	2		none	300	1981	Bulldog brand	$80.00	$160.00
Gunstock	3 1/2	pearl	spay	2		none	300	1981	Bulldog brand	$80.00	$160.00
Gunstock	3 1/2	brown bone	razor	2		banner	300	1981	Pit Bull Trademark	$65.00	$110.00
Gunstock	3 1/2	brown bone	spay	2		banner	300	1981	Pit Bull Trademark	$65.00	$110.00
Gunstock	3 1/2	pearl	clip	2		none	300	1983	Bulldog brand	$85.00	$150.00
Gunstock	3 1/2	pearl	spear	2		none	300	1983	Bulldog brand	$85.00	$150.00
Gunstock	3 1/2	brown bone	clip	2		banner	300	1984	Pit Bull Trademark	$65.00	$110.00
Gunstock	3 1/2	brown bone	spear	2		banner	300	1984	Pit Bull Trademark	$65.00	$110.00
Gunstock/Stockman	3 3/4	stag		3	square	heart	300	1982	Saddle Tramp	$23.50	$100.00
Gunstock/Stockman	3 3/4	stag		3	square	heart	300	1982	Pit Bull Trademark	$22.50	$80.00
Gunstock/Stockman	3 3/4	red sparkly		3	square	heart	300	1982	Pit Bull Trademark	$21.00	$65.00
Gunstock/Stockman	3 3/4	green pearl		3	square	heart	300	1982	Pit Bull Trademark	$21.00	$65.00
Gunstock/Stockman	3 3/4	dark butter & molasses		3	square	heart	300	1982	Pit Bull Trademark	$21.00	$65.00
Gunstock/Stockman	4	stag		3	square	spear	300	1982	Pit Bull Trademark	$23.00	$90.00
Gunstock/Stockman	4	tortoise		3	square	spear	300	1982	Pit Bull Trademark	$21.50	$70.00
Gunstock/Stockman	4	marble		3	square	spear	300	1982	Pit Bull Trademark	$21.50	$70.00
Gunstock/Stockman	4	red sparkly		3	square	spear	300	1982	Pit Bull Trademark	$21.50	$70.00
Stockman	4	stag		3	square	crest	153	1983	S&D Enterprises	$26.50	$80.00
Stockman	4	stag		3	square	spear	296	1983	Pit Bull Trademark	$24.50	$75.00
Stockman	4	stag		3	square	spear	294	1983	Quarter Horseman	$25.00	$90.00
Stockman	4	red sparkly		3	square	spear	312	1983	Pit Bull Trademark	$23.00	$65.00
Stockman	4	tortoise		3	square	spear	294	1983	Pit Bull Trademark	$23.00	$65.00
Stockman	3 3/4	brown bone		3	square	crest	28	1978	Pit Bull Terrier Winchester	$18.00	$500.00
Stockman	3 3/4	brown bone		3	square	crest	138	1979	Pit Bull Trademark	$18.00	$300.00
Stockman	3 3/4	brown bone		3	square	banner	300	1980	Pit Bull Trademark	$14.50	$80.00
Stockman	3 3/4	stag		3	square	banner	300	1980	Pit Bull Trademark	$16.00	$90.00
Stockman	3 3/4	dark butter & molasses		3	square	banner	300	1980	Pit Bull Trademark	$13.50	$75.00
Stockman	3 1/4	brown bone		3	square	crest	428	1980	Pit Bull Trademark	$11.50	$75.00
Stockman	3 1/4	tortoise		3	square	heart	132	1980	Pit Bull Trademark	$13.00	$150.00
Stockman	3 1/4	dark butter & molasses		3	square	heart	180	1980	Pit Bull Trademark	$13.00	$110.00
Stockman	3 1/2	stag		3	square	heart	280	1981	Pit Bull Trademark	$15.50	$110.00
Stockman	3 1/2	brown bone		3	square	heart	300	1981	Pit Bull Trademark	$14.50	$90.00
Stockman	3 1/2	tortoise		3	square	heart	300	1981	Pit Bull Trademark	$13.00	$90.00
Stockman	3 1/2	yellow		3	square	heart	300	1981	Pit Bull Trademark	$13.00	$90.00
Stockman	3 3/4	stag		3	square	banner	511	1982	Bulldog brand	$16.50	$75.00
Stockman	3 3/4	butter & molasses		3	square	banner	321	1982	Bulldog brand	$14.50	$60.00
Stockman	3 3/4	gray slate		3	square	banner	253	1982	Bulldog brand	$14.50	$60.00
Stockman	3 3/4	coon stripe		3	square	banner	284	1982	Bulldog brand	$14.50	$60.00
Stockman	3 3/4	tortoise		3	square	banner	244	1982	Bulldog brand	$14.50	$60.00
Stockman	3 3/4	blue stripe		3	square	banner	304	1982	Bulldog brand	$14.50	$60.00
Stockman	3 3/4	brown bone		3	square	banner	300	1982	Coal miner, pick & shovel	$21.00	$80.00
Stockman	3 7/8	stag ·		3	round	crest	310	1982	S&D Enterprises	$17.50	$85.00
Stockman	3 7/8	stag		3	round	banner	312	1982	Pit Bull Trademark	$16.00	$75.00
Stockman	3 7/8	green pearl		3	round	banner	304	1982	Pit Bull Trademark	$16.00	$65.00
Stockman	3 7/8	butter & molasses		3	round	banner	304	1982	Pit Bull Trademark	$16.00	$65.00
Stockman	3 7/8	tortoise		3	round	banner	172	1982	Pit Bull Trademark	$16.00	$65.00
Stockman	3 7/8	blue stripe		3	round	banner	120	1982	Pit Bull Trademark	$16.00	$80.00
Stockman	3 7/8	black celluloid		3	round	coal miner	300	1982	Coal miner, pick & shovel	$21.00	$80.00
Moose Stockman	4	stag		2	square	diamond	300	1984	Lumber Jack	$24.50	$75.00
Moose Stockman	4	coon stripe		2	square	diamond	288	1984	Lumber Jack	$23.00	$65.00
Moose Stockman	4	purple swirl		2	square	diamond	478	1984	Peacock	$24.00	$225.00
Moose Stockman	4	purple swirl		3	square	crest	144	1984	S&D Peacock	$24.00	$300.00
Stockman	4	stag		3	square	spade	400	1985	Cowboy's Pet	$29.50	$80.00
Stockman	4	greenbone		3	square	spade	400	1985	Cowboy's Pet	$26.50	$75.00
Stockman	4	dark butter & molasses		3	square	spade	300	1985	Cowboy's Pet	$25.50	$70.00
Stockman	4	gray slate		3	square	spade	300	1985	Cowboy's Pet	$25.50	$70.00
Stockman	4	gold dust		3	square	spade	300	1985	Cowboy's Pet	$25.50	$70.00
Stockman	3 1/2	stag		3	square	crest	200	1986	S&D "Our Best"	$28.00	$80.00
Stockman	3 1/2	stag		3	square	spade	300	1986	Pit Bull Trademark	$27.00	$75.00
Stockman	3 1/2	brown bone		3	square	spade	300	1986	Pit Bull Trademark	$25.00	$70.00
Stockman	3 1/2	blue stripe		3	square	spade	300	1986	Pit Bull Trademark	$24.00	$65.00
Stockman	3 1/2	purple stripe		3	square	spade	300	1986	Pit Bull Trademark	$24.00	$65.00
Stockman	3 1/2	pearl		3	square	none	300	1986	Serial No'd Knife Club	$24.00	$125.00
Stockman	4 1/4	stag	clip	3			300	1986	"Cattle King"	$34.50	$110.00
Stockman	4 1/4	bone	clip	3			300	1986	"Cattle King"	$33.00	$80.00

Bulldog Knife Value Guide

Style	Size	Handles	Main Bld	Blds	Bolster	Shield	No.	Year	Etching	Then	Now
Stockman	4 1/4	red sparkly	clip	3			300	1986	"Cattle King"	$31.00	$70.00
Stockman	4 1/4	tortoise	clip	3			300	1986	"Cattle King"	$31.00	$70.00
Serpentine Stock	3 3/8	stag		3	round	horseshoe	804	1984	110th Run For the Roses	$27.00	$90.00
Serpentine Stock	3 3/8	tobacco brown		3	round	horseshoe	420	1984	110th Run For the Roses	$24.50	$60.00
Serpentine Stock	3 3/8	dark butter & molasses		3	round	horseshoe	420	1984	110th Run For the Roses	$24.50	$60.00
Serpentine Stock	3 3/8	gold dust		3	round	horseshoe	432	1984	110th Run For the Roses	$24.50	$60.00
Serpentine Stock	3 3/8	red sparkly		3	round	beer stein	273	1984	Oktoberfest	$23.50	$60.00
Serpentine Stock	3 3/8	dark butter & molasses		3	round	beer stein	297	1984	Oktoberfest	$23.50	$60.00
Serpentine Stock	3 5/8	stag		3	round	tobacco leaf	400	1984	Ohio Tobacco King	$28.50	$75.00
Serpentine Stock	3 5/8	stag		3	round	tobacco leaf	400	1984	N.C. Tobacco King	$28.50	$75.00
Serpentine Stock	3 5/8	stag		3	round	tobacco leaf	400	1984	Kentucky Tobacco King	$28.50	$75.00
Serpentine Stock	3 5/8	stag		3	round	tobacco leaf	400	1984	Virginia Tobacco King	$28.50	$70.00
Serpentine Stock	3 5/8	stag		5	round	crest	204	1984	S&D Our Best	$42.50	$150.00
Serpentine Stock	3 5/8	tortoise		3	round	tobacco leaf	300	1984	Florida Tobacco King	$24.50	$65.00
Serpentine Stock	3 5/8	red sparkly		3	round	tobacco leaf	300	1984	Tennessee Tobacco King	$24.50	$65.00
Serpentine Stock	3 5/8	gold dust		3	round	tobacco leaf	288	1984	S.C. Tobacco King	$24.50	$65.00
Serpentine Stock	3 5/8	coon stripe		3	round	tobacco leaf	200	1984	Georgia Tobacco King	$24.50	$65.00
Serpentine Stock	3 5/8	green pearl		3	round	tobacco leaf	144	1984	Georgia Tobacco King	$24.50	$65.00
Serpentine Stock	3 5/8	stag		5	round	acorn	304	1984	Pit Bull Trademark	$45.00	$125.00
Serpentine Stock	3 7/8	stag		3	round	crest	210	1986	S&D Our Best	$32.50	$150.00
Serpentine Stock	3 7/8	stag		3	round	club	300	1986	Cuttin Horse	$29.50	$125.00
Serpentine Stock	3 7/8	greenbone		3	round	club	300	1986	Cuttin Horse	$28.50	$90.00
Serpentine Stock	3 7/8	red sparkly		3	round	club	300	1986	Cuttin Horse	$27.00	$80.00
Serpentine Stock	3 7/8	tortoise		3	round	club	300	1986	Cuttin Horse	$27.00	$80.00
Serpentine Stock	3 7/8	dark butter & molasses		3	round	club	300	1986	Cuttin Horse	$27.00	$80.00
Trapper	4 1/8	coon stripe		2	round	coon	400	1981	Dog/Coon/Tree 2 B English	$22.00	$85.00
Trapper	4 1/8	coon stripe		2	round	coon	400	1981	Dog/Coon/Tree 2 B English	$22.00	$85.00
Trapper	4 1/8	coon stripe		2	round	coon	400	1981	Dog/Coon/Tree 2 B English	$22.00	$85.00
Trapper	4 1/8	blue stripe		2	round	mountain man	342	1982	Trapper Jack	$21.00	$85.00
Trapper	4 1/8	tortoise		2	round	mountain man	270	1982	Trapper Jack	$21.00	$85.00
Trapper	4 1/8	marble		2	round	mountain man	258	1982	Trapper Jack	$21.00	$85.00
Trapper	4 1/8	butter & molasses		2	round	mountain man	117	1982	Trapper Jack	$21.00	$125.00
Trapper	4 1/8	gray slate		2	round	mountain man	84	1982	Trapper Jack	$21.00	$125.00
Trapper	4 1/8	stag		2	round	banner	156	1981	S&D Buckeye Special	$33.00	$125.00
Trapper	3 7/8	stag		2	round	crest	144	1983	Pit Bull Trademark	$24.50	$85.00
Trapper	3 7/8	stag		3	round	banner	289	1983	Pit Bull Trademark	$28.50	$115.00
Trapper	3 7/8	stag		2	round	banner	294	1983	Pit Bull Trademark	$24.50	$85.00
Trapper	3 7/8	stag		2	round	banner	336	1983	Pit Bull Trademark	$24.50	$70.00
Trapper	3 7/8	red swirl		2	round	banner	294	1983	Pit Bull Trademark	$24.50	$70.00
Trapper	3 7/8	green pearl		2	round	banner	294	1983	Pit Bull Trademark	$23.00	$70.00
Trapper	3 7/8	dark butter & molasses		2	round	banner	297	1983	Pit Bull Trademark	$23.00	$70.00
Trapper	3 7/8	stag		2	round	crest	192	1985	Our Best	$32.00	$90.00
Trapper	3 7/8	stag		2	round	crest	198	1985	Our Best	$32.00	$90.00
Trapper	3 7/8	stag		2	round	acorn	300	1985	Pit Bull Trademark	$29.00	$75.00
Trapper	3 7/8	stag		2	round	acorn	300	1985	Old Reliable	$29.00	$75.00
Trapper	3 7/8	greenbone		2	round	acorn	300	1985	Old Reliable	$28.00	$70.00
Trapper	3 7/8	blue stripe		2	round	acorn	300	1985	Old Reliable	$26.00	$65.00
Trapper	3 7/8	tortoise		2	round	acorn	300	1985	Old Reliable	$26.00	$65.00
Muskrat	3 7/8	coon stripe		2	round	coon	400	1981	Dog/Coon/Tree 2 B English	$22.00	$85.00
Muskrat	3 7/8	coon stripe		2	round	coon	400	1981	Dog/Coon/Tree 2 B English	$22.00	$85.00
Muskrat	3 7/8	coon stripe		2	round	coon	400	1981	Dog/Coon/Tree 2 B English	$22.00	$85.00
Muskrat	3 7/8	gray slate		2	round	muskrat	300	1982	Johnny Muskrat	$21.00	$75.00
Muskrat	3 7/8	butter & molasses		2	round	muskrat	300	1982	Johnny Muskrat	$21.00	$75.00
Muskrat	3 7/8	butter & molasses		2	round	muskrat	300	1982	Johnny Muskrat	$21.00	$75.00
Muskrat	3 7/8	blue stripe		2	round	muskrat	300	1982	Johnny Muskrat	$21.00	$75.00
Muskrat	3 7/8	stag		2	round	banner	150		S&D Buckeye Special	$21.00	$125.00
Copperhead	3 3/4	stag		2	round	crest	132	1983	S&D Our Best	$26.50	$90.00
Copperhead	3 3/4	stag		2	round	heart	296	1983	Rabbit Hound	$25.00	$80.00
Copperhead	3 3/4	old marble		2	round	heart	288	1983	Rabbit Hound	$24.00	$70.00
Copperhead	3 3/4	gold dust		2	round	heart	288	1983	Rabbit Hound	$24.00	$70.00
Copperhead	3 3/4	red sparkly		2	round	heart	288	1983	Rabbit Hound	$24.00	$70.00
Folding Hunter	4 7/8	dark brown bone		2	round tapered	oval	300	1981	Pit Bull Trademark	$18.50	$125.00
Folding Hunter	4 7/8	light brown bone		2	round tapered	oval small	161	1981	Pit Bull Trademark	$18.50	$150.00
Folding Hunter	4 7/8	dark brown bone		2	round tapered	oval	300	1981	Mountain Hunter	$18.50	$110.00
Folding Hunter	4 7/8	dark brown bone		2	round tapered	oval	300	1981	Bull of the Woods	$18.50	$110.00
Folding Hunter	4 7/8	dark brown bone		2	round tapered	oval	300	1981	Hunter's Pride	$18.50	$110.00
Folding Hunter	4 7/8	stag		2	round	spear	384	1983	War Hawk	$24.50	$100.00
Lockback	4 7/8	stag		1	square	none	188	1981	Bulldog brand	$31.00	$200.00
Bowie	15 1/2	stag					204	1984	Simon Kenton's Ride 1785	$105.00	$175.00
Congress	3 7/8	pearl		6	grooved round	none	300	1984	Bulldog Knife Club	$57.50	$125.00
Congress	3 7/8	stag		6	grooved round	heart	300	1984	Bulldog Knife Club	$45.00	$100.00
Congress	3 5/8	pearl		4	round	none	300	1985	Bulldog Knife Club	$52.00	$90.00
Congress	4 1/4	stag		4	round	heart	300	1985	Bulldog Knife Club	$37.00	$85.00
Trapper	4 1/8	stag		2	round	ODKCA	300	1981	Old Dominion	n/a	$90.00
Stockman	4	stag		3	square	ODKCA	300	1982	Old Dominion	n/a	$100.00

Bulldog Knife Value Guide

Style	Size	Handles	Main Bld	Blds	Bolster	Shield	No.	Year	Etching	Then	Now
Hunter	4 7/8	stag		2	round tapered	ODKCA	300	1983	Old Dominion	n/a	$85.00
Congress	3 7/8	stag		4	grooved round	ODKCA	300	1984	Old Dominion	n/a	$90.00
Trapper	3 7/8	stag		3	round	ODKCA	300	1985	Old Dominion	n/a	$100.00
Barlow	3 1/2	stag	spear	2	fancy (tobacco)	S&D Shield	196	1986	S&D Our Best	$25.50	$60.00
Barlow	3 1/2	stag	clip	2	fancy (tobacco)	S&D Shield	214	1986	S&D Our Best	$25.50	$60.00
Barlow	3 1/2	stag	razor	2	fancy (tobacco)	S&D Shield	199	1986	S&D Our Best	$25.50	$60.00
Barlow	3 1/2	stag	spay	2	fancy (tobacco)	S&D Shield	214	1986	S&D Our Best	$25.50	$60.00
Barlow	3 1/2	stag	sheepfoot	2	fancy (tobacco)	S&D Shield	208	1986	S&D Our Best	$25.50	$60.00
Barlow	3 1/2	bone	spear	2	fancy (tobacco)	S&D Shield	142	1986	S&D Our Best	$24.50	$55.00
Barlow	3 1/2	bone	razor	2	fancy (tobacco)	S&D Shield	147	1986	S&D Our Best	$24.50	$55.00
Barlow	3 1/2	bone	spay	2	fancy (tobacco)	S&D Shield	154	1986	S&D Our Best	$24.50	$55.00
Barlow	3 1/2	bone	sheepfoot	2	fancy (tobacco)	S&D Shield	148	1986	S&D Our Best	$24.50	$55.00
Barlow	3 1/2	stag	sheepfoot	2		none	300	1986	Kentucky Barley	$25.50	$65.00
Barlow	3 1/2	stag	spear	2		none	300	1986	Bright Leaf North Carolina	$25.50	$65.00
Barlow	3 1/2	stag	clip	2		none	300	1986	Ohio White Burley	$25.50	$60.00
Barlow	3 1/2	stag	razor	2		none	204	1986	Tennessee Burley	$25.50	$60.00
Barlow	3 1/2	stag	spay	2		none	300	1986	Virginia Bright Leaf	$25.50	$60.00
Barlow	3 1/2	greenbone	razor	2		none	300	1986	Bright Leaf South Carolina	$24.50	$55.00
Barlow	3 1/2	greenbone	sheepfoot	2		none	300	1986	Georgia Bright Leaf	$24.50	$55.00
Barlow	3 1/2	greenbone	spear	2		none	300	1986	Florida Bright Leaf	$24.50	$55.00
Barlow	3 1/2	stag	razor	2		none	96	1986	Misspelled "Tenneffee"	$25.50	$110.00
Boot	3 7/8	stag		1	round	none	300	1982	One-Eyed Jack	$27.50	$85.00
Boot	9 7/8	stag		1	round	none	283	1982	One-Eyed Jack	$27.50	$85.00
Boot	9 7/8	stag		1	round	none	4	1982	Louisville Show Award	n/a	$200.00
Boot	9 7/8	stag		1	round	none	300	1983	Fifth Ace	$29.00	$85.00
Boot	9 7/8	stag		1	round	none	300	1983	Jokers Wild	$29.00	$85.00
Boot	9 7/8	white micarta		1	round	none	300	1983	One-Eyed Jack	$29.00	$70.00
Boot	9 1/2	stag		1	round	none	300	1983	Queen of Hearts	$29.00	$80.00
Letter Opener	9 5/8	gold plated black & red		1	none	none	60	1982	Bulldog brand	$18.00	$60.00
Letter Opener	9 5/8	gold plated black & red		1	none	none	120	1983	S&D Enterprises	$18.00	$50.00
Letter Opener	9 5/8	gold plated black & red		1	none	none	120	1983	S&D Enterprises	$18.00	$50.00
Canoe	3 5/8	stag		2	round	crest	204	1987	S&D Our Best	$32.00	$85.00
Canoe	3 5/8	stag		2	round	leaf	294	1987	Tobacco	$30.00	$75.00
Canoe	3 5/8	greenbone		2	round	leaf	298	1987	Tobacco	$29.00	$70.00
Canoe	3 5/8	red sparkle		2	round	leaf	177	1987	Tobacco	$27.00	$100.00
Canoe	3 5/8	stag		3	round	crest	210	1987	S&D "Our Best"	$35.00	$85.00
Canoe	3 5/8	stag		3	round	leaf	294	1987	Tobacco	$33.00	$75.00
Canoe	3 5/8	greenbone		3	round	leaf	294	1987	Tobacco	$32.00	$70.00
Canoe	3 5/8	gold dust		3	round	leaf	234	1987	Tobacco	$31.00	$70.00
Congress	3 7/8	stag		4	round	bar	300	1982	Pit Bull Trademark	$26.50	$110.00
Congress	3 7/8	stag		4	round	crest	156	1982	S&D Enterprises	$29.00	$150.00
Congress	3 7/8	pearl		4	round	none	292	1982	Tobacco	$37.00	$125.00
Congress	3 7/8	marble		4	round	tobacco leaf	282	1982	Tobacco	$24.00	$85.00
Congress	3 7/8	red sparkly		4	round	tobacco leaf	288	1982	Tobacco	$24.00	$85.00
Congress	3 7/8	tobacco brown		4	round	tobacco leaf	272	1982	Tobacco	$24.00	$85.00
Congress	3 7/8	coon stripe		4	grooved round	tobacco leaf	300	1983	Pride in Tobacco - Ohio	$29.00	$75.00
Congress	3 7/8	tortoise		4	grooved round	tobacco leaf	300	1983	Pride in Tobacco - Kentucky	$29.00	$75.00
Congress	3 7/8	stag		4	grooved round	bar	396	1983	Tobacco	$31.00	$100.00
Congress	3 7/8	pearl		4	grooved round	none note 1	300	1983	Tobacco	$42.50	$115.00
Congress	3 7/8	gray slate		4	grooved round	tobacco leaf	312	1983	Tobacco	$27.00	$75.00
Congress	3 7/8	red swirl		4	grooved round	tobacco leaf	288	1983	Tobacco	$27.00	$75.00
Congress	3 7/8	purple swirl		4	grooved round	tobacco leaf	390	1983	Tobacco	$27.00	$85.00
Congress	3 7/8	dark butter & molasses		4	grooved round	tobacco leaf	384	1983	Tobacco	$27.00	$75.00
Congress	3 7/8	green pearl		4	grooved round	tobacco leaf	396	1983	Tobacco	$27.00	$75.00
Congress	3 5/8	stag		4	round	crest	152	1983	S&D Our Best	$26.50	$85.00
Congress	3 5/8	stag		4	round	diamond	300	1983	Old Chum	$24.00	$70.00
Congress	3 5/8	tobacco brown		4	round	diamond	296	1983	Old Chum	$22.50	$60.00
Congress	3 5/8	purple swirl		4	round	diamond	268	1983	Old Chum	$22.50	$80.00
Congress	3 5/8	old marble		4	round	diamond	296	1983	Old Chum	$22.50	$60.00
Congress	3 5/8	gold dust		4	round	diamond	142	1983	Fulton Hardware	$24.50	$85.00
Congress	3 7/8	stag		2	grooved round	crest	180	1983	S&D Our Best	$26.50	$85.00
Congress	3 7/8	stag		2	grooved round	bar	300	1983	Cut Plug	$26.50	$75.00
Congress	3 7/8	tobacco brown		2	grooved round	tobacco leaf	300	1983	Cut Plug	$23.50	$55.00
Congress	3 7/8	butter & molasses		2	grooved round	tobacco leaf	252	1983	Cut Plug	$23.50	$55.00
Congress	3 7/8	stag		4	grooved round	heart	288	1984	Tenn Walking Horse	$32.50	$110.00
Congress	3 5/8	stag		4	round	spade	300	1985	Pit Bull Tradmark	$31.50	$75.00
Congress	3 5/8	greenbone		4	round	spade	300	1985	Pit Bull Tradmark	$27.00	$65.00
Congress	3 5/8	red sparkly		4	round	spade	300	1985	Pit Bull Tradmark	$25.00	$60.00
Congress	3 5/8	old white		4	round	spade	300	1985	Pit Bull Tradmark	$25.00	$60.00
Congress	4 1/4	torched stag		4	round	crest	192	1985	Our Best	$34.50	$150.00
Congress	4 1/4	torched stag		4	round	tobacco leaf	300	1985	Tobacco	$32.00	$110.00
Congress	4 1/4	greenbone		4	round	tobacco leaf	300	1985	Tobacco	$31.00	$100.00
Congress	4 1/4	tortoise		4	round	tobacco leaf	300	1985	Tobacco	$28.50	$90.00
Congress	4 1/4	purple swirl		4	round	tobacco leaf	300	1985	Tobacco	$28.50	$125.00

Case Stag Sets

While not actually limited editions under my definition, there is reason enough to include Case 1979-80s era stag sets, because they are treated as limited editions by most knife collectors.

The stag handled Case knife was a mainstay in the line until 1970, when due to a reduction on the importation of genuine stag from India, Case discontinued genuine stag handled knives.

A couple of interesting events unfolded. Collectors started chasing down the few stag knives remaining on factory intact displays and buying them for their collections, and Case discovered they had enough discontinued knives laying around to assemble around 1,000 23-knife sets. These sets were allocated to the various salesman based on the dollar volume they produced, and the salesmen in turn allocated the knives to their best customers. At the time there were enough that nearly everyone who wanted one ended up with one. As an added incentive Case added a 5111 1/2 stag lockback in stainless steel with a Cheetah etched on the blade—a knife never before made in that configuration and available only as a part of these sets.

The effect of these stags being released on the market was like pouring gasoline on a fire. Unfortunately a few years later, with the stag available again, Case made up a second set utilizing the few remaining blades and some of the same patterns as the 1970 sets, including more of the Cheetahs.

Those aren't listed here as sets simply because no one I know buys and sells these knives as sets any longer. They bring no more money as a set, and if you tried to assemble a set you would have no way of knowing if the 5254 stag trapper came out of regular production, one of the first series sets or one of the second series sets.

But Case wised up beginning in 1977 with the issuance of what collectors know now as the Grey Etch set. One company even sold a wall plaque to hold a complete set, and because they were sold as sets, usually preserved as sets, and are popular and often traded among commemorative people we did want to add them to this book. We'll deal with each in turn, and I have included a table to assist in this endeavor.

These sets differ from the earlier issues in that they are all stainless steel, other than that it is best to pay close attention to the blade etches.

None of the stag sets described here were serial numbered. However beginning in 1980 there were 1,000 serial numbered sets of each series with engraved bolsters and including the wooden collector box.

The Grey Etch Set

The Grey Etch set was issued in 1977 in a 10,000 set allocation, and is shown under column C. If there is a price corresponding to that pattern number then that pattern was issued with that set. The etch was gray in color and featured the "Case Tested XX" mark with the wavy long tail "C" flowing under the Case.

The Blue Scroll Set

The blue scroll set was issued in 1978 in a 15,000 run, and toward the final end of the run Case changed their 5233 pen knife pattern to a different blade shape with the designation 52033. There were only 2,400 of the 50233's made with blue scroll and are a variation that should be noted. The etching is blue and is in a floral design with no words in the design.

1,000 sets were made with engraved bolsters (similar to the engraving also used on the Moby Dick) and matching serial numbers.

The Red Etch Set

Issued in 1979 in a quantity of 25,000, at a time of a decline in the knife market overall, these knives were issued in different patterns from the two earlier sets, moving toward smaller patterns, and larger quantities. The etching on the knives again featured the Case Tested logo, but this time in red.

1,000 sets were made with engraved bolsters and matching serial numbers.

The Bradford Centennial Set

Issued in 1980 the set changed to an etching honoring the 100th anniversary of Bradford, PA, and is etched with "1880 Bradford Centennial 1980" on the master blades of each knife. An optional wood case with the knives held in by unformed foam on each side of the box was available.

1,000 sets were also made with engraved bolsters and matching serial numbers.

The Case 75th Anniversary Set

Issued in 1981 and also named after the etching on the blades, these sets also had an optional wooden box. One thousand sets were made with engraved bolsters and matching serial numbers.

The Nine Dot Set

The final Case stag set of this era is referred to as the 9 dot set. The knives have the "Lightning S" 8 dot tang markings, and were not etched.

Following the nine dot set Case stags were produced, but in some instances in production run quantities and always available as single purchases. One of the appeals in the seventies and eighties was the knowledge that stag handled knives were going to get scarce—and therefore should be laid back. Case had very clearly stated as far back as the old Dewey Ferguson guides that stag was discontinued, in their words, "at this time," and the Case Kodiak was kept in production throughout the stag high demand days.

The beauty of Case stags today is most of the sets after 1977 were stainless steel blades and were made in plentiful quantities, therefore it is still possible to assemble a complete set, have a decent collection and good chance of appreciation.

There are few segments of knife collecting of which that can be said.

PATTERN	NAME	Issue Year 1977	1978		1979	1980	1981	1982
	Nickname	Grey Etch	Blue Scroll		Red Etch	Bradford Cent.	75th Anniv.	Nine Dot
	Quantity made	10,000 sets	15,000 sets		25,000 sets			
Lockback	5111½ Lssp	68	68					
Clasp	5172 ssp	68	68					
Folding Hunter	5265 sab ssp	65	65					
Trapper	5254 ssp	44	44		42			
Serpentine stock	5347 ssp	44	44 10 dot		42			
Serpentine	52087 ssp	34	34	58	34			
Thirty three pattern	5233 ssp	28	28					
Thirty three pattern	52033 ssp (2,400)			50				
Canoe	52131 ssp		46					
Muskrat					44		45	
Peanut	5220 ssp				32			
Equal end	5279 ssp				28			
Mini-trapper	5207 ssp					34	28	
Two blade stock	52032 ssp				34			
Moose	5275 ssp					38	38	
Texas Jack	5292 ssp					36		
Small serpentine	5381 ssp					36	32	
Copperhead	5249 ssp					36		
Pen	52027 ssp					28		
Two blade stock	5244 ssp						25	
Half whittler	5208 ssp						28	
Swell end	5235 ½ ssp						25	
Baby Copperhead	52109 xssp						25	
One bl. Copperhead	5149 ssp							36
	pockets only	351	397	108	256	208	246	
	Hunters							
	523-5 ssp	38	38			36		
	516-5 ssp	36	36			34		
	5Finn ssp	34	34		34	32		
	M5Finn	28	28		28	26		
	hunters only	136	136		62	128		
	hunters & pocket	487	533		318	336		

Fight'n Rooster Value Chart by Clarence Risner

As of Feb. 1, 1995

From *Edges*, Spring 1995

STYLE	# OF BLADES	HANDLE	ETCHING	QUANT	YEAR	VALUE
MINATURES						
Pen miniature	2 blade	green flake celluloid handle	not etched	200	1983	$25
Pen miniature	2 blade	pick bone handle	not etched	200	1983	$27
Pen miniature	2 blade	black & pearl celluloid handle	not etched	200	1983	$25
Pen miniature	2 blade	yellow celluloid handle	not etched	200	1983	$25
Pen miniature	2 blade	brown & black horn celluloid handle	not etched	200	1983	$25
Pen miniature	2 blade	pink Christmas celluloid handle	not etched	200	1983	$25
Pen miniature	2 blade	blue & black pearl celluloid handle	not etched	200	1983	$25
Pen miniature	2 blade	yellow celluloid handle	not etched	200	1983	$23
Pen miniature	2 blade	pick bone handle	etched	500	1976	$28
Pen miniature	2 blade	crystal white celluloid handle	not etched	200	1983	$25
Pen miniature	2 blade	black horn celluloid handle	not etched	200	1983	$23
Pen miniature	2 blade	smooth bone handle	not etched	200	1983	$23
Pen miniature	2 blade	crystal white celluloid handle	not etched	125	1983	$27
Pen miniature	2 blade	black & pearl celluloid handle	not etched	200	1984	$25
Pen miniature	2 blade	black celluloid handle	not etched	125	1983	$30
Pen miniature	2 blade	stag handle	not etched	300	1983	$25
Pen miniature	2 blade	red celluloid handle	not etched	125	1983	$27
Pen miniature	2 blade	horn celluloid handle	not etched	200	1984	$25
Pen miniature	2 blade	white on white celluloid handle	not etched	125	1983	$27
Pen miniature	2 blade	pearl handle	not etched	200	1984	$25
Pen miniature	2 blade	pearl handle	not etched	200	1983	$45
Miniature	1 blade	black striped celluloid handle	not etched	200	1983	$23
Miniature	1 blade	gray pearl celluloid handle	not etched	200	1983	$23
Miniature	1 blade	ivory celluloid handle	not etched	200	1983	$23
Miniature	1 blade	horn celluloid handle	not etched	200	1983	$23
Miniature	1 blade	yellow celluloid handle	not etched	200	1983	$23
Miniature	1 blade	pearl handle Fight'n Rooster etched on handle	not etched	300	1983	$40
Miniature Trapper	2 blade	pearl handle	not etched	600	1983	$40
LADIES BANTY						
Ladies banty	1 blade	amber celluloid handle	not etched	300	1980	$25
Ladies banty	1 blade	pink Christmas celluloid handle	not etched	300	1980	$25
Ladies banty	1 blade	amber celluloid handle	not etched	300	1980	$25
Ladies banty	1 blade	gold flake celluloid handle	not etched	300	1980	$25
Ladies banty	1 blade	pearl handle	not etched	300	1980	$40
Ladies banty	1 blade	pink Christmas celluloid handle	not etched	500	1980	$20
Ladies banty	1 blade	gold flake celluloid handle	not etched	300	1980	$23
Ladies banty	1 blade	pearl handle	not etched	300	1980	$40
SODBUSTERS						
Sodbuster miniature	2 blade	brown & black celluloid handle	not etched	200	1983	$25
Sodbuster miniature	2 blade	black & pearl celluloid handle	not etched	200	1983	$25
Sodbuster miniature	2 blade	yellow celluloid handle	not etched	200	1983	$25
Sodbuster	1 blade	pearl handle	CAPTAIN'S ROOSTER	300	1980	$75
SOUTHERN STYLE						
Sodbuster	1 blade	black & pearl celluloid handle	etched	300	1978	$50
Sodbuster	1 blade	old Christmas celluloid handle	etched	300	1978	$50
Sodbuster	1 blade	butter & molasses celluloid handle	etched	300	1978	$50
Sodbuster	1 blade	red & black celluloid handle	etched	300	1978	$50
Sodbuster (rare)	1 blade	yellow celluloid handle	etched	15	1977	$115
Sodbuster	1 blade	black celluloid handle (English made)	etched	15	1981	$150
Sodbuster	1 blade	imitation pearl celluloid handle (English made)	etched	15	1981	$150
Sodbuster	1 blade	blue celluloid handle (English mdade)	etched	15	1981	$150
Sodbuster	1 blade	pearl handle	ALBEMARLE CLUB	200	1980	$75
Sodbuster	1 blade	pearl handle	IDEAL HARDWARE	30	1981	$115
Sodbuster	1 blade	yellow celluloid handle-FIGHT'N ROOSTER logo	not etched	150	1987	$180
Sodbuster	1 blade	light blue celluloid handle-FIGHT'N ROOSTER logo	not etched	150	1987	$180
Sodbuster	1 blade	black celluloid handle-FIGHT'N ROOSTER logo	not etched	150	1987	$180
Sodbuster	1 blade	brown celluloid handle-FIGHT'N ROOSTER logo	not etched	150	1987	$180
Sodbuster	1 blade	light green celluloid handle-FIGHT'N ROOSTER logo	not etched	150	1987	$180
Sodbuster	1 blade	dark green celluloid handle-FIGHT'N ROOSTER logo	not etched	150	1987	$180
Sodbuster (rare)	1 blade	wood handle	FIGHT'N ROOSTER		1984	$45
STOCKMAN						
Stockman	3 blade	yellow celluloid handle	reverse etched	100	1977	$75
Stockman	3 blade	feather white celluloid handle	reverse etched	300	1977	$75
Stockman	3 blade	tortoise shell celluloid handle	reverse etched	300	1977	$45
Stockman	3 blade	pick bone handle	etched	100	1978	$85
Stockman	3 blade	black & pearl celluloid handle	etched	300	1978	$45
Stockman	3 blade	red & black celluloid handle	etched	300	1978	$45

Fight'n Rooster Price Guide

STYLE	# OF BLADES	HANDLE	ETCHING	QUANT	YEAR	VALUE
Stockman	3 blade	tortoiseshell	etched	600	1978	$45
Stockman	3 blade	butter & molasses celluloid handle	etched	300	1978	$45
Stockman	3 blade	old Christmas celluloid handle	etched	300	1978	$45
Stockman	3 blade	gold flake celluloid handle	etched	300	1978	$45
Stockman	3 blade	green, pearl & black striped celluloid handle	etched	36	1986	$65
Stockman (rare)	3 blade	gold & black check celluloid handle	etched		1983	$60
Stockman	3 blade	yellow & white vertical striped celluloid handle	etched	300	1985	$40
Stockman	3 blade	gray spider celluloid handle	etched	600	1984	$40
Stockman	3 blade	blue quartz celluloid handle	etched	200	1985	$40
Stockman	3 blade	wine & pearl swirl celluloid handle	etched	300	1985	$40
Stockman	3 blade	blue, black & orange celluloid handle	etched	200	1985	$40
Stockman	3 blade	orange & black ripple celluloid handle	etched	50	1986	$40
Stockman	3 blade	green pearl & black celluloid handle	etched	300	1986	$40
Stockman	3 blade	black celluloid handle	ACE IN THE HOLE	600	1984	$55
Stockman (rare)	3 blade	new Christmas celluloid handle	EASY MONEY		1986	$50
Stockman	3 blade	pick bone handle		18	1986	$50
Stockman	3 blade	black & blue pearl celluloid handle	WEST COAST TURNAROUND	600	1985	$50
Stockman	3 blade	red & black striped celluloid handle	FOLSOM PRISON	600	1985	$45
Stockman	3 blade	end of day celluloid handle	JOKERS WILD	600	1985	$125
Stockman	3 blade	gold, pearl & black celluloid handle	BROWN SUGAR	600	1986	$40
Stockman	3 blade	gold peacock on green celluloid handle	etched	50	1987	$50
Stockman	3 blade	gold peacock on red celluloid handle	etched	50	1987	$50
Stockman	3 blade	silver peacock on blue celluloid handle	etched	50	1987	$50
Stockman	3 blade	silver peacock on black celluloid handle	etched	50	1987	$50
Stockman	3 blade	silver peacock on green celluloid handle	etched	50	1987	$50
Stockman	3 blade	pick bone handle	gold etched	100	1987	$65
Stockman	3 blade	tortoise shell celluloid handle	gold etched	100	1987	$65
Stockman	3 blade	stag handle	gold etched	100	1987	$65
Stockman	3 blade	gold & black damasters celluloid handle	etched	100	1987	$45
Stockman	3 blade	gold roosters with red celluloid handle	etched	100	1987	$40
Stockman	3 blade	gold roosters with black celluloid handle	etched	100	1987	$40
Stockman	3 blade	black roosters with gold celluloid handle	etched	100	1987	$40
Stockman	3 blade	gold scrolled with red celluloid handle	etched	100	1987	$40
Stockman	3 blade	gold scrolled with black celluloid handle	etched	100	1987	$40
Stockman	3 blade	gold scrolled with blue celluloid handle	etched	100	1987	$40
Stockman	3 blade	Hitler on red celluloid handle	etched	100	1987	$40
Stockman	3 blade	black celluloid handle	BLACK DIAMOND	1200	1979	$40
Stockman	3 blade	green peacock on silver celluloid handle	etched	50	1987	$40
Stockman	3 blade	red peacock on gold celluloid handle	etched	50	1987	$40
Stockman	3 blade	black peacock on silver celluloid handle	etched	50	1987	$40
Stockman	3 blade	blue peacock on gold celluloid handle	etched	50	1987	$40
Stockman	3 blade	green peacock on gold celluloid handle	etched	50	1987	$40
Stockman	3 blade	blue peacock on silver celluloid handle		50	1987	$40
Stockman	3 blade	roaring twenties celluloid handle	etched	600	1987	$40
Stockman	3 blade	roaring twenties celluloid handle	etched	600	1987	$40
Stockman	3 blade	roaring twenties celluloid handle	etched	600	1987	$40
Stockman	3 blade	roaring twenties celluloid handle	etched	600	1987	$40
Stockman	3 blade	roaring twenties celluloid handle	etched	600	1987	$40
Stockman	3 blade	roaring twenties celluloid handle	etched	600	1987	$40
Stockman	3 blade	pick bone handle	TENNESSEE MOTOR VEHICLE	600	1987	$85
Stockman	3 blade	genuine horn handle	GOLD COAST CHAPTER	100	1983	$85
Stockman	3 blade	stag handle	TENNESSEE KENTUCKY CLUB	100	1980	$75
Stockman	3 blade	smooth bone handle	TENNESSEE KENTUCKY CLUB	100	1982	$60
Stockman	3 blade	pick bone handle	TENNESSEE KENTUCKY CLUB	100	1983	$60
Stockman	3 blade	blue & black celluloid handle	reverse etched INDIAN TERRITORY	100	1986	$60
Stockman	3 blade	red pearl celluloid handle	reverse etched SWEET SIXTEEN	100	1986	$50
Stockman	3 blade	smooth bone handle	reverse etched stainless blade	200	1986	$40
Stockman	3 blade	stag handle	reverse etched stainless blade	200	1986	$40
Stockman	3 blade	bone stag handle	reverse etched stainless blade	200	1986	$40
Stockman	3 blade	stag handle	etched	200	1986	$40
Stockman	3 blade	black pearl celluloid handle	ROUGH CUT	1200	1986	$40
Stockman	3 blade	blue & silver celluloid handle	DEATH & TAXES	ltd.	1987	$45
Stockman	3 blade	art noveau lady on red celluloid handle	etched	100	1987	$40
Stockman	3 blade	art noveau lady on green celluloid handle	etched	100	1987	$40
Stockman	3 blade	art noveau lady on blue celluloid handle	etched	100	1987	$40
Stockman	3 blade	gold deer on green celluloid handle	etched	500	1987	$40
Stockman	3 blade	gold ducks on green celluloid handle	etched	500	1987	$40
Stockman	3 blade	gold wild boar on green celluloid handle	etched	500	1987	$35
Stockman	3 blade	gold grouse on green celluloid handle	etched	500	1987	$35
Stockman	3 blade	gold elk on green celluloid handle	etched	500	1987	$35
Stockman	3 blade	gold small deer on green celluloid handle	etched	500	1987	$35
Stockman	1 blade	pick bone handle	etched	12	1981	$60
Stockman	1 blade	brown black pearl celluloid handle	etched	12	1981	$60
Stockman	1 blade	blue black pearl celluloid handle	etched	24	1981	$60
Stockman	3 blade	waterfall celluloid handle	etched	300	1988	$40

Fight'n Rooster Price Guide

STYLE	# OF BLADES	HANDLE	ETCHING	QUANT	YEAR	VALUE
Stockman	3 blade	pick bone handle	etched	100	1978	$50
Stockman	3 blade	frosted amber celluloid handle	etched	250	1984	$40
Stockman	3 blade	gold & black striped celluloid handle	DOUBLE TROUBLE	1200	1986	$50
Stockman	3 blade	brown black pearl vertical striped celluloid handle	etched	200	1984	$45
Stockman	3 blade	gray pearl celluloid handle	KENTUCKY STATE POLICE	400	1985	$45
Stockman	3 blade	pick bone handle	reverse etched	rare	1978	$80
Stockman	3 blade	new Christmas celluloid handle	gold etched	12	1987	$75
Stockman	3 blade	blue marble celluloid handle	WILDCAT FEVER	600	1985	$60
Stockman	3 blade	black celluloid handle	etched	24	1980	$80
Stockman	3 blade	brown & black striped celluloid handle	THE TENNESSEAN	300	1978	$60
Stockman	3 blade	blue & black striped celluloid handle	THE VIRGINIAN	300	1978	$60
Stockman	3 blade	gold & black striped celluloid handle	THE KENTUCKIAN	300	1978	$60
Stockman	3 blade	green & black striped celluloid handle	THE CAROLINIAN	150	1978	$60
Stockman	3 blade	feather white celluloid handle	THE CAROLINIAN	150	1978	$65
Stockman	3 blade	gold flake celluloid handle	TWENTY DOLLAR GOLD PIECE	600	1978	$45
Stockman	3 blade	black & pearl celluloid handle	NICE & EASY	300	1978	$45
Stockman	3 blade	black celluloid handle	EASTERN KENTUCKY CLUB	100	1984	$45
Stockman	3 blade	red & black celluloid handle	WILD FIRE	300	1978	$45
Stockman	3 blade	red & black celluloid handle	TILL DEATH DO US PART	1200	1979	$45
Stockman	3 blade	black & orange celluloid handle	GRIT & STEEL	1200	1979	$45
Stockman	3 blade	black celluloid handle	BLACK DIAMOND	1200	1979	$45
Stockman	3 blade	crystal white celluloid handle	MOONSHINE SPECIAL	1200	1979	$45
Stockman	3 blade	tortoise shell celluloid handle	BLACK WIDOW	unlimited	1979	$35
Stockman	3 blade	pick bone handle	BLACK WIDOW	1	1979	$100
Stockman	3 blade	gold flake celluloid handle	TWENTY DOLLAR GOLD PIECE	unlimited	1979	$40
Stockman	3 blade	new Christmas celluloid handle	EASY MONEY	1200	1979	$40
Stockman	3 blade	gold & black striped celluloid handle	THE KENTUCKIAN	600	1980	$50
Stockman	3 blade	smooth bone handle	TENNESSEE HIGHWAY PATROL	600	1980	$150
Stockman	3 blade	crystal white celluloid handle	TENNESSEE HIGHWAY PATROL	12	1980	$100
Stockman	3 blade	genuine horn handle	etched	150	1980	$45
Stockman	3 blade	golden fluff celluloid handle	etched	400	1980	$40
Stockman	3 blade	butterscotch celluloid handle	etched	400	1980	$40
Stockman	3 blade	smokey gray celluloid handle	etched	400	1980	$40
Stockman	3 blade	mint green celluloid handle	etched	400	1980	$40
Stockman	3 blade	new Christmas celluloid handle	EASY MONEY	600	1982	$40
Stockman	3 blade	yellow brown celluloid handle (no bolsters)	etched	300	1982	$35
Stockman	3 blade	tortoise shell celluloid handle (no bolsters)	etched	300	1982	$35
Stockman	3 blade	old Christmas celluloid handle (no bolsters)	etched	300	1982	$35
Stockman	3 blade	new Christmas celluloid handle (no bolsters)	etched	300	1982	$35
Stockman	3 blade	gold gilded rooster handle	reversed gold etching	300	1982	$50
Stockman	3 blade	gold gilded blue & black pearl peafowl handle	reversed gold etching	300	1982	$50
Stockman	3 blade	gold gilded blue & white art noveau lady handle	reversed gold etching	300	1982	$50
Stockman	3 blade	gold gilded black & white climbing rose handle	reversed gold etching	300	1982	$50
Stockman	3 blade	pearl gray celluloid handle	GREYHOUND	200	1982	$40
Stockman	3 blade	gold gilded rooster handle	reversed gold etching	300	1982	$50
Stockman	3 blade	gold gilded gold & green peafowl handle	reversed gold etching	300	1982	$50
Stockman	3 blade	gold gilded black & white art nouveau lady handle	reversed gold etching	300	1982	$50
Stockman	3 blade	gold gilded black & red climbing rose handle	reversed gold etching	300	1982	$50
Stockman	3 blade	crystal white celluloid handle	LEADER DOG	1000	1982	$40
Stockman	3 blade	gold gilded black handle	reversed etching	500	1983	$50
Stockman	3 blade	gold gilded red & black handle	reversed etching	500	1983	$50
Stockman	3 blade	gold & black striped celluloid handle	THE KENTUCKIAN	100	1983	$60
Stockman	3 blade	brown & gold striped celluloid handle	THE TENNESSEAN	100	1983	$60
Stockman	3 blade	blue & black striped celluloid handle	THE VIRGINIAN	125	1983	$60
Stockman	3 blade	green pearl & black celluloid handle	etched	100	1983	$60
Stockman	3 blade	wine & pearl celluloid handle	etched	600	1983	$40
Stockman	3 blade	spider web red celluloid handle	etched	125	1983	$60
Stockman	3 blade	blue on blue flame celluloid handle	etched	200	1983	$35
Stockman	3 blade	dark lilac celluloid handle	etched	100	1983	$60
Stockman	3 blade	butter & molasses celluloid handle	etched	200	1983	$40
Stockman	3 blade	dark red & black celluloid handle	etched	600	1983	$40
Stockman	3 blade	brown & white pearl celluloid handle	etched	150	1983	$40
Stockman	3 blade	blue black pearl celluloid handle	etched	200	1983	$40
Stockman	3 blade	white & black celluloid handle		50	1983	$50
Stockman	3 blade	red gold celluloid handle	etched	300	1983	$40
Stockman	3 blade	black & white celluloid handle	COAL DIGGER	1000	1983	$45
Stockman	3 blade	blue slate celluloid handle	etched	250	1983	$40
Stockman	3 blade	blue & white celluloid handle	BRUSHY MOUNTAIN	600	1983	$50
Stockman	3 blade	snakeskin pearl celluloid handle	etched	300	1984	$40
Stockman (very rare)	3 blade	pick bone handle	TENNESSEE KNOCKDOWN		1979	$75
Stockman	3 blade	genuine horn handle	etched	200	1985	$40
Stockman	3 blade	smooth brown bone handle	etched	250	1988	$40
Stockman	3 blade	genuine horn handle	not etched	35	1978	$70
Stockman	3 blade	smooth brown bone (no shield)	THE INVISIBLE EMPIRE	12	1983	$60
Stockman	3 blade	orange & black celluloid handle	etched	200	1985	$40
Stockman	3 blade	smooth brown bone handle	THE INVISIBLE EMPIRE	1000	1983	$50

Fight'n Rooster Price Guide

STYLE	# OF BLADES	HANDLE	ETCHING	QUANT	YEAR	VALUE
Stockman	3 blade	new Christmas celluloid handle	etched	150	1983	$40
Stockman	3 blade	old Christmas celluloid handle	etched	150	1983	$40
Stockman	3 blade	red & black celluloid handle	etched	150	1983	$40
Stockman	3 blade	brown, black & pearl celluloid handle	etched	24	1984	$45
Stockman	3 blade	green sparkle celluloid handle	etched	50	1986	$45
Stockman	3 blade	white on white celluloid handle	etched	50	1986	$45
Stockman	3 blade	black & white striped celluloid handle	etched	300	1986	$40
Stockman	3 blade	new Christmas celluloid handle	etched	300	1986	$40
Stockman	3 blade	old Christmas celluloid handle	etched	300	1986	$40
Stockman	3 blade	red & black celluloid handle	etched	300	1986	$40
Stockman	3 blade	yellow & white striped celluloid handle	etched	100	1986	$40
Stockman	3 blade	crystal white celluloid handle	WILDCAT FEVER	600	1986	$50
Stockman	3 blade	blue & black pearl celluloid handle	WILDCAT FEVER	600	1987	$50
Stockman	3 blade	crystal white celluloid handle	WILDCAT FEVER	600	1987	$50
Stockman	3 blade	blue & black pearl celluloid handle	STRUT'N WITH SUTTON	300	1987	$80
Stockman	3 blade	blue marble celluloid handle	WILDCAT FEVER	600	1987	$50
Stockman	3 blade	tortoiseshell celluloid handle	BLACK WIDOW	1200	1979	$50
Stockman	3 blade	crystal white celluloid handle	etched	300	1985	$40
Stockman (Small)	3 blade	old Christmas celluloid handle	not etched	300	1983	$40
Stockman (Small)	3 blade	pick bone handle	not etched	300	1983	$35
Stockman (Small)	3 blade	tortoiseshell celluloid handle	not etched	300	1983	$35
Stockman (Small)	3 blade	stag handle	not etched	300	1983	$35
Stockman	6 blade	stag handle	etched	250	1984	$65
Stockman	6 blade	genuine horn handle	etched	250	1984	$65
Stockman	4 blade	new Christmas celluloid handle	etched	200	1986	$40
Stockman	4 blade	stag handle	etched	200	1986	$40
Stockman	4 blade	orange & black celluloid handle	etched	200	1986	$40
Stockman	4 blade	pick bone handle	etched	200	1986	$40
Stockman	4 blade	old Christmas celluloid handle	etched	200	1986	$60
Stockman (Small)	3 blade	red, brown & pearl celluloid handle	etched	unlimited	1981	$32
Stockman (Small)	3 blade	butter & molasses celluloid handle	etched	unlimited	1981	$32
Stockman (Small)	3 blade	red & black celluloid handle	etched	unlimited	1981	$32
Stockman (Small)	3 blade	gold flake celluloid handle	etched	200	1982	$32
Stockman (Small)	3 blade	black & white striped celluloid handle	etched	200	1982	$32
Stockman (Small)		red & gold celluloid handle	etched	unlimited	1981	$32
Stockman (Small)	3 blade	blue & black celluloid handle	etched	200	1982	$32
Stockman (Small)	3 blade	tortoise shell celluloid handle	etched	200	1982	$32
Stockman (Small)	3 blade	red & black celluloid handle	etched	200	1982	$32
Stockman (Small)	3 blade	old Christmas celluloid handle	etched	200	1982	$32
Stockman (Small)	3 blade	black celluloid handle	BLACK DIAMOND	400	1982	$40
Stockman	3 blade	red, brown & pearl celluloid handle	RED FOX	400	1982	$35
Stockman (Small)	3 blade	crystal white celluloid handle	MOONSHINER	400	1982	$45
Stockman (Small)	3 blade	alligator celluloid handle	etched	200	1986	$30
Stockman (Small)	3 blade	pick bone handle	reverse etched-stainless blade	200	1986	$55
Stockman (Small)	3 blade	stag handle	etched	200	1986	$35
Stockman (Small)	3 blade	end of day celluloid handle	LITTLE JOKER	200	1986	$110
Stockman (Small)	3 blade	smooth brown bone handle	etched	600	1986	$35
Stockman (Small)	3 blade	pick bone handle	etched	200	1986	$37
Stockman (Small)	3 blade	stag handle	etched	200	1986	$39
Stockman (Small)	3 blade	new Christmas celluloid handle	etched	200	1986	$35
Stockman (Small)	3 blade	smooth bone handle	reverse etched-stainless blade	200	1986	$45
Stockman	2 blade	gold flake celluloid handle	THE COAL MINER	600	1978	$175
Stockman	2 blade	black & pearl celluloid handle	THE COAL MINER'S DAUGHTER	600	1978	$175
Stockman (Small)	1 blade	red & black celluloid handle	etched	12	1982	$170
Stockman (Small)	1 blade	old Christmas celluloid handle	etched	12	1982	$170
Stockman (Small)	1 blade	gold flake celluloid handle	etched	12	1982	$170
Stockman (Small)	1 blade	yellow celluloid handle	not etched	rare	1981	$170
Stockman (Fancy)	3 blade	genuine horn handle	etched	100	1988	$240
Stockman (Fancy)	3 blade	black & pearl celluloid handle	etched	100	1988	$240
Stockman (Fancy)	3 blade	stag handle	etched	100	1988	$240
Stockman (Fancy)	3 blade	blue slate celluloid handle	etched	100	1988	$240
Stockman (Fancy)	3 blade	gray spider celluloid handle	etched	100	1988	$240
Stockman (Fancy)	3 blade	green & black celluloid handle	etched	100	1988	$240
Stockman (Small)	3 blade	pearl handle	CAPTAIN'S ROOSTER	600	1982	$60
Stockman	3 blade	pearl handle	CAPTAIN'S ROOSTER	24	1980	$120
Stockman	3 blade	pearl handle-center bolster	not etched	12	1984	$125
Stockman	3 blade	pearl handle	CAPTAIN'S ROOSTER	300	1986	$80
Stockman	3 blade	pearl handle	KNIFE FOUNDERS	2600	1980	$75
Stockman	3 blade	pearl handle	INVISIBLE EMPIRE	1000	1981	$90
Stockman	4 blade	pearl handle	CAPTAIN'S ROOSTER	300	1984	$70
Stockman	3 blade	pearl handle	CAPTAIN'S ROOSTER	12	1982	$150
Stockman	3 blade	pearl handle	KNIFE CITY-1980	100	1980	$125
Stockman	3 blade	pearl handle	CAPTAIN'S ROOSTER	?	1980	$70
Stockman	3 blade	pearl handle	TENNESSEE MOTOR VEHICLE	12	1982	$200
Stockman	3 blade	pearl handle	FLORIDA KNIFE COLLECTORS-1980	300	1980	$80
Stockman	3 blade	pearl handle	FLORIDA KNIFE COLLECTORS-1981	300	1981	$80
Stockman (Display)	3 blade	waterfall celluloid handle-etching illustrates sequence of American History				$750

Fight'n Rooster Price Guide

STYLE	BLADES	HANDLE	ETCHING	QUANT	YEAR	VALUE
Stockman	1 blade	smooth white bone handle-narrow frame	etched	6	1986	$250
Stockman	1 blade	pick bone handle-narrow frame	etched	6	1986	$250
Stockman	1 blade	blue flame celluloid handle-narrow frame	etched	6	1986	$250
Stockman	1 blade	pick bone handle-round bolsters	not etched	24	1982	$250
Stockman	1 blade	new Christmas celluloid handle-short bolster	WILD FIRE	6	1977	$250
Stockman	1 blade	crystal white celluloid handle-short bolster	WILD FIRE	6	1977	$250
Stockman	1 blade	tortoise shell celluloid handle-short bolster	etched	60	1988	$60
Stockman	1 blade	genuine horn handle-no bolster	etched	60	1988	$60
Stockman	3 blade	imitation ivory handle-short bolster	stainless blades reverse etched	12	1984	$110
Stockman	3 blade	pick bone handle-round bolsters	not etched	12	1981	$65
Stockman	3 blade	snakeskin celluloid handle-long bolsters	etched	6	1984	$85
Stockman	3 blade	black comp. handle no bolst., pick/tweezers in handle	etched	24	1978	$80
Stockman	3 blade	tort. shell cell. handle-long-bolsters-round shield	BLACK WIDOW	24	1978	$80
Stockman	3 blade	front handle wine and pearl celluloid-back handle, purple and black cell., short bolsters-stainless	reverse etched	12	1984	$75
Stockman	3 blade	yellow celluloid handle-short bolsters	etched	300	1977	$45
Stockman	3 blade	pickbone handle-round bolsters	PREMIUM STOCK KNIFE	rare	1977	$100
Stockman	3 blade	butter and molasses celluloid handle, short bolsters-no shield	etched	6	1982	$80
Stockman	3 blade	red and black celluloid handle on front, red and gold cell. handle, short bolst., stainless	reverse etched	12	1984	$60
Stockman	3 blade	smooth brown bone handle-long bolsters	FLORIDA KNIFE COLLECTORS	300	1982	$60
Stockman	3 blade	blue, black and silver striped celluloid handle, long bolsters	etched	rare	1983	$60
Stockman	3 blade	gray celluloid handle-long bolsters-no shield	reverse etched GREYHOUND	rare	1983	$60
Stockman	3 blade	smooth brown bone handle-long bolsters	ALLEGHENY MOUNTAIN	100	1984	$60
Stockman	3 blade	black celluloid handle-long bolsters	etched	24	1980	$65
Stockman	3 blade	stag handle-long bolsters	FLORIDA KNIFE COLLECTORS	200	1979	$55
Stockman	3 blade	smooth bone handle-short bolsters	WILLIAMSON COUNTY	100	1985	$80
Stockman	3 blade	smooth brown bone handle-long bolsters	MOORE COUNTY LAW ENFORCEMENT	100	1981	$80
Stockman	3 blade	blue quartz celluloid handle-long bolsters	etched	100	1986	$50
Stockman	3 blade	blue flame celluloid handle-long bolsters	WILDCAT FEVER	600	1988	$45
Stockman	3 blade	blue velvet celluloid handle-long bolsters	3 etched BREAKFAST OF WILDCATS	150	1988	$75
Stockman	3 blade	pink snakeskin celluloid handle-long bolsters	HUMMINGBIRD	1000	1988	$60
Stockman	3 blade	Christmas knife-green, gold and red cell. handle with MERRY CHRISTMAS	not etched	100	1988	$50
Stockman	3 blade	red celluloid handle-long bolsters	KENTUCKY	300	1988	$40
Stockman	3 blade	blue snakeskin celluloid handle-long bolsters	BLUE MOON OF KENTUCKY	600	1988	$50
Stockman	3 blade	red bone handle-long bolsters	HAYWOOD KNIFE CLUB	100	1988	$55
Stockman	3 blade	silver sparkle celluloid handle-long bolster	SILVER DOLLAR	1000		$35
Stockman	3 blade	blue snakeskin celluloid handle-long bolsters	PEACE OF MIND	1000	1988	$40
Stockman	3 blade	yellow, black and white celluloid handle, long bolsters	BUMBLE BEE	300	1988	$150
Stockman	3 blade	orange snakeskin celluloid handle-long bolsters	SON OF A GUN	600	1988	$40
Stockman	3 blade	cajun marble celluloid handle-long bolsters	INDIANA HOOSIERS	300	1988	$75
Stockman	3 blade	gold gilded-red rose handle-no bolsters	gold gilded reverse etched blades	300	1982	$65
Stockman	3 blade	gold gilded-red rose handle-no bolsters	gold gilded reverse etched blades	300	1982	$65
Stockman	3 blade	gold gilded-blue and red peacock handle-no bolsters	gold gilded reverse etched blades	300	1982	$65
Stockman	3 blade	green and white art nouveau lady handle-no bolsters	gold gilded reverse etched blades	300	1982	$65
Stockman	3 blade	smokey gray celluloid handle-long bolsters	KENTUCKY STATE POLICE	400	1988	$40
Stockman	3 blade	black and orange celluloid handle-long bolster	etched	5 or less	1988	$150
Stockman	3 blade	smoke gray celluloid handle-long bolsters	etched	5 or less	1988	$150
Stockman	3 blade	cajun marble celluloid handle-long bolsters	etched	5 or less	1988	$150
Stockman	3 blade	red and gold celluloid handle-long bolsters	etched	5 or less	1988	$150
Stockman	3 blade	tortoiseshell celluloid handle-long bolsters	not etched	5 or less	1988	$150
Stockman	3 blade	pink snakeskin celluloid handle-long bolsters	etched	5 or less	1988	$150
Stockman	3 blade	blue snakeskin celluloid handle-long bolsters	etched	5 or less	1988	$150
Stockman	3 blade	orange snakeskin celluloid handle-long bolsters	etched	5 or less	1988	$150
Stockman	3 blade	yellow, black & pearl celluloid handle-long bolsters	etched	5 or less	1988	$150
Stockman	3 blade	rose wood handle-long bolsters	etched	300	1988	$40
Stockman	3 blade	red, pearl & black celluloid handle-long bolsters	etched	12	1985	$70
Stockman (Sowbelly)	3 blade	stag handle-large shield	etched	125	1989	$50
Stockman (Sowbelly)	3 blade	waterfall celluloid handle-large shield	etched	125	1989	$50
Stockman (Sowbelly)	3 blade	cajun marble celluloid handle-large shield	etched	125	1989	$50
Stockman (Int'l)	3 blade	green black celluloid handle-3 blades in one end, no bolsters	etched	125	1983	$50
Stockman (Sowbelly)	1 blade	blue smoke celluloid handle-bird wing shield	etched	6	1988	$75
Stockman (Sowbelly)	3 blade	pearl handle-fancy pulls	INTERNATIONAL FIGHT'N ROOSTER	300	1988-II	$75
Stockman (Sowbelly)	3 blade	pearl handle-fancy pulls	KENTUCKY CUTLERY ASSN.	120	1989	$75
Stockman (Small)	3 blade	pearl handle Merry Christmas 1983	CAPTAIN'S ROOSTER	50	1983	$70
Stockman (Small)		pearl handle	ALBEMARLE KNIFE CLUB	100	1983	$65
Stockman (Small)	3 blade	pearl handle	not etched	12	1983	$60
Stockman	3 blade	pearl handle-stainless blades-long bolsters	not etched	12	1984	$85
Stockman	5 blade	pearl handle-short bolsters with center bolster	not etched	12	1982	$90
Stockman	5 blade	pearl handle-round bolsters FORT CITY KNIFE COLLECTOR'S CLUB FIFTH ANNIVERSARY		35	1986	$90
Stockman	3 blade	pearl handle-round bolsters-bolsters etched	INVISIBLE EMPIRE	1000	1981	$80
Stockman	5 blade	stag handle-no shield	EASY MONEY	rare	1982	$100

Fight'n Rooster Price Guide

STYLE	BLADES	HANDLE	ETCHING	QUANT	YEAR	VALUE
Stockman (Small)	1 blade	brown & yellow celluloid handle, saber blade-bird wing shield	etched	100	1986	$100
Stockman (Small)	1 blade	orange & black celluloid handle, saber blade-bird wing shield	etched	100	1986	$100
Stockman (Small)	1 blade	black & pearl celluloid handle, saber blade-bird wing shield	etched	100	1986	$100
Stockman	1 blade	horn handle-saber blade-no bolster, bird wing shield	etched	100	1987	$45
Stockman	3 blade	end of the day handle	E. KENTUCKY KNIFE CLUB	50	1986	$125
Stockman (Small)	3 blade	end of the day handle	END OF THE DAY	200	1989	$100
Stockman	1 blade	stock pattern-brown bone handle	etched premium stock very, very rare knife		1978	$80
Stockman	1 blade	round bolster-pick bone (very rare)	no etch very rare		1978	$75
Stockman	3 blade	long bolsters-has pick bone handle-round shield	WATTS BAR	200	1986	$45
Stockman		long bolsters-dog bone shield-pick bone handle	Tennessee Highway	500	1986	$50
Stockman	3 blade	long bolsters-orange & black striped handle	no etch	1	1990	$50
Stockman (Proto.)	3 blade	slant bolsters-green and brown striped celluloid, acorn shield	BLUE MOON OF KENTUCKY	1	1990	$60
Stockman (Proto.)	3 blade	slant bolsters-silverfish celluloid-acorn shield	BLUE MOON OF KENTUCKY	1	1990	$60
Stockman (Proto.)	3 blade	slant bolsters-brown straw celluloid handle, acorn shield	BLUE MOON OF KENTUCKY		1990	$60
Stockman	3 blade	crest shield-black celluloid, Buck Creek stamped on master blade	BLACK DIAMOND	1	1983	$85
Stockman	3 blade	crest shield-brown & pearl celluloid handle, matchstriker pulls	FIGHT'N ROOSTER	4	1989	$50
Stockman (Large)	3 blade	dog bone shield-mother of pearl handle, scrimshawed	CAPTAIN'S ROOSTER	15	1985	$85
Stockman (Small)	3 blade	pearl handle are scrimshawed	no etch	20	1982	$90
Stockman	3 blade	crest shield-red bone handle-matchstriker pulls	GRANDAD	1000	1990	$40
Stockman	3 blade	dog bone shield-red and black striped celluloid, matchstriker pulls	FOLSOM PRISON	600	1986	$40
Stockman	3 blade	black and orange celluloid handle, dog bone shield-matchstriker pulls	BROWN SUGAR		1986	$40
Stockman	3 blade	black and pearl celluloid handle, dog bone shield-matchstriker pulls	KLAN	300	1989	$40
Stockman	3 blade	long bolsters-dog bone shield, imitation pearl handle	FIGHT'N ROOSTER	6	1985	$40
Stockman	3 blade	blue mosaic celluloid-crest shield, matchstriker pulls	PEACE OF MIND	1000	1990	$40
Stockman	3 blade	crest shield-copper mosaic handle, matchstriker pulls	SON OF A GUN	1000	1988	$40
Stockman	3 blade	red & gold celluloid-dog bone shield, matchstriker pulls	SWEET SIXTEEN	limited	1986	$45
Stockman	3 blade	large crest shield-crushed velvet celluloid, matchstriker pulls	CHRISTMAS 1990	200	1990	$40
Stockman (Large)	3 blade	crest shield-black & silver celluloid, matchstriker pulls	NO PAIN, NO GAIN	1000	1988	$40
Stockman	3 blade	silver fish cell.-matchstriker pulls-acorn shield	HOOK, LINE, AND SINKER	800	1990	$40
Stockman	3 blade	acorn shield-black and straw gold handle, matchstriker pulls	LIVE HARD, DIE YOUNG	800	1990	$40
Stockman	3 blade	brown plastic celluloid	LEATHER-LACE	800	1991	$40
Stockman	3 blade	orange and black celluloid, matchstriker pulls-acorn shield	PARADISE	800	1991	$40
Stockman	3 blade	pick bone handle	TRUCK BUILDERS	100		$40
Stockman	6 blade	stag handle	WHEELER BASIN KNIFE CLUB	100	1984	$75
Stockman	6 blade	stag handle	WHEELER BASIN KNIFE CLUB	100	1982	$75
Stockman	3 blade	Buck Creek handle-mint green celluloid	FIGHT'N ROOSTER	75	1981	$50
Cattleman	3 blade	burnt bone handle	FLINT RIVER KNIFE CLUB	75	1985	$50
Cattleman	3 blade	green bone handle	HAYWOOD KNIFE CLUB	135	1986	$55
Stockman	3 blade	mother of pearl handle	WILLIAMSON COUNTY CLUB KNIFE	100	1987	$85
Stockman	3 blade	green and pearl handle	BLUEGRASS STATE	1000	1989	$40
Stockman	3 blade	black celluloid handle	SUPREME SACRIFICE	1000	1989	$45
Stockman	3 blade	slant bolsters-snakeskin celluloid handle	FIGHT'N ROOSTER	200	1989	$40
Stockman	3 blade	slant bolsters-black & brown pearl cell.	FIGHT'N ROOSTER	200	1989	$40
Stockman	3 blade	slant bolsters	FIGHT'N ROOSTER-New Xmas	200		$40
Stockman	3 blade	slant bolsters	FIGHT'N ROOSTER-waterfall	200	1989	$45
Cattleman (Proto.)	3 blade	pearl handle	GEM CAPITAL			$85
Stockman (Proto.)	3 blade	pearl handle	GEM CAPITAL			$85
Stockman (rare)	3 blade	long bolster	FIGHT'N ROOSTER-waterfall handle		1988	$55
Stockman	3 blade	slant bol.-red bone handle	TENN-KY CLUB KNIFE	100	1989	$45
Stockman		long bols.-white bone	FIGHT'N ROOSTER		1984	$45
Stockman	3 blade	stag handle	FLORIDA KNIFE CLUB	2	1982	$85
Stockman	3 blade	gold blades-had blue sparkle handle	reverse etched FIGHT'N ROOSTER	1	1980	$85
Stockman	3 blade	2 tone green handle	FIGHT'N ROOSTER	12	1983	$60
Stockman (Proto.)	3 blade	fancy bolsters-pearl	FIGHT'N ROOSTER		1989	$90
Stockman (Proto.)	6 blade	gem capital club knife-no jewels in handle-pearl handle		rare		$100
Stockman	3 blade	has pink fractured pearl handle	CAPTAIN'S ROOSTER	24	1990	$100
Stockman	5 blade	has pink fractured pearl handle-very rare	CAPTAIN'S ROOSTER	6	1990	$100
Stockman	5 blade	has white fractured pearl handle-very rare	CAPTAIN'S ROOSTER	6	1990	$100
Stockman	3 blade	green bone	HAYWOOD KNIFE CLUB	100	1989	$50
Cattleman	3 blade	smooth bone handle	FLINT RIVER KNIFE CLUB	75	1985	$50
Stockman		gold blades-black and pearl handle	FIGHT'N ROOSTER	6	1981	$75
Stockman	3 blade	has green striped handle	NO GUTS, NO GLORY	1000	1990	$40
Stockman		bright green striped handle	FISHERMAN'S LUCK	1000	1990	$40
Stockman	3 blade	yellow celluloid	reverse FIGHT'N ROOSTER	100	1977	$65
Stockman	3 blade	feather white celluloid	reverse FIGHT'N ROOSTER	300	1977	$65
Stockman	3 blade	red, black & pearl celluloid handle-long bolsters	LOUISVILLE CARDINALS	200	1989	$45
Stockman	3 blade	red & black celluloid handle-long bolsters	CAT STOMPER	125	1989	$45
Stockman	3 blade	tan & white striped celluloid handle	TRUCK BUILDERS KNIFE CLUB	1	1984	$75
Stockman	3 blade	cajun marble celluloid handle	DEAD MAN'S HAND	400	1989	$45
Stockman	3 blade	pickbone handle	SWAN LAKE	200	1985	$40
Stockman	3 blade	crystal white celluloid handle-long bolsters	etched	12	1985	$50
Stockman	3 blade	black & pearl swirl celluloid handle-long bolsters	NO PAIN NO GAIN	1000	1989	$35
Stockman (Small)	3 blade	tortoiseshell celluloid handle-bar shield	not etched	7	1982	$225
Stockman (Small)	3 blade	old Christmas celluloid handle-bar shield	not etched	7	1982	$225

242

Fight'n Rooster Price Guide

STYLE	BLADES	HANDLE	ETCHING	QUANT	YEAR	VALUE
Stockman (Small)	3 blade	blue flame celluloid handle-bar shield	not etched	7	1982	$225
Stockman (Small)	3 blade	gold flake celluloid handle-bar shield	not etched	7	1982	$225
Stockman (Small)	3 blade	red & black celluloid handle-bar shield	not etched	7	1982	$225
Stockman (Small)	3 blade	rosewood handle-crest shield	etched	200	1989	$25
Stockman (Small)	3 blade	waterfall celluloid handle-crest shield	etched	200	1989	$30
Stockman (Small)	3 blade	cajun marble celluloid handle-crest shield	etched	200	1989	$25
Stockman (Small)	3 blade	end of day celluloid handle-dog bone shield	reverse etched stainless blade	12	1986	$75
Stockman	3 blade	stag handle-medium serpentine pattern	etched	200	1989	$35
Stockman	3 blade	green bone handle-medium serpentine pattern	TENNESSEE KENTUCKY KNIFE CLUB	100	1988	$40
Stockman	2 blade	pickbone handle-short bolsters	etched	rare	1983	$55
Stockman	3 blade	white crystal celluloid	JACKSON COUNTY MOONSHINE SPECIAL	100	1979	$100
Stockman (Proto.)	2 blade	black and orange	FIGHT'N ROOSTER		1983	$55
Stockman (Proto.)	3 blade	with groove on bolster-gold flake handle	$20 gold piece		1982	$55
Stockman (Proto.)	3 blade	2 grooves on bolster-gold flake handle	$20 gold piece		1982	$50
Stockman (Proto.)	3 blade	3 grooves on bolster-gold flake handle	$20 gold piece		1982	$50
Stockman (Proto.)	1 blade	no bolsters-green celluloid handle	no etch		1983	$45
Stockman (Proto.)	2 blade	tortoiseshell	FIGHT'N ROOSTER		1983	$45
Stockman (Proto.)	3 blade	one handle is silver-other is red, white & blue	reverse etched Silver dollar		1988	$45
Stockman (Proto.)	3 blade	one handle is silver-other is red, white & blue	reverse etched Silver dollar	12	1988	$45
Stockman (Proto.)	3 blade	one handle is silver-other is red, white & blue	FIGHT'N ROOSTER	6	1988	$45
Stockman	3 blade	silver flake handle	Gold Silver Dollar	1000	1988	$40
Stockman	3 blade	silver flake handle	reverse etched silver dollar	1000	1988	$40
Stockman	3 blade	silver flake handle	rev. etch Sterling Frank W. Buster	300	1988	$60
Stockman	3 blade	crushed blue velvet handle	FIGHT'N ROOSTER	5 or less	1988	$60
Stockman	3 blade	blue snake skin handle	FIGHT'N ROOSTER	5 or less	1988	$60
Stockman	3 blade	tan & white striped handle	no etch	1	1982	$75
Stockman	3 blade	red & black cell. handle-long bolsters	FIGHT'N ROOSTER		1983	$45
Stockman	3 blade	red marble handle	WHAT GOES AROUND	1000	1989	$40
Stockman		matchstriker pulls, blue snakeskin plastic handle	BLUE MOON OF KENTUCKY	600	1989	$45
Stockman	5 blade	acorn shield-red pick bone	FIGHT'N ROOSTER	70	1990	$50
Stockman	5 blade	acorn shield-green pick bone	FIGHT'N ROOSTER	70	1990	$50
Stockman	5 blade	acorn shield-stag handle	FIGHT'N ROOSTER	50	1990	$55
Stockman	6 blade	Buck Creek shield-worked bolsters, black composition handle	FIGHT'N ROOSTER	1	1989	$125
Stockman	3 blade	blue and black celluloid handle	LIKE FATHER, LIKE SON	1000	1989	$60
Stockman	3 blade	match striker pulls-black & orange cell. handle	TIGER EYE	600	1989	$110
Stockman	3 blade	plain pulls-black & orange celluloid handle	TIGER EYE	600	1989	$110
Stockman	3 blade	black and white plastic handle	INVISIBLE EMPIRE	1000	1989	$45
Stockman	3 blade	plain pulls-gold or brown & purple handle	GUNS & ROSES	1000	1989	$65
Stockman	3 blade	red & gold handle-plain pulls	hand-etched COCA-COLA	1000	1989	$45
Stockman	3 blade	matchstriker pulls-brown and pearl handle	WIN SOME, LOSE SOME	1000	1989	$45
Stockman	3 blade	red & gold handle	Rose of Sharon	300	1989	$65
Stockman (Proto.)	2 blade	tiger brown & orange cell. handle-screwdriver	FIGHT'N ROOSTER		1989	$45
Cattleman (Proto.)	3 blade	burnt bone	unetched		1989	$65
Cattleman (Proto.)	3 blade	roaring 20's handle	no etch		1988	$65
Cattleman (Proto.)	3 blade	horn handle-no shield-stamped prototype	cattleman etch		1985	$65
Stockman	3 blade	violet and gold celluloid handle-matchstriker pulls	GUNS & ROSES	1000	1989	$50
Stockman	3 blade	matchstriker pulls	Coca Cola etch in red & gold	1000	1989	$45
Stockman	3 blade	matchstriker pulls-pearl & green cell.	Merry Christmas	200	1989	$50
Stockman	3 blade	matchstriker pulls-long bolster, green bone handle-dog bone shield	FIGHT'N ROOSTER	100	1990	$45
Stockman	3 blade	long bolster-dog bone shield-red bone handle, matchstriker pulls	FIGHT'N ROOSTER	100	1990	$45
Stockman	3 blade	long bolster-stag handle, dog bone shield-matchstriker pulls	FIGHT'N ROOSTER	100	1990	$45
Stockman	3 blade	acorn shield-stag handle, slant bolsters-matchstriker pulls	FIGHT'N ROOSTER	100	1990	$45
Stockman	3 blade	acorn shield-red bone handle, slant bolsters-matchstriker pulls	FIGHT'N ROOSTER	100	1990	$45
Stockman	3 blade	acorn shield-green bone handle, slant bolsters-matchstriker pulls	FIGHT'N ROOSTER	100	1990	$45
Stockman	3 blade	round bolsters-mother of pearl handle, stainless blades	no etch	6	1985	$80
Cattleman	3 blade	end of the day handle, Tennessee-Kentucky club knife		100	1985	$125

Knives Of Thunder!

NASCAR commemorative fever is spreading

From *Edges*, Fall 1991.

Some of the more popular and valuable commemoratives are the ones saluting the exploits of 10 Million Dollar Bill Elliott, King Richard Petty, Handsome Harry Gant and the other pedal-to-the-metal superstars who burn up the NASCAR racing circuit.

Among the more lucrative NASCAR commemoratives are those honoring Elliott. As reported in the November 1989 *Edges*, Little River Knife Sales, Case and Taylor Cutlery teamed to produced 1,000 coke bottle patterns celebrating Elliott's selection by fan vote as the most popular driver over five consecutive years (1985-89). Sold for a suggested retail of $225 in '89, the knives are now valued at $350 by *Collectors World Racing Magazine*.

Little River's at it again, this time with the "10 Million Dollar Bill" Elliott commemorative. Designed by Jim Gullette and Theresa Thomas, it's another coke bottle pattern set in an elaborate presentation box with pewter inlay of Elliott's car in cloisonne, and with a color metal photo plate of Elliott on the inside cover. "People are saying the box is worth the price without the knife in it," Gullette said.

Now for the best part—the knife sold out before the first one was made! Of course, the commemorative is available from selected retailers—or at least it was when *Edges* went to press. "We don't know what it will do as far as increasing in value," Gullette noted. "But as fast as it went to the retailers, the secondary market will probably jump out of sight."

The new Elliott piece is but a sample of the NASCAR commemorative fever that is gripping knife buffs.

NASCAR Knife Value Update

Name/Commemorates	NASCAR Knife	Quantity	Value*
Bobby Allison The Legend	Case Big Coke	1,200	$275
Bobby Allison '88 Daytona 500	Case 5254	1,000	$180
Davey Allison '87 Rookie of Year	Case 5254	n/a	$150
Davey Allison Hard Charger	Case BK61050	1,000	$500
Davey Allison Hard Charger	Case Imi. Ivory 5254	2,000	$200
Davey Allison Champ To All	Case Black 5254	2,000	$200
Buddy Baker 1st To Break 200	Case 5254	1,200	$85
Geoff Bodine '86 Daytona 500	Case 52131	1,000	$140
Case/Little River Collectors Edition Davey Allison	Case 3⅛" LB/Maxx card	unlimited	$19.95**
Case/Little River Collectors Edition Dale Earnhardt	Case 3⅛" LB/Maxx card	unlimited	$19.95**
Case/Little River Collectors Edition Bill Elliott	Case 3⅛" LB/Maxx card	unlimited	$19.95**
Case/Little River Collectors Edition Jeff Gordon	Case 3⅛" LB/Maxx card	unlimited	$19.95**
Case/Little River Collectors Edition Jimmy Hensely	Case 3⅛" LB/Maxx card	unlimited	$19.95**
Case/Little River Collectors Edition Ernie Irvan	Case 3⅛" LB/Maxx card	unlimited	$19.95**
Case/Little River Collectors Edition Alan Kulwicki	Case 3⅛" LB/Maxx card	unlimited	$19.95**
Case/Little River Collectors Edition Mark Martin	Case 3⅛" LB/Maxx card	unlimited	$19.95**
Case/Little River Collectors Edition Ken Schrader	Case 3⅛" LB/Maxx card	unlimited	$19.95**
Case/Little River Collectors Edition Kyle Petty	Case 3⅛" LB/Maxx card	unlimited	$19.95**
Case/Little River Collectors Edition Richard Petty	Case 3⅛" LB/Maxx card	unlimited	$19.95**
Case/Little River Collectors Edition Rusty Wallace	Case 3⅛" LB/Maxx card	unlimited	$19.95**
Case/Little River Collectors Edition Darrell Waltrip	Case 3⅛" LB/Maxx card	unlimited	$19.95**
Case/Little River Winston Motor Sports Set	21 Case knives in cherry chest	1,500	$5,500
Dale Earnhardt Top Gun	Case 6240RPB	1,000	$250
Dale Earnhardt '86, '87 Winston Cup	Case 6265	2,000	$180
Dale Earnhardt '86, '87 Winston Cup	Hen & Rooster trapper	2,000	$75
Dale Earnhardt '80, '86, '87 Winston Cup	Case 5254	2,000	$140
Dale Earnhardt '90 Winston Cup	Case 6251 RPB	1,500	$180
Dale Earnhardt Back in Black	Frost Scrimshaw	10,000	$20
Dale Earnhardt 5-Time Champ	Frost Scrimshaw	10,000	$20
Dale Earnhardt '90 Winston Cup	Frost Scrimshaw	5,000	$25
Dale Earnhardt '91 Winston Cup	Frst Scrimshaw	5,000	$25
Dale Earnhardt Signature #3	Frost U.S.A.	unlimited	$50
Dale Earnhardt '91 Winston Cup & 5-Time Champ	Keen Kutter Set	2,500	$75
Dale Earnhardt '91 Winston Cup	Case 6254RSB	2,000	$125
Dale Earnhardt 5-Time Champ	Case 6265RPB	2,000	$225
Dale Earnhardt 5-Time Champ	Case 5-piece 6254/1-piece white Bowie	1,000	$800
Dale Earnhardt '90 Winston Cup	Frost Stainless	10,000	$10
Dale Earnhardt Signature #3	Frost Ink Pen	unlimited	$25
Dale Earnhardt Back in Black	Frost Stainless	10,000	$20
Dale Earnhardt '90 Winston Cup	Frost Stainless	10,000	$20
Dale Earnhardt '91 Winston Cup	Frost Stainless 3"	10,000	$20
Dale Earnhardt '91 Winston Cup	Frost Stainless 4"	10,000	$20
Bill Elliott Driver of the Year	Case Big Coke	1,000	$400
Bill Elliott '88 Winston Cup	Case Red 6254	3,500	$150
Bill Elliott Winston Million	Case 6254	1,200	$400
Bill Elliott Awesome Bill	Case 5254	600	$500
Bill Elliott '85 Coca-Cola 500	Frost lockback	n/a	$40
Bill Elliott #9 Car (red top, white bottom)	Frost scrimshaw	n/a	$40
Bill Elliott #9 (red top & bottom)	Frost scrimshaw	n/a	$40
Bill Elliott 10 Million Dollar Bill	Case Big Coke	1,500	$350
Elliot/Johnson Set	Case BWC61050 & ROG61050	1,500 sets	$400
Harry Grant Handsome Harry	Case 6254	1,000	$150
Harry Grant - Bush	Case 6254	n/a	$150***
Harry Grant - Winston Cup	Case Green 5254	250	$250***
Jeff Gordon	Case Blue 5254	100	$250
Jay Hedecock Mod. Champ '90 & '92	Case Blue Copperhead	43	$600
Ernie Irvan	Case Green Big Coke	250	$140
Ned Jarrett	Case Blue 5254	500	$125
Flossie Johnson	Case Red 5254	97	$225***
Flossie Johnson	Case Red Canoe	97	$150***
Junior Johnson Last American Hero	Case 5254	2,000	$150
Junior Johnson Ford	Case 5254	1,000	$150
Alan Kulwicki Tribute To Champ	Case Orange 5254	1,000	$250
Alan Kulwicki '92 Winston Champ	Case White Trapper	1,000	$250
Alan Kulwicki '92 Winston Champ	Case Golden Bowie	250	$800
Bobby Labonte	Case Red 5254	100	$150
Fred Lorenzen '60 Golden Boy	Case 5254	500	$200
JD McDuffie Last of Independents	Case R61072	350	$250
Mark Martin Rising Star	Case 5254	1,000	$150
Sterling Marlin 2-Time Winston Winner	Case 5254	500	$85
Myers Brothers Set	Case 5254 and ROG 6200	500 each	$165
David Pearson Racing Legend	Case 6240	n/a	$25
David Pearson '60 Rookie of Year	Case 5254	1,200	$75
The Petty Legend (Lee, Richard, Kyle)	3 knife set	1,500	$400
Richard Petty King (bluebone)	Case Big Coke	1,500	$450
Richard Petty King (redbone)	Case Big Coke	1,000	$600
Richard Petty Ultra-Limited Edition	Case Coke Bottle	32	$2,000
Robert Pressley Future Champ	Case 5254	59	$500
Fireball Roberts Purple People Eater	Case 5254	1,000	$85
Stock Car Legend (Lee, Richard, Kyle)	3 knife set	1,000	$110
Stock Car Legend (Lee Petty)	Case 5254	2,000	$75
Stock Car Legend (Lee Petty)	Hen & Rooster trapper	2,000	$70
Stock Car Legend (Lee Petty)	Case folding hunter	500	$100
Tribute To A Legend (Cale Yarborough)	Case 5254	2,000	$75
Tribute To A Legend (Cale Yarborough)	Hen & Rooster trapper	2,000	$70
Kenny Wallace	Case Green 5254	100	$100
Rusty Wallace Winston Cup Champ	Case Big Coke	1,000	$275
Darrell Waltrip Top Money History	Case 5254	2,000	$120
Darrell Waltrip 3-Time Winston Cup Champ	Case BK61060	1,500	$200
Wood Brothers	Case Red 5254	1,000	$100***
Glen Wood	Case Brown 5254	500	$125***

* Based on an average of values submitted by a number of NASCAR knife authorities.
** Suggested retail: Little River Knives' Jim Gullette says the knives are so new that they haven't had enough time to hit the secondary market and appreciate yet
*** The value of a matched serial number set of these two knives: $500
**** The value of a matched serial number set of these two knives: $450
***** The value of a matched serial number set of these two knives: $275

Schrade Scrimshaw:
15 Years Of Pocketknife Values

From *Edges* Summer, 1991

Begun in 1976, the Schrade Scrimshaw Series of the Great American Outdoors is one of the longer ongoing scrimshaw knife series available to collectors/investors. It contains a wide range of knife styles with scrimshaw scenes of various wildlife animals.

Herein are the current collector values of the series through 1989.

Schrade Great American Outdoors Scrimshaw Series

Year	Pattern	Scrimshaw	Price	Collector Value
1976	502 Sharp Finger	Whales/Ship	$40	$35
1977	508 Folding Hunter	Eagle/Banner	$50	$45
1977	502 Sharp Finger	Eagle/Banner	$30	$25
1978	508 Folding Hunter	Bear	$40	$35
1978	505 Stockman	Canada Geese	$30	$25
1978	506 Barlow	Raccoons	$20	$18
1978	502 Sharp Finger	Bear	$25	$22
1979	508 Folding Hunter	Bear/Hunter	$35	$30
1979	500 Large Lockblade	Buffaloes	$30	$27
1979	503 Small Lockblade	Trout	$20	$18
1979	505 Stockman	Seagulls	$25	$22
1979	506 Barlow	Raccoon	$18	$15
1979	501 Drop Point	Buck	$20	$18
1980	508 Folding Hunter	Turkeys	$35	$25
1980	500 Large Lockblade	Rams	$20	$18
1980	503 Small Lockblade	Trout	$18	$15
1980	505 Stockman	Raccoons	$20	$18
1980	506 Barlow	Ducks	$15	$12
1980	502 Sharp Finger	Pronghorn	$18	$15
1981	507 Lockback	Bear	$30	$25
1981	508 Folding Hunter	Raccoons	$35	$30
1981	500 Large Lockblade	Bucks	$20	$18
1981	503 Small Lockblade	Gar	$16	$14
1981	505 Stockman	Dog & Pheasant	$20	$18
1981	506 Barlow	Fox	$15	$13
1981	502 Sharp Finger	Ram	$18	$16
1981	509 Little Finger	Canada Geese	$18	$16
1982	507 Lockback	Bighorn	$30	$26

Year	Pattern	Scrimshaw	Price	Collector Value
1982	508 Folding Hunter	Bison	$30	$26
1982	500 Large Lockblade	Deer	$20	$18
1982	503 Small Lockblade	Trout	$16	$15
1982	505 Stockman	Mallards	$18	$16
1982	506 Barlow	Squirrel	$15	$13
1982	502 Sharp Finger	Cougar	$16	$15
1982	509 Little Finger	Raccoon	$18	$16
1983	507 Lockback	Mustang	$30	$27
1983	508 Folding Hunter	Rams	$30	$27
1983	500 Large Lockblade	Raccoons	$20	$18
1983	503 Small Lockblade	Catfish	$16	$13
1983	505 Stockman	Rabbit	$18	$15
1983	506 Barlow	Owl	$12	$12
1983	502 Sharp Finger	Bear & Dog	$16	$15
1983	509 Little Finger	Eagle	$18	$15
1984	507 Lockback	Raccoons	$28	$25
1984	500 Large Lockblade	Moose	$18	$15
1984	503 Small Lockblade	Trout	$16	$15
1984	505 Stockman	Duck Decoy	$18	$15
1984	506 Barlow	Boar/Dogs	$12	$11
1984	511 Cub Lockback	Chipmunk	$18	$15
1984	502 Sharp Finger	Elk Bugling	$16	$15
1985	507 Lockback	Bears	$28	$25
1985	500 Large Lockblade	Beavers	$18	$15
1985	503 Small Lockblade	Alligator	$16	$15
1985	505 Stockman	Weasel	$18	$15
1985	506 Barlow	Pheasant	$12	$12
1985	511 Cub Lockback	Raccoon	$18	$15
1985	502 Sharp Finger	Fawn	$16	$15
1986	507 Lockback	Turkeys	$28	$25
1986	500 Large Lockblade	Mallards	$15	$15
1986	503 Small Lockblade	Steelhead	$14	$14
1986	505 Stockman	Coyotes	$18	$16
1986	506 Barlow	Pup/Decoy	$12	$12
1986	511 Cub Lockback	Opossum	$16	$15
1986	502 Sharp Finger	Raccoon	$16	$15
1987	507 Lockback	Wolves	$26	$25
1987	503 Small Lockblade	Otters	$14	$14
1987	524 Tradesman	Badger	$16	$15
1987	505 Stockman	Retriever	$18	$16
1987	511 Cub Lockback	Frog	$16	$15
1987	513 Bearhead L'back	Mallards	$16	$15
1987	502 Sharp Finger	Polar Bear	$16	$15
1988	507 Lockback	Cougar	$26	$25
1988	503 Small Lockblade	Sunfish/Perch	$14	$14
1988	524 Tradesman	Grizzlies	$16	$15
1988	505 Stockman	Skunks	$16	$15
1988	511 Cub Lockback	Weasel	$16	$15
1988	513 Bearhead L'back	Beaver	$16	$15
1988	502 Sharp Finger	Pheasant	$16	$15
1989	507 Lockback	Bear & Cub	$26	$23
1989	503 Small Lockblade	Two Bass	$14	$14
1989	505 Stockman	Wood Ducks	$16	$15
1989	513 Bearhead L'back	Eagle	$16	$15
1989	515 4-inch Lockback	Dog & Rabbit	$21	$17
1989	502 Sharp Finger	Coon Hunting	$16	$14
1989	518 Guthook Hunter	Ram	$18	$15

Schrade's Latest Scrimshaw Editions

Schrade has offered two more installments in addition to those listed on the previous page. Those installments—the 1990 and '91 editions—are listed by model and scrimshaw scene below. This set continues to be issued every year—but because prices are in such flux we are listing only those through 1991. We are not listing any collector value because people still have large inventories.

Year	Pattern	Scrimshaw
1990	502SC Fixed Blade	Mare & Colt
1990	503SC Lockblade	Brown Trout
1990	505SC Pocketknife	Pointer & Bobwhite Quail
1990	507SC Lockback	Foxes
1990	513SC Lockback	Raccoon
1990	515SC Lockback	Wild Turkey
1990	518SC Fixed Blade Guthook	Whitetail Deer
1991	502SC Sharp Finger	Hunter & Beagle
1991	515SC Guthook	Grizzly Bear
1991	513SC Lockback	Eagle
1991	515SC Lockback	Raccoons
1991	507SC Lockback	Elk
1991	503SC Lockblade	Fly Fisherman
1991	505SC Stockman	Canada Geese

Winchester Value Chart by Clarence Risner

From *Edges,* Spring 1995

As of Feb. 1, 1995

PATTERN	RELEASE	HANDLES	SHIELD	BLADES	STAMP	ETCH	NO.	YEAR	THEN	NOW
W15 1924	1	Old Rogers	Heraldic	1	-Org. Winchester stamping in two straight lines	Winchester	4,173	1987	$43.99	$100
W15 1924		Lt. Old Rogers	Heraldic	1	-No Pattern no. date stamped in a curve	Winchester	400	1987	$43.99	$550
W15 1924		Old Rogers	Heraldic	1	-Pattern no. & date stamped in a curve	Winchester	600	1987	$43.99	$375
W15 1924		Pearl	Heraldic	1	-Org. Winchester stamping in two straight lines	Mason Dixon Club	100	1987		$200
W15 1924		Pearl	Heraldic	1	-Org. Winchester stamping in two straight lines & CC	Fort City Club	160	1987		$250
W15 1924	41	Goldstone	Oval	1	-Org. Winchester stamping in two straight lines	Winchester	544	1992	$59.99	$85
W15 3964	2	Old Rogers	Heraldic	3	-Org. Winchester stamping in two straight lines	High Polish Winchester	2,578	1987	$49.99	$95
W15 3964		Old Rogers	Sm. Heraldic	3	-Org. Winchester stamping in two straight lines	Satin Finish Winchester	800	1987	$49.99	$250
W15 3964		Old Rogers	Lg. Heraldic	3	-Org. Winchester stamping in two straight lines	Satin Finish Winchester	600	1987	$49.99	$325
W15 3964		Old Rogers	Sm. Heraldic	3	-Org. Winchester stamping in two straight lines	High Polish Winchester	150	1987	$49.99	$750
W15 1901	3	Old Rogers	Heraldic	1	-Org. Winchester stamping in two straight lines	Winchester	3,308	1987	$44.99	$100
W15 1901		Old Rogers	Heraldic	1	-Sm. Winchester stamping in two straight lines	Winchester	841	1987	$44.99	$175
W15 1901	42	Goldstone	Oval	1	-Org. Winchester stamping in two straight lines	Winchester	502	1992	$59.99	$70
W15 1901		Pearl	Heraldic	1	-Org. Winchester stamping in two straight lines	Winchester	317	1992	$129.99	$175
W15 1987-1	4	Cast Bronze	None	2	-Org. Winchester stamping in two straight lines	Winchester	10,640	1987	$27.49	$40
W15 1987-1		Cast Bronze	None	2	-Org. Winchester stamping in two straight lines misstamped 88	Winchester	553	1987	$27.49	$90
W15 2921	5	Old Rogers	Heraldic	2	-Org. Winchester stamping in two straight lines	Winchester	3,272	1987	$54.99	$100
W15 2921	43	Goldstone	Oval	2	-Org. Winchester stamping in two straight lines	Winchester	542	1992	$65.99	$85
W15 2921		Pearl	Heraldic	2	-Org. Winchester stamping in two straight lines	Winchester	296	1992	$159.99	$300
W15 2904	6	Old Rogers	Heraldic	2	-Org. Winchester stamping in two straight lines	Winchester	3,387	1987	$49.99	$100
W15 2857	7	Old Rogers	Heraldic	2	-Org. Winchester stamping in two straight lines	Winchester	3,070	1987	$49.99	$90
W15 2967	8	Peach Seed	Heraldic	2	-Org. Winchester stamping in two straight lines	Winchester	2,587	1988	$54.99	$105
W15 2967	46	Goldstone	Oval	2	-Org. Winchester stamping in two straight lines	Winchester	488	1992	$66.99	$75
W15 2967		Pearl	Heraldic	2	-Org. Winchester stamping in two straight lines	Winchester	280	1992	$169.99	$200
W15 3904	9	Old Rogers	Heraldic	3	-Org. Winchester stamping in two straight lines	Winchester	2,964	1988	$59.99	$120
W15 3904		Pearl	Heraldic	3	-Org. Winchester stamping in two straight lines	Winchester	296	1991	$159.99	$250
W15 3904		Stag	Heraldic	3	-Org. Winchester stamping in two straight lines	Winchester	580	1991	$99.99	$130
W15 2851	10	Old Rogers	Heraldic	2	-Org. Winchester stamping in two straight lines	Winchester	3,234	1988	$44.99	$85
W15 2851		Stag	Heraldic	2	-Org. Winchester stamping in two straight lines	Winchester	511	1991	$79.99	$115
W15 2851		Pearl	Heraldic	2	-Org. Winchester stamping in two straight lines	Winchester	317	1991	$124.99	$160
W15 2851	44	Goldstone	Heraldic	2	-Org. Winchester stamping in two straight lines	Winchester	504	1992	$59.99	$75
W15 1927	11	Peach Seed	Propeller	1	-Org. Winchester stamping in two straight lines	Winchester	3,248	1988	$79.99	$110
W15 1927		Peach Seed	Propeller	1	-Org. Winchester stamping in two straight lines but Stamped 1950	Winchester	889	1988	$79.99	$250
W15 2935	12	Old Rogers	Bar	2	-Org. Winchester stamping in two straight lines	Winchester	2,782	1988	$49.99	$75
W15 2935		Pearl	Bar	2	-Org. Winchester stamping in two straight lines	Winchester	332	1991	$139.99	$240
W15 2935		Stag	Bar	2	-Org. Winchester stamping in two straight lines	Winchester	529	1991	$99.99	$140
W15 2991	13	Old Rogers	Propeller	2	-Org. Winchester stamping in two straight lines	Winchester	2,439	1988	$53.99	$75
W15 2991		Pearl	Heraldic	2	-Org. Winchester stamping in two straight lines	Winchester	287	1992	$149.99	$250
W15 1988-1	14	Cast Bronze	None	1	-Org. Winchester stamping in two straight lines	Winchester	6,921	1988	$32.99	$40
W15 2880-1/2	15	Peach Seed	Balloon	2	-Org. Winchester stamping in two straight lines	Winchester	2,468	1988	$56.99	$75
W15 2913-1/2	16	Peach Seed	Heraldic	2	-Org. Winchester stamping in two straight lines	Winchester	2,410	1988	$59.99	$75
W15 3971	17	Rogers	Heraldic	3	-Org. Winchester stamping in two straight lines	Winchester	2,409	1989	$54.99	$80
W15 3971	47	Goldstone	Oval	3	-Org. Winchester stamping in two straight lines	Winchester	561	1992	$66.99	$75
W15 3971		Pearl	Heraldic	3	-Org. Winchester stamping in two straight lines	Winchester	254	1992	$159.99	$225
W15 2978	18	Old Rogers	Heraldic	2	-Org. Winchester stamping in two straight lines	Winchester	2,457	1989	$47.99	$70
W15 2978		Old Rogers	Heraldic	2	-Org. Winchester stamping in two straight lines	Forkland Festival	75	1989	$49.99	$85
W15 2978	45	Goldstone	Oval	2	-Org. Winchester stamping in two straight lines	Winchester	524	1992	$59.99	$75
W15 2978		Stag	Heraldic	2	-Org. Winchester stamping in two straight lines	Winchester	581	1992	$79.99	$135
W15 2978		Pearl	Heraldic	2	-Org. Winchester stamping in two straight lines	Winchester	250	1992	$139.99	$200
W15 3949	19	Peach Seed	Heraldic	3	-Org. Winchester stamping in two straight lines	Winchester	2,185	1989	$56.99	$75
W15 3949	36	Stag	Heraldic	3	-Org. Winchester stamping in two straight lines	Winchester	982	1991	$99.99	$115
W15 3949	39	Goldstone	Oval	3	-Org. Winchester stamping in two straight lines	Rifle & Yellow Boy	482	1991	$68.99	$95
W15 3049 1/2		Christmas Tree	Oval	3	-Org. Winchester stamping in two straight lines	Winchester	250	1992	$69.99	$80
W15 3049 1/2		Christmas Tree	Oval	3	-Org. Winchester stamping in two straight lines	Fancy Winchester	250	1992	$69.99	$85
W15 3049 1/2		Goldstone	Oval	3	-Org. Winchester stamping in two straight lines	Winchester	250	1992	$69.99	$80
W15 3049 1/2		Goldstone	Oval	3	-Org. Winchester stamping in two straight lines	Winchester	250	1992	$69.99	$85
W15 3049 1/2		Waterfall	Oval	3	-Org. Winchester stamping in two straight lines	Winchester	250	1992	$69.99	$80
W15 3049 1/2		Waterfall	Oval	3	-Org. Winchester stamping in two straight lines	Fancy Winchester	250	1992	$69.99	$85
W15 3049 1/2		Candy Stripe	Oval	3	-Org. Winchester stamping in two straight lines	Fancy Winchester	250	1992	$69.99	$85
W15 3049 1/2		Candy Stripe	Oval	3	-Org. Winchester stamping in two straight lines	Winchester	250	1992	$69.99	$80
W15 2904 1/2	20	Peach Seed	Heraldic	2	-Org. Winchester stamping in two straight lines	Winchester	2,639	1989	$54.99	$75
W15 2904 1/2		Lt. Rogers	Heraldic	2	-Org. Winchester stamping in two straight lines	Winchester	147	1989	$68.99	$300
W15 2904 1/2		Lt. Peach Seed	Heraldic	2	-Org. Winchester stamping in two straight lines	Winchester	71	1989	$68.99	$550
W15 2904 1/2	38	Stag	Heraldic	2	-Org. Winchester stamping in two straight lines	Winchester	730	1992	$94.99	$115
W15 1989-1	21	Cast Bronze	None	1	-Org. Winchester stamping in two straight lines	Winchester	980	1989	$32.99	$40
W15 1950	22	Stag	Propeller	1	-Org. Winchester stamping in two straight lines	Winchester	2,511	1989	$104.99	$125
W15 1950		Stag	Propeller	1	-Org. Winchester stamping in two straight lines	Mason Dixon Club #ed	110	1989	$104.99	$175
W15 3902	23	Rogers	Heraldic	3	-Org. Winchester stamping in two straight lines	Winchester	1,392	1990	$58.99	$70
W15 3902		Rogers	Heraldic	3	-Org. Winchester stamping in two straight lines	Forkland Festival	125	1990	$58.99	$70
W15 3902	37	Stag	Heraldic	3	-Org. Winchester clamping in two straight lines	Winchester	894	1991	$99.99	$115

Winchester Knife Price Guide

PATTERN	RELEASE	HANDLES	SHIELD	BLADES	STAMP	ETCH	NO.	YEAR	THEN	NOW
W15 1936	24	Rogers Brown Bone	Heraldic	1	-Org. Winchester stamping in two straight lines	Winchester	1,566	1990	$49.99	$60
W15 1036 1/2		Christmas Tree Cell	Oval	1	-Org. Winchester stamping in two straight lines	Winchester	250	1992	$64.99	$75
W15 1036 1/2		Christmas Tree Celluloid	Oval	1	-Org. Winchester stamping in two straight lines	Fancy Winchester	250	1992	$64.99	$75
W15 1036 1/2		Waterfall Celluloid	Oval	1	-Org. Winchester stamping in two straight lines	Winchester	250	1992	$64.99	$75
W15 1036 1/2		Waterfall Celluloid	Oval	1	-Org. Winchester stamping in two straight lines	Fancy Winchester	250	1992	$64.99	$75
W15 1036 1/2		Goldstone Celluloid	Oval	1	-Org. Winchester stamping in two straight lines	Winchester	250	1992	$64.99	$75
W15 1036 1/2		Goldstone Celluloid	Oval	1	-Org. Winchester stamping in two straight lines	Fancy Winchester	250	1992	$64.99	$75
W15 1036 1/2		Candy Stripe Celluloid	Oval	1	-Org. Winchester stamping in two straight lines	Winchester	250	1992	$64.99	$75
W15 1036 1/2		Candy Stripe Celluloid	Oval	1	-Org. Winchester stamping in two straight lines	Fancy Winchester	250	1992	$64.99	$75
W15 1936 1/2		Rogers Brown Bone	Oval	1	-Org. Winchester stamping in two straight lines	Winchester	250	1992	$68.99	$80
W15 1036 1/2		Rogers Brown Bone	Oval	1	-Org. Winchester stamping in two straight lines	Fancy Winchester	250	1992	$68.99	$80
W15 2903	25	Rogers Brown Bone	Heraldic	2	-Org. Winchester stamping in two straight lines	Winchester	1,186	1990	$52.99	$55
W15 1990-1	26	Cast Bronze	None	1	-Org. Winchester stamping in two straight lines	Winchester	2,315	1990	$33.99	$40
W15 0670	27	Pakkawood	None	1	-Org. Winchester stamping in two straight lines	Winchester	1,114	1990	$62.99	$70
W15 0680	28	Pakkawood	None	1	-Org. Winchester stamping in two straight lines	Winchester	1,057	1990	$64.99	$70
W15 1920	29	Peach Seed Brown Bone	Lg. Boat	1	-Org. Winchester stamping in two straight lines	Winchester	1,594	1990	$89.99	$110
W15 1920		Peach Seed Brown Bone	Lg. Boat	1	-Org. Winchester stamping in two straight lines	Southern California Blades Club	55	1990	$89.99	$150
W15 1920	33	Genuine Stag	Lg. Boat	1	-Org. Winchester stamping in two straight lines	Winchester	969	1991	$119.99	$140
W15 1991-1	30	Cast Bronze	None	2	-Org. Winchester stamping in two straight lines	Winchester	2,690	1991	$33.99	$40
W15 4935	31	Old Rogers Brown Bone	Bar	4	-Org. Winchester stamping in two straight lines	Winchester	1,380	1991	$69.99	$80
W15 4935		Genuine Stag	Bar	4	-Org. Winchester stamping in two straight lines	Winchester	486	1992	$109.99	$120
W15 4935		Genuine Pearl	Bar	4	-Org. Winchester stamping in two straight lines	Winchester	360	1992	$169.99	$200
W15 3995	32	Peach Seed Brown Bone	Heraldic	3	-Org. Winchester stamping in two straight lines	Winchester	1,440	1991	$67.99	$80
W15 3907	34	Peach Seed Brown Bone	Heraldic	3	-Org. Winchester stamping in two straight lines	Winchester	966	1991	$69.99	$80
W15 1991-2	35	Cast Bronze	None	2	-Org. Winchester stamping in two straight lines	"125th Anniv. of Winchester"	2,650	1991	$34.99	$40
W15 1991-2		Sterling Silver	None	2	-Org. Winchester stamping in two straight lines	"125th Anniv. of Winchester"	454	1991	$109.99	$140
W15 1950 SR-89	40	Genuine Stag	Rifle	1	-Org. Winchester stamping in two straight lines	Winchester	980	1991 (stamped 89)	$109.99	$150
W15 1992-1	48	Cast Bronze	None	2	-Org. Winchester stamping in two straight lines	Winchester	New Release	1992	$34.99	New Release
W15 29103 1/2	49	Burnt Orange Bone	Rifle	2	-Org. Winchester stamping in two straight lines	Winchester	New Release	1992	$109.99	New Release
W18 39101	51	Burnt Orange Bone	Cartridge	3	-Org. Winchester stamping in two straight lines	Cartridge Series	New Release	1992	$109.99	New Release
W15 1001 1/2		Christmas Tree Celluloid	Oval	1	-Org. Winchester stamping in two straight lines	Fancy Winchester	500	1992	$59.99	New Release
W15 1001 1/2		Candy Stripe Celluloid	Oval	1	-Org. Winchester stamping in two straight lines	Fancy Winchester	500	1992	$59.99	New Release
W15 1001 1/2		Waterfall Celluloid	Oval	1	-Org. Winchester stamping in two straight lines	Fancy Winchester	500	1992	$59.99	New Release
W15 1001 1/2		Abalone Celluloid	Oval	1	-Org. Winchester stamping in two straight lines	Fancy Winchester	500	1992	$59.99	New Release
W15 1901 1/2		Rogers Green Bone	Oval	1	-Org. Winchester stamping in two straight lines	Fancy Winchester	500	1992	$64.99	New Release
W15 1901 1/2		Genuine Stag	Oval	1	-Org. Winchester stamping in two straight lines	Winchester	500	1992	$79.99	New Release
W15 1992-3		Cast Bronze	None	2	-Org. Winchester stamping in two straight lines	"100th Anniv. of Olin Corp"	New Release	1992	$35.00	New Release
W15 1992-3		Sterling Silver	None	2	-Org. Winchester stamping in two straight lines	"100th Anniv. of Olin Corp"	New Release	1992	$100.00	New Release
W07 0537		Rogers Brown Bone	Heraldic	2	-Org. Winchester stamping in two straight lines	Rifle, Gauge #, Model 37	2,000	1988	$199.99	$250
W07 0528		Peach Seed Brown Bone	Rifle	2	-Org. Winchester stamping in two straight lines	"Wild Bill Hickok"	2,500	1988	$149.99	$175

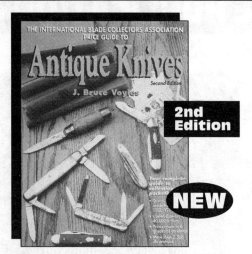

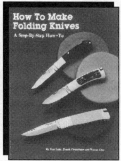